BASKETBALL — FIVE PLAYER

FRANCES H. EBERT

Associate Professor, Department of Women's
Physical Education, Western Michigan University,
Kalamazoo, Michigan

BILLYE ANN CHEATUM

Associate Professor, Department of Women's
Physical Education, Western Michigan University,
Kalamazoo, Michigan

1972
W. B. SAUNDERS COMPANY
Philadelphia • London • Toronto

W. B. Saunders Company: West Washington Square
Philadelphia, Pa. 19105

12 Dyott Street
London, WC1A   1DB

1835 Yonge Street
Toronto 7, Ontario

Basketball—Five Player   ISBN 0-7216-3305-6

Print No.:   9   8   7   6   5   4   3   2   1

DEDICATED TO

our parents,
who provided us not only with the education,
but also the opportunities
to play and coach Basketball.

PREFACE

Written for physical education majors, as well as non-majors enrolled in basketball classes, this book was designed to lead the student through simple, individual skills to more complicated defensive and offensive techniques. Since the rules of basketball have recently changed and five players are used on a team instead of six, the offensive and defensive strategies used by women players and coaches must be radically altered. The authors have therefore kept the following aims in mind:

To present the basic individual offensive and defensive skills included in beginning basketball classes. To simplify the transition from six player to five player basketball. To offer coaching suggestions and drill techniques for players who are now required to alternate between offensive and defensive tactics instead of playing a single position.

To present a brief chapter on coaching, including such topics as qualifications of the coach, duties of the student manager, team selection, duties of the captain, planning home–away events, and coaching during competition.

Throughout the book, emphasis has been placed on giving a detailed explanation of the skills (accompanied by approximately 330 illustrations and over 200 drills), and the methods used in conditioning athletes during pre-season, season, and post-season periods. The conditioning exercises are combined with skill techniques used throughout the game.

As women coaches enter into state, regional, and national competition, their knowledge must expand to include treatment of injuries to athletes, the legal implications of emergency first-aid, and the duties of trainers giving aid to injured players.

Anyone reading Five Player Basketball should systematically progress through the individual playing techniques, conditioning programs, and shooting and rebounding skills, to knowledge of the more advanced zone and man-to-man defense, the offensive strategies effective against various methods of defense, treatment of injuries, and coaching strategy.

FRANCES H. EBERT
BILLYE ANN CHEATUM

ACKNOWLEDGMENTS

We are indebted to numerous coaches, students, and future teachers who have contributed to our knowledge and understanding of the game of basketball. We are especially grateful to

Pat Ashby for her contributions to Chapter 2, "Conditioning," and the countless hours she spent proofreading and posing for pictures.

Jean Buning for her assistance in typing the manuscript.

James Smith and the photography department of Western Michigan University for photographing the various plays.

Jan Ellinger and Phyllis Cupp, physical education majors at Western Michigan University, who posed for the pictures.

Ken Nehring, who gave Fran Ebert her background in five player basketball.

Thomas Little, Hurstene Pickey, Sally Knight, Lina Cull and Lucille Williamson, who coached, supported and assisted Billye Ann Cheatum throughout her training in basketball.

CONTENTS

ix

5

6

7

8

9

HISTORY AND DEVELOPMENT OF BASKETBALL

HISTORY

Basketball, one of the few sports originated in America, was perhaps the only game that was consciously invented to meet a recognized need. Dr. Luther Gulick, a professor at the YMCA college in Springfield, Massachusetts, directed Dr. James Naismith to design a vigorous activity to be played indoors during the winter months enabling students to remain in good condition between football and baseball seasons, and appealing to even more students. Consequently, in 1892, limited by the restraints of a gymnasium, Dr. Naismith conceived a sport which emphasized skill and excluded personal contact and running with the ball. Originally, an Association (round) football was employed; however, it was soon replaced by a more functional soccer ball. The goals, peach baskets measuring fifteen inches across the top and fifteen inches deep, were suspended ten feet from the floor. Some of the more imaginative coaches attached backboards made of wire screening to the baskets.

Original Rules

Although the official rules were simple, teams could consist of three to 40 players. Nine players were recommended: one goalie, two guards, three centers, two wings and a home man. Understandably, players seldom needed to sit on the bench hoping for a substitution.

The following 13 rules governing basketball before the turn of the century made no provisions for strategy or technique:

1. The ball could be thrown in any direction with one or both hands.

1

2. The ball could be batted in any direction with one or both hands (never with the fist).

3. A player could not run with the ball; he had to throw it from the spot where he caught it. Allowance was made for catching the ball while running at a good speed if an attempt was made to stop.

4. The ball had to be held between the hands, not placed between the arm and body.

5. Shouldering, holding, pushing, tripping or striking an opponent was not allowed: the first infringement of this rule counted as a foul; the second disqualified a player until the next goal was made, and if there was intent to injure, the player was disqualified for the whole game and no substitute was allowed to take his place.

6. A foul was committed by striking at the ball with the fist or violation of Rules 3, 4, or 5.

7. Three consecutive fouls by a team counted as a goal for the opponents. ("Consecutive meant the opponents did not make a foul in the meantime.)

8. A goal was made when the ball was thrown or batted from the ground into the basket and stayed there, providing that those defending the goal did not touch or disturb it. If the ball rested on the edges of the basket and an opponent moved it, it counted as a goal.

9. When the ball went out of bounds, it was thrown into the field of play by the first person touching it. In case of a dispute, the umpire threw it straight into the field. The player who took the throw in was allowed five seconds; if he held the ball longer it went to his opponent. If any side persisted in delaying, the umpire called a foul.

10. The umpire was judge of the players; he noted fouls and notified the referee when three consecutive fouls had been made. He had the power to disqualify.

11. The referee was judge of the players; he decided when the ball was in-bounds and in play, and to which side it belonged. He determined when a goal had been made, kept an account of the goals, kept time, and performed other duties assigned to him.

12. There were two 15-minute halves, with five minutes' rest in between.

13. The side making more goals was the winner. In case of a draw, the captains could agree to continue the game until another goal was made.

To start the game, the teams were placed at opposite ends of the court, the ball was tossed in the center, and the players rushed for the ball. A horizontal line was later drawn across the court separating it into halves. Team size was reduced to seven, but by 1893 each team was officially restricted to five players. Frank Mahan, a student of Dr. Naismith, referred to the new game as "basketball" since the essential equipment included only baskets and a ball. The first rings were attached to the basket in 1898 but the open bottom net was not permitted until 1908, compelling a team to retrieve the ball from the basket each time a goal was scored.

The game, enthusiastically received by Springfield College students, spread rapidly throughout the United States. Extensive acceptance of basketball can be attributed to the many graduates of Springfield College, the training center of the YMCA, who took the game to YMCA's throughout the United States. Ultimately, the international influence of the YMCA enabled other countries to learn the game with the result that basketball was featured in the Olympic games of 1904 and was officially recognized as an Olympic sport in 1936.

International Basketball Federation

Although the first set of rules published in 1893 was used by the YMCA, the Amateur Athletic Union, the National Collegiate Athletic Association, and the professional leagues adopted separate sets of rules and this tended to hinder the uniform progress of the game. To resolve the problems caused by the use of several sets of official rules, a Joint Committee for Rules composed of representatives from each of these associations met in 1915 and formulated a uniform code of rules to govern basketball in the United States. Seventeen years later the International Basketball Federation (F.I.B.A.), with 80 member countries, was established as the international controlling organization for basketball. Responsibilities of the F.I.B.A. included: (1) establishing and standardizing the rules of play; (2) sponsoring the principal tournaments of International competition; and (3) safeguarding the best interests of the game.

Despite rule changes throughout the years, the modern game retains Dr. Naismith's fundamental requirements: a large light ball (manufactured according to Dr. Naismith's specifications soon after the game was developed); no running with the ball; a horizontal goal; and avoidance of personal contact. Contemporary exponents of basketball have altered and expanded the rules in a continuous effort to perpetuate maximal activity for all players. For instance, at the start of play a tall person could assume a position three feet from the basket and immediately score a goal with a minimal amount of effort. Today all free throws are considerably restricted, although a tall person stationed near the basket maintains an advantage.

History of Basketball for Women

Women became interested in basketball two weeks after the game was inaugurated. A group of women teachers from Buckingham Grade School in Springfield, Massachusetts, observed men in a physical education class playing the game. The women immediately made arrangements to use the gymnasium and receive a lesson from Dr. Naismith. The ladies arrived for instruction attired in uniforms of high-topped shoes and long trailing dresses with bustles and leg of mutton sleeves.

National Rules Committee

Mrs. Sandra Abbott Berenson, an instructor of physical education at Smith College, introduced basketball to Smith College women in 1892. By the following March, two teams had been organized and a contest scheduled between them. Although the game was well-received, the women realized that modification of the rules would be necessary for the safety, health, and enjoyment of girls and women. Smith College students played the game under modified rules in 1892; thereafter, various groups of girls and women adopted the game with individual modification of the rules. In June, 1899, at the Conference of Physical Training held in Springfield, a National Rules Committee composed of women in physical education was appointed to investigate and establish a set of rules based on the official basketball rules but more suitable for girls. In an effort to make the game more appropriate for women the committee instituted the three division court and prohibited any player from touching a ball held by an opponent. While most teams adhered to the rules established by the National Committee, some teams continued to follow modified or men's rules.

The second rules committee meeting was held in 1905, and the third in 1908; since then, with the exception of 1915, the meetings have been held annually. Their purpose is to discuss the rules, to consider requests and suggestions for changes, and to make revisions when warranted. Each state has a chairman who heads its committee. The chairman is responsible for submitting an annual report of conditions within her state, including recommendations for rule changes. The requests are based on communication with teachers, coaches, and officials in the state. Individuals are also encouraged to submit suggestions to the national committee.

Amateur Athletic Federation

A serious conflict in women's basketball occurred in 1923 with the formation of the Amateur Athletic Federation, which later became the Amateur Athletic Union. The AAU and the National Basketball Committee under the auspices of the American Physical Education Association (currently the American Association for Health, Physical Education and Recreation), elected separate governing bodies and consequently established separate rules. The AAU endorsed competition and leagues for highly skilled women, and encouraged competition at the national level. The NSWA, now the DGWS (Division for Girls' and Women's Sports), stressed team activity for women and discouraged any form of competition for the skilled individual. The differences between the two associations continued to flourish until 1958 when a directive from the DGWS Executive Council compelled the National Basketball Committee to adopt rules identical to those followed by the AAU. At that time a minimum of seven different sets of rules were used by women in various parts of the United States. These included the rules of the Amateur Athletic Union, the Division for Girls and Women's Sports, the Texas High School Girls, the Oklahoma High School Girls, the Iowa High School Girls, those published by the Girls' National Basketball Rules Committee for secondary schools, and the Women's Basketball Association. The cooperation of the AAU and the DGWS in devising a common set of rules enabled the two organizations to control basketball play for women in the majority of high schools, colleges and universities, and in virtually all the private and public recreational agencies.

Major rule changes

A summary of some of the most important changes that have been made in the rules will illustrate the development of the game.

I. **Size and Type of Court**
- 1907   100' × 60' for nine players
-          72' × 50' for five players
- 1922   90' × 45'
- 1932   two court game made as important as three court game (optional)
- 1938   two court game becomes official
- 1947   90' × 50'
- 1949   94' × 50'
- 1953   Max: 94' × 50'
- 1970   Min: 74' × 42'
-          two-inch division line concentric circles at center

II. **Playing Time**
- 1907   15 minute halves
- 1924   8 minute quarters
- 1953   8 minute quarters plus overtime periods (2 minutes)

III. **Number of Players**
- 1907   5 to 9 players
- 1922   6 to 9 players
- 1924   6 players
- 1968   5 players—optional

6

HISTORY AND DEVELOPMENT OF BASKETBALL

IV. **Officials**
    1907   1 referee, 2 umpires, 2 scorers, 2 timekeepers, 4 linesmen
    1914   1 referee, 1 umpire, 1 scorer, 1 timekeeper, 2 linesmen
    1922   linesmen dropped
    Before 1931   2 scorers and 2 timers
    1932   2 card officials added for Center Throw Game
    1942   card officials dropped
    1953   1 referee, 1 umpire, 1 timer, 1 scorer
    1964   home team selects both officials

V. **Baskets and Backboards**
    1908   open bottom net approved
    1940   backboards to be placed four feet in from end lines
    1941   fan-shaped backboards allowed
    1953   fan-shaped or rectangular backboard of plate glass, wood, or any other rigid material permitted

VI. **Tactics and Techniques**
  A. The Bounce
    1907   player may bounce ball on floor three times
    1911   bounced ball must be caught with only one hand
    1914   bounced ball caught legally in one or both hands but only one bounce permitted
    1933   bottom of bounced ball no longer must come to knee height to be legal
    1935   ball may bounce more than once with original impetus and be legally regained
  B. The Dribble
    1948   limited dribble allowed on optional basis
    1949   limited dribble becomes official
    continuous dribble allowed on experimental basis, not optional
    1951   continuous dribble not allowed even on experimental basis
    1961   three bounce dribble legal
    1966   continuous dribble permitted
  C. Bounce Pass
    1917   bounce pass allowed but only if unintentional on attempt at a regular pass
    1918   bounce pass becomes legitimate play
  D. Juggle
    1917   juggle approved but bottom of ball must go above head of player
    1936   height of juggle no longer stipulated
    1964   term "air dribble" replaces "juggle"
  E. Pivot
    1925   first time maneuver officially called "pivot"
    1934   player allowed to pivot only on rear foot following two-count stop

1939 pivot defined so that player may pivot on either foot

1940 at end of a run player may drag or lift pivot foot up to other foot

1953 player must use rear foot after two-count stop, either foot when catching ball while standing still, or after one-count stop

F. Guarding

1907 guarding permitted only with arms in vertical plane

1932 arm position in any plane permitted so long as there is no bodily contact

1933 if out-of-bounds space limited, guard must stay at least 3 feet away from opponent out of bounds

1939 either one or two hands may tie ball

1948 use of legs, arms, body, legal in guarding

1955 player may use two hands to tie ball in possession of another player

1960 ball may be tied with one or two hands

1962 player may tap or take ball from another player

G. Jump balls taken in center of nearest restraining circle

VII. **Out-of-Bounds**

1907 player not out-of-bounds if only one foot goes over line and is immediately brought back

1933 players encouraged to take balls out-of-bounds without waiting for whistle

1944 player taking ball out-of-bounds must enter court within three feet on either side of spot where ball is put back into play

1948 player out-of-bounds if any part of foot or body touches line; in playing ball in from out-of-bounds feet must be entirely behind the line

1953 playing ball in from out-of-bounds all parts of body must be behind boundary line until ball crosses line

1962 player without ball may run out-of-bounds provided return is approximately three feet from where he left court

1964 player without ball running out-of-bounds may re-enter at position not at an advantage (no longer restricted to three feet)

ceiling, apparatus, and obstruction over court are out-of-bounds

roving player, one guard and one forward initiated

VIII. **Center Jump and Center Throw**

1907 game started with toss between two center players who could bat or catch ball on jump

1914 catching ball not allowed on jump

1918 player jumping had to keep one hand behind and in contact with back

1926 hand behind back no longer required

1932   center throw-in to start game and quarters given equal emphasis with center toss up. Both optional
1934   no whistle required on center play unless time-in taken (general tendency to lessen unnecessary blowing of whistle)
1936   center jump eliminated; center throw-in official method; ball alternately awarded to teams during each quarter
1942   center throw awarded to team not scoring previous goal, still awarded alternately each quarter
1953   overtime periods started by jump ball
       tapping ball more than twice on jump ball a violation
       time-in commenced by jump ball thrown by referee
1956   time-in called on jump ball as soon as ball tapped by a player
1962   center throw may be made to forward or roving guard allowing either balanced or unbalanced court
1963   on center jump court may be balanced or unbalanced
1964   center jump replaces center throw as method of starting play each quarter

IX. **Violations**

1910   player with ball must be standing with body vertical
1911   body need not be vertical but player must stand on both feet when throwing ball
1923   handing, rolling, kicking ball are violations instead of fouls
1924   holding ball over three seconds and traveling with ball violations rather than fouls; penalty for violation is a throw-in from out-of-bounds by opposing team
1951   rolling or handing ball to another player becomes legal
1953   handing ball to another player illegal
       player may hold ball three seconds in-bounds
1956   three second lane violation
1959   player may touch or cross free throw lane boundaries during free throw
1960   on free throw ball must touch rim or enter basket
       failure to jump on toss-up when ordered by official a violation not a foul
1961   player may hand ball to teammate
1963   violation to extend arms sideward during free throw
1964   player may hold ball indefinitely if no opponent is within three feet
       player may hold ball five seconds if opponent is within three feet
       goal tending rule added (interference with ball on downward flight toward basket)
1966   teammates may not pass ball back and forth behind end line

player guarding opponent who is out of bounds must allow three feet of space to put ball in play. Repeated violation is a foul

no player may step on or over boundary line while guarding an opponent taking a throw-in

player guarding opponent who is out of bounds must allow three feet of space to put ball in play

1968 air dribble a violation

X. Fouls

1918 delaying game, snatching ball become technical fouls; other fouls used in modern play added later

holding, blocking, tripping, charging, pushing, and unnecessary roughness classified as personal fouls

1919 blocking carefully defined

1924 tagging defined

1930 obstruction defined

ingoing substitute for captain takes over all technical team fouls

1932 if forward was fouled in act of shooting and basket was made, goal counted and player awarded one free throw; if basket was missed forward awarded two free throws

1934 threatening the eyes of an opponent becomes a technical foul

1936 four personal fouls allowed instead of three before player disqualified

1949 captain not to have technical fouls charged against own disqualification

1951 coaching during time-out and at intermission permissible at or near coach's bench

1953 five personal fouls allowed before player disqualified

blocking defined as personal contact which impedes progress of an opponent who does not have the ball

after double foul ball put in play by center jump following last free throw

1955 overguarding a player without the ball becomes a foul

1959 foul for "boxing up" not called if player can shoot or pass

1960 foul for "boxing up" deleted from rules

1962 personal foul for spinning or pulling opponent off balance while tying the ball

interference with ball after a goal to delay throwing and gain an advantage considered a foul

foul for intentional fumble on center throw deleted

1964 during last two minutes of game and all overtime periods individual foul penalized by two free throws; if goal scored one free throw awarded

team fouls not counted toward disqualification of the team

1966 unsportsmanlike tactics given a more severe penalty;

free throw awarded and whether made or missed, ball
is given out-of-bounds at the division line to team
taking free throw

fouls on follow through in shot for goal no longer interfere with scoring of goal

coaching from side lines not a team foul

XI. **Free Throws**
1914   free throw must be taken by forward
1935   forward who is fouled must take free throw
1945   instead of free throw, optional to take throw-in from
        side line any time a foul is made during the game
1946   free throw, not throw-in, must be taken as award fol-
        lowing a foul
1949   in time-out during free throw shooting forward to take
        ball out on sideline whether basket made or missed
1953   ten seconds allowed from time referee places ball at
        free throw line or hands ball to player
1957   free throw lane widened to twelve feet
1959   ball in play after free throw missed. If made, awarded
        out-of-bounds at side line opposite free throw line
        to forward taking free throw
1962   players line-up in alternate positions on lanes.
        Each team has responsibility for one endline lane spot
1963   free throw taken at wrong basket repeated at correct
        basket
1964   free throw must be taken within free throw circle
1966   additional line mark adapted to assist players in posi-
        tioning for free throw

XII. **Time-Out**
1934   time-out within one minute or less of quarter time
        ends quarter and that time is added to following quarter
1935   rest time-out shortened from two minutes to one
1938   time-out not allowed between two free throws
1939   each team allowed three time-out periods for rest in-
        stead of two
1940   time-out for rest may be requested by any player not
        just captain
1949   time-out taken when foul is called until ball is put in
        play at sideline following a free throw
1953   time-out taken for jump balls; one additional time-out
        taken for each extra period of a tie game
1957   team time-outs increased to four
1959   time-out for free throws until ball touches ring or
        backboard, providing goal is not made
1960   time-in on unsuccessful free throw as soon as ball
        touches player on the court
        coach may call time-out
1964   team time-outs increased to five

XIII. **Substitutions**
1937   substitute going into game allowed to talk with team-
        mates before ball put in play

1939   two re-entries into game allowed each player

player may not re-enter the game during the same quarter in which he leaves the game

1940   player may go back into game during same quarter in which he leaves the game

1949   unlimited number of substitutions; no longer a requirement for substitute to report to referee or umpire; substitute to report only to scorekeeper

1953   substitute must report to scorekeeper and be recognized by official, except at intermission

1953-1959   substitutions made before free throw attempted

1962   substitutions allowed between two consecutive free throws

1963   substitutions no longer need to be recognized by official between quarters

1964   time-out for substitution may be taken any time ball is dead

XIV. **Scoring**

1907   two points awarded for field goals, one point for free throws

if forward was fouled in act of shooting for third time, team automatically received one point as well as free throw

1917   previous rule repealed

1921   one point awarded for field goals difficult to guard in a vertical plane, such as two-hand overhead shot, one-hand overhead shot, hook shot, shots made with player's back to basket and all one-hand shots

1932   two points awarded for all field goals because guards allowed to guard with arms in horizontal plane

1951   goal scored by player throwing ball into basket of opponent credited to opponents although not to a specific player

1961   after goal scored ball put in play from any point beyond end line

XV. **Tie Games**

1907   tie games continue until one team has two points more than opponents

1922   tie games stand as such

1953   tie games continue without change of baskets; first period two minutes long and additional periods two minutes long or less. Game terminates (1) if either team is ahead by one point *at the end of any period,* or (2) a team scores a total of two points after the first extra period

1954   tie games may stand by mutual agreement of captains before game starts

1964   sudden death eliminated—each extra period three minutes long with two minute intermission

2

CONDITIONING FOR
BASKETBALL

INTRODUCTION

Today, an unprecedented emphasis is placed on the development of highly skilled women athletes. There is an increasing need for participants to attain a state of maximal physical conditioning. An athlete must perform efficiently from the beginning of the game until the final seconds, and, if necessary, in overtime periods. Training programs, therefore, should be designed to develop the essential components of fitness, strength, flexibility, cardiorespiratory endurance, agility, balance, speed and power, if the basketball player is to display the best possible individual and team assets.

To attain a level of physical fitness, the body must undergo a series of physical, chemical and physiological changes. Muscles developed to a state of maximum size and efficiency use a minimal number of muscle fibers to accomplish an assigned task. Numerous fibers in a muscle contract to perform a movement and if any of them becomes fatigued additional fibers in the muscle continue to contract to complete the desired movement.

A well-designed strengthening program not only increases the bulk of a muscle but will simultaneously increase the number of capillaries that supply the muscle with "fuel," food and oxygen, and remove waste products. Chemically, fuel becomes more readily available and is stored in greater amounts, and the speed at which nerves are able to stimulate the muscle is increased. The circulatory system is more developed, increasing the volume of oxygen taken into the respiratory system, and oxygen is more abundant. Although the heart beat of a trained athlete may be slower, the increased stroke volume pumps a greater amount of blood throughout the body.

Year-Round Conditioning Program

In order to develop an athlete to a high level of physical efficiency, a year-round conditioning program should be devised and enforced. The year-round program may be divided into phases such as pre-season, early season, mid-season, late-season, and post-season exercises. Pre-season and post-season conditioning programs are more individualized while the early, mid- and late-season exercises are based on team needs.

The success of a conditioning program depends upon the willingness of the players to exert determination and self-discipline. Each player should be aware that she must be in excellent physical condition if she is to offer the greatest contribution to a team. There is an improvement in individual achievements and in the total game performance of the team when all players are in top physical condition.

Fatigue

Starting conditioning programs slowly helps to prevent fatigue, soreness, or any serious damage to muscles. Individuals sustaining muscular injuries or pain are often tempted to quit before giving the program an adequate trial. An individual who has been ill may be gradually reconditioned to top performance. During practice, sideline a player who shows signs of sluggishness or fatigue. If recovery is not evident within a few minutes, send the player home to rest. Continuing practice in a weakened state may be more harmful to the individual than the initial illness. When a player returns to competition following a serious illness, permission from a team doctor or a school nurse is necessary. With their consent the player may resume full practice and finally ease into the added stress of a game situation. It is the responsibility of the coach or athletic trainer to examine the player prior to daily practice. A satisfactory examination consists of checking temperature and pulse-rate and inquiring about fatigue symptoms.

Symptoms of Fatigue
1. Local tiredness in active muscles
2. General feeling of bodily tiredness
3. General feeling of sleepiness
4. Pain and soreness in muscles
5. Stiff joints
6. Dragging
7. Swollen hands and feet
8. Nausea, vomiting or profuse sweating
9. Pain in the abdomen
10. Pain in the back of the head

Staleness

Athletes sometimes encounter staleness, a condition related to fatigue. Staleness may result when an individual attempts to improve but unconsciously sets personal goals too high. When a plateau is reached and improvement is not readily observed the player becomes frustrated. The coach should prescribe a period of rest away from the sport after observing any symptoms of staleness.

Symptoms of Staleness
1. Player's performance does not improve
2. General feeling of tiredness
3. Restlessness
4. Inability to sleep well
5. Sleep does not refresh the individual
6. Nightmares
7. Loss of appetite
8. Loss of weight
9. Disturbed digestion
10. Constipation
11. Sunken eyes
12. Dark rings under the eyes
13. Occasional headaches
14. Back pains
15. Paleness and coldness of extremities
16. Poor muscular control and balance
17. Slow return of pulse rate to normal and a rapid rise of the pulse rate
18. Low blood pressure

EXERCISES FOR A CONDITIONING PROGRAM

It is imperative for the coach and players to faithfully adhere to the conditioning program. Through various methods the coach must communicate to team members a deep belief in the benefits of a healthy body. Both high school and college players desire a program in which they can believe, thus the coach's methods must be effective and of obvious benefit to the students. Players who are convinced of the necessity of the program will exert maximal effort to achieve a well-toned body. The coach should motivate students by continually recognizing improvement and offering encouragement. As soon as the results become apparent to teammates, they will consistently reinforce one another in the conditioning program.

Flexibility Exercises

Flexibility, the stretching ability of a muscle, aids in muscular efficiency and increases its range of motion. The following exercises develop flexibility in the legs, hips, lower back, upper back and arms. SP indicates starting positions; EX indicates exercise.

Leg Flexibility (Stretching)
1. *Straddle Sit and Leg Bounce*
   SP: Sitting—legs apart, knees extended

FIGURE 2–1   Closed pike bounce.

      EX: Bend the trunk down and forward, touch the chest to the right leg and reach for the right foot with both hands. Repeat with the left leg. Until the muscles have been properly conditioned, avoid bouncing to touch the chest to the legs.

2. *Closed Pike Bounce*
      SP: Sitting position—legs together and flat on the floor, toes pointed.
      EX: Bring the arms forward, elbows extended, then slowly touch the chest to the legs.

3. *Straddle Lean*
      SP: Stand, side stride position—feet approximately eighteen inches apart, hands on hips
      EX: Keep the upper back straight and the head up, bend the trunk forward as far as possible. Avoid bending the knees.

4. *Straddle Jump*
      SP: Standing—feet together
      EX: Jump in the air, simultaneously lifting the legs to the sides. Keep the head up, the trunk straight and reach up, as though catching a ball for a rebound. Land with the feet together.

5. *Bleacher Stretch*
      SP: Stand on the left leg—place the right foot on a bleacher step
      EX: Extend the elbows forward, grasp the right ankle with the hands and place the chest on the right leg. Keep the right knee extended throughout the movement. Repeat using the left leg. For variety, move the supporting

FIGURE 2-2 Bleacher stretch.

leg further back and the upper leg to a lower bleacher step.

6. *Front Scale*
SP: Tall standing position—feet together
EX: Keep the back straight, the head up, arms raised side-

FIGURE 2-3   Front scale.

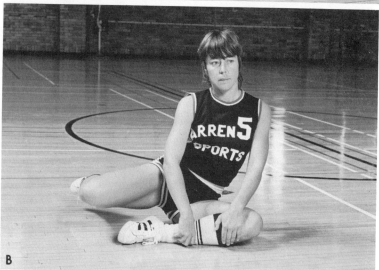

FIGURE 2–4 Pretzel sit. Leg lifts.

ward; lean forward and lift the left leg backward and upward to a position parallel with the floor. The right leg and left knee are alternately extended.

Hip Flexibility

1. *Pretzel Sit and Leg Lifts*
   SP: Pretzel sit
   EX: Lift the back leg off the floor as high in the air as possible, extend the back leg to the side and then return to the original position. Repeat with the opposite leg.

2. *Heel Reach*
   SP: Standing—feet shoulder width apart
   EX: Turn the trunk to the left, keep the hips in a stationary position and reach back toward the right heel with both hands. Focus the eyes on the right heel. Hold the position for five seconds. Repeat to the right.

3. *Side Bends*
   SP: Standing—feet shoulder width apart, arms raised above the head
   EX: Flex the spine laterally to the left while reaching toward the left and down with both arms. A stretching sensation should be apparent in the upper rib area on the right side of the body. Repeat to the right.

FIGURE 2–5   Heel reach.

FIGURE 2-6   Pretzel bend.

Lower Back
1. *Pretzel Bend*
   SP: Supine lying—arms extended, palms on the floor
   EX: Lift the feet upward and over the head, touching the
        toes to the floor above the head. Throughout the exer-
        cise, maintain the knees in an extended position and the
        hands in contact with the floor.
2. *Chest Lift*
   SP: Prone lying—arms at side, palms up, legs straight and
        together
        Raise the chest and shoulders off the floor as high as
        possible, hold for five seconds. Keep the head in line
        with the spine, the eyes focused on the floor and the
        shoulder blades pulled together. (Aids in developing
        back strength.)
3. *Thigh Lift*
   SP: Prone lying—arms at side, palms up, legs extended and
        together
   EX: Raise the chest and shoulders off the floor as high as
        possible and hold for five seconds. The pelvis should re-
        main in contact with the floor. (Also develops strength in
        the lower back and thighs.)
Upper Back
1. *Straddle-Lean Scapula Pull*
   SP: Standing—legs in side-stride position, hands on hips
   EX: Bend forward and down as far as possible, pulling the
        scapula toward the spine. The back and legs should re-
        main straight.

FIGURE 2-7   Chest lift.

2. *Tailor-Sitting Arm Lift*
   SP: Tall sitting position—legs crossed in tailor position, hands on back of neck, elbows shoulder level
   EX: A partner standing behind places the lateral side of his lower leg against the spine and slowly lifts the sitting partner's arms as high as possible.

FIGURE 2-8   Thigh lift.

3. *Arm Circle*

SP: Standing—feet shoulder width apart, arms shoulder level, elbows extended

EX: Circle the arms forward using the shoulder joint as the pivot. Progressively increase the size of the circle.

Strength Exercises

Strength exercises, designed to tone or strengthen the muscles of the body, are more beneficial when combined with flexibility exercises. The following strength exercises are for parts of the body requiring additional strength for improving basketball skill.

Arm and Shoulder Strength

1. *Wall Push-ups*

SP: Stand two feet from a wall—feet flat on the floor, elbows extended forward, place finger tips and thumbs on the wall

EX: Keep the body straight, flex the elbows and lean toward the wall. Try to touch the chest to the wall, then return

FIGURE 2–9 Wall push-ups.

the body to the starting position by extending the elbows. (Also increases ankle flexibility.)

2. *Modified Push-ups*

SP: Prone lying—elbows and knees flexed, hands on floor at mid-chest position

EX: Extend the elbows until the arms are straight and the body weight rests on the hands and knees. Return to the starting position by flexing the elbows.

3. *Modified Finger Tip Push-up*

SP: Same as modified push-ups except the pads of the thumbs and fingers are placed on the floor

EX: Perform the same as modified push-ups.

4. *Push-ups*

SP: Prone lying—elbows flexed, hands on floor at mid-chest position, toes resting on floor

EX: Extend the elbows until the arms are straight and the weight of the body rests on the hands and toes. The body and head stay in a straight line throughout the

FIGURE 2–10   Pull-ups.

movement. Flex the elbows to return to starting position.

5. *Pull-ups*
   SP: Long hanging position—palms turned toward body. Adjust height of bar so that the feet may be lifted six inches from the ground
   EX: Flex the arms and elbows, raise the body until the chin is over the bar. Slowly return to long hanging position. Repeat the exercise with the palms facing away from the body.

6. *Wall Pass*
   SP: Stand in a front stride position holding a basketball—face the wall, extend elbows forward until the hands are approximately six inches from the wall
   EX: Push the basketball repeatedly against the wall, flexing the arms and completely extending the elbows on each pass.

7. *Door Isometrics*
   SP: Stand in the center of a doorway—place the back of the hands against the frame at hip level
   EX: Push sideward and upward for six seconds, then re-

FIGURE 2–11 Door isometrics.

lease. Variations: (1) Repeat the exercise with the palms resting on the door frame above waist level. Push sideways. (2) Repeat the exercise with the palms against the door frame above the head. Push sideways.

Wrist Strength

1. *Volleying*
   SP: Stand approximately two feet in front of a wall—hold a basketball above the head
   EX: Use the wrists and finger tips to volley the ball against the wall. Individuals who have weak wrists should begin with a volleyball, progress to a soccer ball and then a basketball.

2. *Medicine Ball Passing*
   SP: Stand approximately seven to ten feet in front of a partner
   EX: Chest pass the medicine ball back and forth.

3. *Low Dribble*
   SP: Knees bent—head up, feet forward stride position, trunk inclined forward, body balanced
   EX: Dribble the ball for two minutes using the right hand and keeping the ball as close to the floor as possible. Repeat with the left hand.

4. *Hand Squeeze*
   SP: Standing—feet shoulder width apart, hands in a fist in front of chest
   EX: Squeeze the hands, hold for six seconds. Variation: Repeat the exercise holding tennis balls.

Abdominal Strength

1. *Sit-ups*
   SP: Hook lying position—hands behind the head. (A player with weak abdominals may fold the arms in front of the body and have a partner hold her feet.)
   EX: Curl upward to a sitting position by slowly lifting the head, the upper back and lower back from the floor. Return to the starting position with the lower back touching the floor first followed by the upper back and the head. Keep the chin on the chest when the body is moving.

2. *V-Sit (or Jack Knife)*
   SP: Sitting position—palms placed on floor next to hips
   EX: Raise the feet from the floor and simultaneously reach toward the toes with the fingers. Hold five seconds then return to the starting position. Variations: Extend elbows to the side and parallel to floor.

3. *L-Lift*
   SP: Hang from a pull-up bar—palms face body
   EX: Raise the legs until the body forms an "L" with the legs parallel to the floor. Players who are unable to perform the exercise may lift the legs to a tuck position, then extend the knees to the "L" position.

A

B

C

FIGURE 2-12   V-Sit.

FIGURE 2-13   L-Lift.

Leg Strength and Power Development
1. *Run in Place*
   SP: Standing—feet together
   EX: Run in place lifting each knee to the chest. Variation: Repeat the same exercise with weights attached to the ankles.
2. *Toe Raises (Heel Lifts)*
   SP: Standing—feet together
   EX: Raise the heels from the floor standing on toes, then lower heels but do not allow heels to touch the floor. (Also helps strengthen the ankles.)
3. *Tuck Jumps*
   SP: Standing—feet together, hands on hips
   EX: Jump in the air, simultaneously tucking the knees to the chest and wrapping the arms around them.
4. *Wall Sit*
   SP: Sitting—back placed against a flat surface—thighs and back form a right angle
   EX: Hold the sitting position for 30 to 60 seconds.
5. *Bench Step-ups*
   SP: Standing—face a two foot bench or a bleacher step

FIGURE 2–14   Heel lifts.

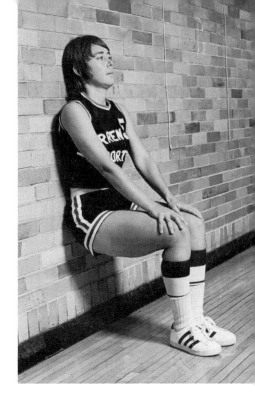

FIGURE 2–15   Wall sit.

EX: Step up with the right leg, fully extending the body, then step down. Repeat with the left leg.

6. *Side Bench Step-up*
   SP: Standing—right side of the body facing a two-foot bench
   EX: Step on the bench with the right leg, extend the body and place the left foot on the bench. Then step down on the opposite side of the bench, right leg first followed by the left. Repeat stepping with the left leg leading the movement and stepping to the left.

7. *Jumping*
   SP: Standing—feet slightly apart.
   EX: Jump in the air as high as possible. Repeat with a partner resisting the jump by pressing down on the shoulders. (Also improves agility.)

8. *Bear Hug*
   SP: Standing—feet slightly apart
   EX: Lunge forward diagonally, the arms around the thigh. Repeat with the opposite leg.

9. *Squat Thrusts*
   SP: Standing—hands on hips
   EX: Lower the body to a squat position, place the hands on the floor and simultaneously extend the legs backward. Return to the squat position and finish in the original standing position.

10. *Treadmill*
    SP: Runner start

EX: Run in place from the starting position until completing a full leg rotation.

11. *Jump Rope*
    SP: Standing—feet together, arms raised sideward and parallel to the floor
    EX: Jump in the air, circle the arms and land on the balls of the feet each time the rope travels under them.

12. *Hill Climb*
    SP: Standing at the bottom of a hill
    EX: Sprint up the hill and back down. Variation: Sprint up and down the bleachers.

Ankle Strength

1. *Walk*
    SP: Standing—weight on the outside of the feet
    EX: Walk around the gymnasium with the weight on the outer edges of the feet.

2. *Flex and Extend Feet*
    SP: Long sitting—legs together, knees extended
    EX: Point the toes toward the body then in the opposite direction.

3. *Foot Resisters*
    SP: Long sitting—legs together, partner holding the outside of each foot
    EX: Push against the hand of the partner. Variation: Repeat the exercise with the partner holding the top of each foot, medial side of the foot, and the ball of the foot.

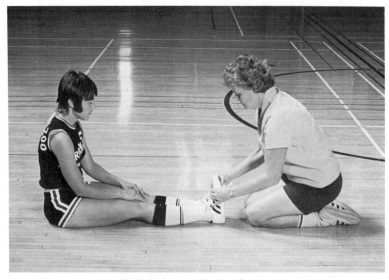

FIGURE 2–16   Foot resisters.

Agility Exercises

Agility, the ability to move quickly in all directions, is essential for any basketball player who strives to be physically fit and contribute fully to a team. A player lacking agility is in poor condition for receiving a pass, evading opponents, or intercepting passes. The following exercises, designed to improve agility, lead to more successful game participation.

Jumping Series

1. *Forward and Backward Jumping*
   SP: Standing—feet together, hands on hips
   EX: Jump forward and backward with a smooth continuous action, feet leaving the ground and landing at the same time.
2. *Side to Side Jumping*
   SP: Standing—feet together, hands on hips
   EX: Same as exercise 2, except jump from side to side.
3. *Standing Long Jump*
   SP: Standing—feet together, arms at sides
   EX: Bend the knees, throw the arms forward to assist in jumping as far forward as possible. Leave the ground and land with feet together.

Shuffle Series

1. *Lateral Shuffle*
   SP: Standing—feet slightly apart
   EX: Step laterally to the right with the right foot, place the left foot beside the right and transfer the weight to the left foot. Repeat several times then reverse direction.
2. *Diagonal Shuffle*
   SP: Standing—feet slightly apart
   EX: Same as the lateral shuffle except the movement is performed diagonally forward or backward.

Sprint Series

1. *Sprint and Stop*
   SP: Standing—feet slightly apart
   EX: Run forward as fast as possible, stop. Repeat the action.
2. *Sprint, Stop and Jump*
   SP: Standing—feet slightly apart
   EX: Run forward, stop and jump as high as possible. Repeat the action.
3. *Backward Run*
   SP: Standing—feet slightly apart
   EX: Run backward looking over the right shoulder. Repeat the exercise looking over the left shoulder.
4. *Diagonal Backward Run*
   SP: Standing—feet slightly apart
   EX: Run three to five steps diagonally backward to the right, pivot on the right foot and change directions. Run three to five steps diagonally left and pivot on the left foot.

Hop Series
1. *Forward Hop*
   SP: Standing on one foot—hands on hips
   EX: Hop around the outside of the basketball court. Repeat
        the exercise using the other foot. Variation: Same posi-
        tion, hop backward.
2. *Sideward Hop*
   SP: Standing on right foot—right side facing in the direction
        the body will move
   EX: Hop sideward to the right around the outside of the
        basketball court. Repeat using the left foot and hopping
        to the left.

Run Series and Jump Rope
1. *Supine Run*
   SP: Supine lying—top of head pointed in the direction of
        the intended run
   EX: Turn over on the right or left side, stand and start run-
        ning rapidly. Variation: Repeat the exercise with a
        diagonal or forward run, or a combination of move-
        ments such as a backward run, a jump to a squat posi-
        tion and a diagonal run.
2. *Coach's Hand Signal Drill*
   SP: Standing on endline
   EX: Run forward until the coach uses a hand signal indi-
        cating a directional change. Signals may indicate a for-
        ward or backward run, diagonal jump up, or shuffle to
        the right or left.
3. *Shuttle Run*
   SP: Standing on endline
   EX: Run forward five yards and run back to the starting line,
        turn around and run ten yards forward, returning to
        touch the starting line. Run fifteen yards forward and
        return to the starting line. Variation: In the gymnasium
        players may run from the endline to the top of the
        closest circle, to the center line, to the top of the oppo-
        site circle and the opposite endline, returning after each
        run to touch the starting point on the endline.
4. *Reverse Turn and Run*
   SP: Stand in one corner of a basketball court
   EX: Sprint forward to the first corner, stop, plant the inside
        foot and turn backward to face the second corner and
        run to it. Repeat the reverse turn in each corner then
        run the course in the opposite direction.
5. *Mirror Drill*
   SP: Standing—face a partner
   EX: Shuffle laterally to the right or left, stop quickly, then
        shuffle in the opposite direction, stopping and starting
        several times. Partner watches the waist and attempts to
        duplicate the movement.
6. *Jump Rope*
   SP: Standing

      EX: A. Jump forward over a rope with feet together.
            B. Jump forward and backward.
            C. Jump sideward.
            Inexperienced students may practice jumping without the rope.

7. *Four Corner Run*
    SP: Standing in one corner of the basketball court
    EX: Sprint forward to the second corner, shuffle, run across to the third, backward run to the fourth and shuffle run back to starting place. The four corners of either the entire basketball court or half-court may be used.

Speed and Endurance

Speed and endurance are the products of training that improves cardiovascular fitness by increasing the ability of the body to consume and utilize oxygen and dispose of waste products. Perform the following list of exercises at least four times a week.

Speed and Endurance Exercises (Training)

1. *Jog.* Jog with heel-toe foot placement ½ mile in five minutes. Increases the distance to 1½ miles within the first three weeks. Gradually reduce the time required to jog the distance and begin running on the balls of the feet. Attempt to run the distance at an even pace. In four to five weeks jog the first quarter mile to warm up, run the mile in eight minutes or less then jog a quarter mile to recover.

2. *Sprint.* Sprint three 50 yard dashes with a two minute recovery period between each dash. Gradually reduce the recovery period to one minute or less. When the pulse rate returns to 120 beats per minute (30 beats per 15 seconds) after sprinting, increase the number of dashes and distance to be run to 150 to 220 yards.

3. *Sprint Stop.* Sprint forward and stop. Alternate stopping and starting for a distance of 75 yards.

4. *Shuttle Runs.* See Page 32, exercise number 3.

5. *Hill Sprint.* Sprint up a hill or the bleachers.

6. *Jump Rope.* Jump rope for two minutes with feet together.

7. *Run in Place.* Run in place for six to 10 minutes without stopping.

8. *Grassroot Drill.* Jog around the outside edge of a basketball court or a track and *between* each exercise. While the players are jogging, the coach gives commands such as shuffle backward, push-up, grapevine-run right, or treadmill. Players stop jogging, perform the exercise, and immediately return to jogging.

Pre-Season Program

The pre-season exercise program is divided into the fitness areas described previously on page 13. Primarily its objective is to condition the individual before the additional stress of a game situation is encountered.

Flexibility

1. Straddle Sit Bounce—bounce slowly toward each leg four times, three repetitions
2. Closed Pike Bounce—10 repetitions
3. Pretzel Bends—hold for six seconds, three repetitions
4. Pretzel Sit Leg Lifts—two repetitions on each side of the body
5. Chest Lifts—three repetitions
6. Thigh Lifts—three repetitions
7. Arm Circles—10 repetitions forward and 10 repetitions backward.

Strength

1. Sit-ups—25 to 50
2. Wall Push-Ups or Modified Finger Tip Push-Ups—15 to 25
3. Wall Sit—hold 30 to 45 seconds, two repetitions
4. Pull-Ups—underhand grip, as many as possible. Repeat using the overhand grip
5. Heel Lifts
6. Heel Lifts using ankle weights

Agility

1. Jump Series
   A. Jump forward and backward with both feet for 30 seconds.
   B. Alternately jump to the left and right sides with both feet for 30 seconds.
2. Sprint Series
   A. Run backward for 50 yards.
   B. Run five steps diagonally backward to the right, then five steps to the left. Repeat for 30 yards.
   C. Run five steps diagonally forward to the left, plant the outside foot, change direction quickly then run five steps diagonally to the right following the same procedure. Repeat for 50 yards.
   D. Spring forward, stop and start as quickly as possible for 50 yards.
   E. Sprint forward, stop quickly and jump as high as possible. Repeat five times in 50 yards.
3. Shuffle Series
   A. Shuffle diagonally forward.
   B. Shuffle diagonally backward.
   C. Shuffle laterally to the right and left.
   D. Shuffle run 30 yards to the right and 30 yards to the left.
   E. Shuttle run touching four lines within 30 yards.

Speed and Endurance

1. Jog ½ mile—pre-season goal should be to increase the distance to 1½ miles within the first three weeks. See exercise 1, page 33 for procedure.
2. Sprint 50 yards—three repetitions with a two-minute recovery period between each sprint. The length of the recovery period may be longer at the beginning of the program; however,

players should strive to reduce the recovery period and simultaneously increase the distance.

3. Stretching—exercises such as the straddle lean, heel reach, side bend or toe touch should be performed after each jog or sprint.

Early Season Program

Flexibility
1. Straddle Sit Bounces—four toward each leg, three repetitions
2. Arm Circles—50 repetitions forward and backward
3. Pretzel Bend—work up to 10 repetitions
4. Pretzel Sit Leg Lifts—three repetitions on each side of the body.
5. Straddle Jump—three repetitions

Strength
1. Low Dribble—two minutes with each hand
2. Wall Volley—30 to 60 seconds
3. Wall Pass—30 to 60 seconds
4. Modified Push-Ups—15 to 25 repetitions
5. Modified Finger Tip Push-Ups—15 ro 25 repetitions
6. Bench Step-Up—facing the bench, 30 to 60 seconds
7. Side Bench Step-Up—30 to 60 seconds
8. Foot Resisters—hold for six seconds on each exercise. Three repetitions.

Agility
1. Jump Rope—60 to 120 seconds
2. Mirror Drill—20 to 30 seconds
3. Shuttle Run—two to three repetitions
4. Sprint Series—length of the gymnasium
5. Shuffle Series—length of the gymnasium
6. Hand direction drill by the coach
7. Supine Run—two repetitions
8. Four Corner Run—two repetitions

Speed and Endurance
1. Spring-step forward the length of a basketball court, run backward the same distance. Two repetitions
2. Run in place eight minutes or run 10 dashes of 30 to 40 yards
3. Scrimmage five to seven minutes without stopping

Mid-Season

By mid-season a team is in good physical condition and will need only a few of the exercises in each series to maintain fitness.

Flexibility
1. Straddle Lean—four bounces, three repetitions
2. Heel Reach—four times to each heel, three repetitions
3. Closed Pike Bounce—10 repetitions

Strength
1. Wall Volley—use the backboard and perform team formation for two minutes. Count the number of times the ball is volleyed before a miss occurs.

Agility
1. Mirror Drill—30 seconds
2. Grassroot Drill—two to five minutes
3. Shuttle Run—three to four repetitions

Speed and Endurance
1. Bleacher Run—two repetitions with no rest period
2. Scrimmage—eight to 10 minutes with no rest period

Late Season

Late season training requires few exercises for maintaining strength, agility, speed or endurance; however, flexibility is quickly lost if a planned exercise program is not continued.

Flexibility
1. Bleacher Stretch—four bounces on each leg, three repetitions
2. Pretzel Bends—10 repetitions
3. Straddle Bounce—four on each leg, three repetitions

Strength
Strength exercises may be individually assigned if it is necessary to strengthen a specific section of the body.

Agility
1. Shuttle Run—four times each practice session
2. Grassroot Drill—once or twice a week

Speed and Endurance
1. Scrimmage—10 to 15 minutes with no rest periods

Post Season

1. Players should rest for at least three weeks after the season is over
2. A few exercises from each fitness category can be followed. Begin light practice sessions
3. Player should jog one to two miles daily. Run several 50 to 100 yard sprints along with jogging
4. Participation in other sports should be encouraged
5. Players should rest for two weeks prior to the pre-season training program
6. A weight training program on the Universal Gym Set may be started

BODY CONTROL

INTRODUCTION

One of the most difficult aspects to develop in basketball is the ability to control the body in all situations, such as accelerating rapidly, stopping without traveling, jumping to maximal height, and keeping the body in balance. A player skilled in running, pivoting, turning, faking, and jumping is usually well coordinated and may learn subsequent techniques more readily. Body control skills do not seem to provide the same motivation or pleasure as activities practiced with the basketball. Therefore, players find it necessary to exert more self-discipline in acquiring them. Practice sessions may be more enjoyable if the teacher or coach strives to excite and challenge the players with a variety of drills and provides them with an appreciation for a highly coordinated body.

Relaxation and balance

Relaxation and balance, the two most important elements of body control, provide a player with the ability to execute any skill requiring speed. Relaxation is important because a player who cannot relax on the court will often be unduly tense, consequently lowering the efficiency of the neuromuscular system and hindering performance. Good balance is essential for reacting and executing a move quickly. Both offensive and defensive players frequently need to rely on the fast reaction proper balance allows in attaining a more strategic position. Although running speed is an asset, fast reaction time and quickness, the ability to accelerate rapidly, are even more advantageous in a game situation. Since the defensive player must react to the movements of the offensive player, a quick start gives the offensive player the advantage. On the other hand, a quick defensive player who makes a mistake often has sufficient time to recover and assume a proper guarding position.

To accelerate rapidly the principles of balance and body control should be observed:
1. Weight is equally distributed on both feet;
2. Weight is on the balls of the feet and the base of the toes;
3. Slight forward lean of the body;
4. Head up;
5. Arms relaxed.

A balanced position may be obtained by spreading the feet in a slightly forward stride stance with the weight equally distributed over the balls of the feet and the base of the toes. Flex the knees in a semi-crouched position with the shoulders slightly forward, the head up, and the arms relaxed and away from the body. React quickly without disturbing the balance of the body by shuffling the feet forward, sidewards, and backwards without taking long steps. In defensive play move the arms to discourage passing, to block passes and shots, and to steal the ball when the opponent dribbles.

BODY CONTROL IN GAME SITUATIONS

Change of Direction

Change of direction is an elusive technique often utilized by an offensive player. To execute a change of direction while running the player forcefully plants the outside foot, simultaneously bends the knees and lowers the hips, and turns the inside foot in the direction the play will go. The player pushes off with the outside foot and shifts weight in the direction of the inside foot. In other words, a player moving to the right shifts weight to the right foot, bends the knees, pushes off with the right foot and executes a quick long step to the left followed by short running steps. Maximal running speed is achieved within the first few steps after every change of direction.

Change of Pace

A change of pace that varies running speed every few steps is a valuable offensive tactic. Players who possess the ability to move quickly or slow the pace, who can stop without losing their balance or telegraphing their intentions to their opponent will more likely be able to elude their opponents and obtain scoring opportunities.

Cutting

A thorough discussion of running strategy must include cutting, a technique combining change of direction and change of pace.

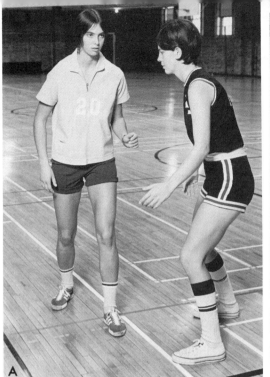

FIGURE 3–1 Player demonstrating change of direction.

Offensively, the two purposes of a cut are to enable a forward to evade a guard in order to receive the ball and dribble toward the basket and to provide a forward with an opportunity to establish a play for a teammate. Four methods of cutting are the straight cut, the reverse cut, the criss-cross or scissors cut, and the pick and roll cut. Players should begin with the simplest method, the straight cut, and practice the skills involved until each is performed effectively. The straight cut depends upon speed or running the defensive player into a teammate in order to free the player with the ball. An effective method of executing the straight cut is to use the change of direction maneuver with a player running in one direction quickly shifting to another, hopefully leaving the opponent behind or away from the intended pass.

The reverse cut is a technique in which the forward and defensive player move in the same path toward the ball; however, the forward quickly turns and travels in the opposite direction. Defensive players guarding too closely set up ideal situations for using the reverse cut.

Cutting patterns related to definite offensive strategy include the criss-cross or scissors and the pick and roll. The criss-cross, the most effective cut, involves a pivot player offense with one player cutting off a teammate. For example, two offensive players criss-cross around a teammate in the pivot-post position. The first forward cuts off the hip of the pivot-post, while the second forward cuts off the opposite hip of the first forward and the pivot-post (Figure 3-3).

The pick and roll is used most frequently against player-to-player defense (See chapter on offense). The cutter establishes a screen on the guard of a teammate, the teammate dribbles past the

FIGURE 3-2 The reverse cut.

FIGURE 3–3   The criss-cross.

screen, the cutter rolls, blocking the guard, and cuts in a direction to receive a pass (Figure 3-4).

In any method of cutting, if the teammate with the ball fails to make a pass, the player executing the cut continues the pattern until another cutting position is achieved. Avoid initiating cutting patterns until a teammate is in position to pass the ball.

Stopping

In girls' basketball the violation called most often seems to be traveling, or failure to stop correctly. An offensive player receiving the ball on the move should first transfer weight to the rear foot and then to the base of support over both feet. Shifting weight over the base of support assists the player in maintaining balance. Theoretically, the faster a player runs the lower the weight is transferred as she comes to a stop.

Running stride stop

The running stride stop (one-two stop) is the most natural and commonly performed stop. Its use is determined by the player's speed and by the intended action after the player stops. The stop is executed by placing one foot down firmly and stopping on the second step. The two steps allow a player additional time to gain

FIGURE 3-4 Pick and roll.

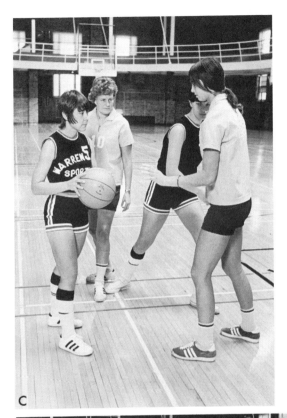

FIGURE 3–4 Continued.

FIGURE 3–5   Running stride stop.

control of the body and maintain balance by placing the hips midway between both feet (Figure 3-5). Technically, any type of offensive maneuver can be executed by a player with the ball, using the rear foot as a pivot foot.

Jump stop

The jump stop is most effective when the player moves at a slower speed or when the choice of either foot as the pivot foot is desired. In the jump stop the player's feet leave the ground and return simultaneously, with body weight absorbed in the heels as they contact the floor. The knees are flexed and the follow-through brings the center of gravity low and over both feet (Figure 3-6).

DRILL

1. Form a large circle covering the length of the gymnasium and allow each individual sufficient room to move. Concentrate on running and changing pace. All the players start running slowly, gradually increasing and alternating speed.

2. Use verbal signals to change the direction in which the players are running; for example, left, right, backward, forward.

3. Indicate a change of pace with verbal signals; for example, run, walk, trot.

4. Add a stopping technique to the running patterns by giving the players a verbal or whistle command to stop. Each player

FIGURE 3–6 Jump stop.

counts the number of steps required to stop. To test reaction time signal the group to run, have someone call jump stop or one-two stop and then give the cue to stop.

5. Have each player observe a partner to determine whether or not she travels in the act of stopping.

6. Place a leader in front of the group. The players imitate the leader's actions, or follow her verbal commands or hand signals.

7. Have the players assume a prone position at one end of the gymnasium. On a signal each player quickly stands and runs until the signal to stop is given.

8. Set up a sequence the players must follow, such as run, change of direction to left, change of pace to slow walk, and jump stop. On a signal, each skill is performed in succession.

Pivot

Although the rules of basketball state that it is illegal to progress in any direction while holding the ball inbounds, a player may change body position by pivoting. In pivoting a player holding the ball may step one or more times in any direction with the same foot while the other foot, the pivot, remains fixed to the floor. The player's previous action officially determines the pivot foot. Either foot is legal when the player comes to a standstill on the first step of a two-step stop or catches the ball from a stationary position or a jump stop. Only the rear foot may pivot when a player catches the ball and comes to a two-step stop

45

following a run, a dribble, or an air dribble. Frequently the pivot is performed by a closely guarded player who attempts to protect the ball or elude a guard prior to shooting for the basket or stopping for a dribble.

Although each type of pivot, the rear, front and reverse, has a specific purpose, the mechanics of performance are similar. The player bends both knees, places the weight of the body on the pivot foot, leans the head and shoulders into the turn, and assumes a new position as quickly as possible. The back of the body leads the body backward in a rear pivot, the front of the body initiates the forward movement in the front pivot.

Rear pivot

Generally, the *rear pivot* is used by an offensive player whose forward motion is impeded by a defensive player. The player establishes a pivot foot then swings the other foot to the rear or to an open area away from the defensive player. The ball is protected by keeping the body low, the feet shoulder width apart and the elbows spread. When a forward is guarded too closely from the front she can easily perform a screen pass by a half pivot to the rear and passing to a trailing teammate. If the defensive player is

FIGURE 3–7   Rear pivot.

exceptionally close an offensive player may occasionally use the rear pivot as an evasive tactic. Pivoting may also clear an area for a pass. The offensive player maneuvers the guard away from the area where the ball will be passed then pivots into the area.

Front pivot

The front pivot enables an offensive player to protect the ball when the defensive player is approaching from the side. The player pivots on the foot away from the approaching guard, shifts the other foot forward and turns her back toward the defensive player. When the defensive player is directly in front of the offensive player the front pivot should be avoided. The principle difference between the rear and front pivot is in the direction that the moving foot and body will travel.

Reverse pivot

The reverse pivot is an offensive tactic that enables a player to evade an opponent, cut toward the basket or receive a pass. A reverse pivot is most effective when a player has her back to the basket after an unexpected stop. When a guard is near, the post player pushes off with the pivot foot, the foot closest to the defensive player, turns and rolls toward the basket while taking a long deep step toward the basket with the opposite foot. The reverse turn is often successfully used by: (1) an offensive player without the ball who is guarded too closely. The forward feints

FIGURE 3–8 Front pivot.

FIGURE 3–9   Reverse pivot.

reception of a pass, reverse turns and moves toward the basket to receive the ball; (2) a defensive player to elude the offense; and (3) a guard in a switching player-to-player defense who has been blocked by a screen. The pivot, reverse turn, fake, change of direction, change of pace, run and stop seem to be even more successful when combined in efficient and deceptive patterns that conceal a player's plan of action.

DRILLS

1. Have the students in mass formation with or without the ball. On a command given by a leader the entire group pivots in the manner indicated. Commands include: *right-rear* or *right-front*, a pivot on the right foot to the back or front; *left-rear* or *left-front*, a pivot on left foot to the back or front.

2. Station the students in pairs along the sideline of the court. The first person in each line, player 1, stands approximately three feet in front of the person who is second in line, player 2. Player 1 pivots, 2 runs past the right side of 1, receives the hand-off, jump stops, and pivots. The jump stop places 2 ahead of 1 who runs past the left side of 2 for a hand-off, jump stop and pivot. (Figure 3-1.)

3. Set up practice situations in which the students practice pivots from all possible angles. For example, to practice the half turn divide the group into parallel columns facing the center of the court. Player 1, the first person in each line, dribbles 12 feet toward the center of the court, executes a rear pivot to face 2, the second person in line, then passes to 2. Each person repeats the drill until

△ or ▲   Offensive player

      ▲   Offensive player's previous position

☐ or ■   Defensive player

      ▤   Defensive player's previous position

●→ or ●   Ball's final position

⊘→ or ⊘   Ball's previous position

·········   Path of the ball

‒ ‒ ‒ ‒ ‒   Path of a player without the ball

〰〰〰   Path of a player with the ball, indicating dribbling

✕   Extra player to set ball in motion

⟶   Direction of motion

▶   Pivot

An explanation of the symbols used in the diagram of this book is given in this chart.

DIAGRAM 3–1 **Pivot and jump stop drill for partners.**
DIAGRAM 3–2 **Drill for pivoting from all angles.**

every member of the squad has practiced the half turn. After the players successfully perform the right rear pivot and the left rear pivot, practice front pivots.

4. Reinforce the skills of pass receiving, pivoting, and stopping by practicing a three-corner pivot drill. Students are arranged in three lines forming a triangle with considerable distance between lines. The first player in line one starts the drill by passing to the first player in line two, who runs to meet the pass, receives the ball, stops immediately without dribbling, and pivots to the right.

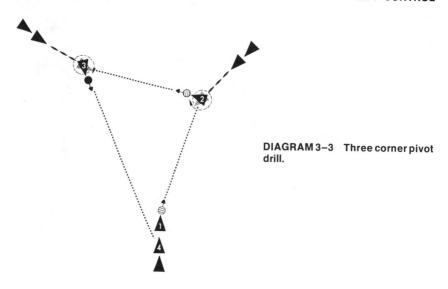

DIAGRAM 3-3   Three corner pivot drill.

Player 2 passes to the first person in line three who executes the same movements as the previous player. Continue in the same manner around the triangle until each student performs the drill (Figure 3-3).

5. The four-corner drill combines the pivot and dribble. Arrange the group in four lines 20 feet apart and facing the center of a square. The first player in each line dribbles the ball into the center of the square, jump stops, rear pivots, and passes the ball to the person at the front of the line. After completing the drill, players move clockwise around the square to the end of the next line. The same drill may also be practiced counterclockwise. There is less confusion if all four players dribble into the center of the square at the same time.

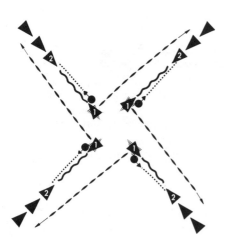

DIAGRAM 3-4   Four corner pivot drill.

Feinting

The feint, involving faking movement in one direction then shifting to another, is useful to players with or without the ball. A fake is used to place a player in the clear for a dribble, pass, cut or shot at the goal. A closely guarded forward takes a step toward the basket while retaining most of the weight on the rear foot, then quickly transfers all the weight to the rear foot in order to receive a pass. If the guard fails to shift with the fake the forward transfers weight to the forward foot and cuts toward the goal. Unusually successful feints include feinting toward the player with the ball then cutting toward the basket for a pass. Faking tiredness until the guard relaxes then cutting rapidly into the open, or refraining from raising the arms when face guarded until the pass is near, can prevent a guard's early detection of a pass.

Players should practice faking in front of a mirror or with a partner until it becomes automatic. Fakes should be practiced before every drill! Although each person develops a distinct feinting style, those who are unable to out-maneuver a defensive player are not only easy to guard but also of little value to a team.

Feinting hints

1. A player possessing the ball may fake using any combination of head, shoulder, eye, feet or ball movement.
2. A successful fake must be realistic enough to force the guard to move.
3. Faking with the feet does not require as great a movement as a fake with another part of the body.
4. A fake performed too rapidly will not allow the guard sufficient time to react.
5. A player who feints low should pass the ball at ear level if the guard reacts. A high fake is passed low if the guard reacts.
6. A fake may have to be performed more than once to pull the guard out of position.
7. An effective feint—but one which requires practice—is to turn the body to the left, fake left and then pass the ball to the right.
8. A protective measure when faking a pass is to shield the ball with the hand nearest the guard.

Techniques of Feinting

After a fake the action of the offensive player depends upon the guard's reaction. During the feint the offensive player observes the guard's movements for any improper action such as a shift in weight, a jump or a slow reaction. The offensive player facing a guard may fake a shot by moving the head and shoulders upward as the ball is raised for the shot. If the guard reacts to the fake by jumping or by moving in too close the forward can drive around the guard. Faking with the head, shoulders, or ball to the left or right until the guard responds, then dribbling around the guard on the side opposite the successful fake would be another effective maneuver. If the guard fails to react to the feint the offensive player moves in the direction of the fake.

Some of the most difficult faking techniques include the rocker step, the hesitation and the cross-over step. The rocker motion, which has a fake step toward the basket and a step back to the original position, provides the basis for the hesitation and the cross-over. To be convincing, a strong step is made forward or toward the goal transferring the weight forward. The player protects the ball by moving it to the side of her body. In the *rocker motion* the forward steps first to the right side of the defensive player, moves her foot back in place, steps forward to the left side of the guard and then back again. Players practice the rocker motion with and without an opponent, and concentrate on faking and maintaining balance.

ROCKER STEP

The rocker step, a variation of the rocker motion, includes a step toward the basket followed by a step backward. The offensive player steps forward, fakes the step back with the head and shoulders then shifts her weight to the back foot releasing the forward foot for a drive toward the goal (Figure 3-11).

HESITATION OR WALKING STEP

The hesitation or walking step draws the defensive player out of position long enough for the forward to make a quick jump shot or for a teammate to set a screen. The step entails maintaining weight on the pivot foot, taking a small step forward and letting the heel contact the floor first as in a normal walking motion. There is usually little reaction from the defensive player; therefore, the

FIGURE 3–10 The cross-over.

forward raises the front foot to complete the full stride, leaving the defensive player behind.

CROSS OVER

The cross-over relies on good balance, footwork and rhythm and is the most difficult fake to execute. The cross-over is done in one motion starting with a half step slightly to one side of the body, with body weight carried toward the inside of the ball of the foot. Often referred to as the jab step, the initial lay step allows the player to push off vigorously with the foot and cross it over in front of the body in preparation for a drive in the opposite direction.

Post players stationed between defensive players and the basket are accomplished in a variety of fakes in order to deceive the defense and score. Feinting with the head, shoulders and ball frequently lures the guard too far forward on her toes. The forward adds to the credibility of the feint by turning her head toward the goal. The forward will have more success with the feint if she watches the guard's position and reaction. Another effective faking technique is feinting or stepping in one direction followed by a turn in the opposite direction.

Planning the feint

These questions will assist players in analyzing the position and reaction of the defensive player:

1. Does the defensive player retreat with the fake or go for the ball?

   A defensive player who does not retreat is vulnerable to a drive with the rocker step.

2. Does the guard assume a parallel or a forward stride stance?

   If the stance is parallel, the guard is in poor position to retreat. If the stance is forward stride, the guard will have difficulty protecting a move to the side of the forward foot.

3. Does the guard play too loose or too close to the forward with the ball?

   When the guard is playing too close, and the shoulder of the forward is even with the body of the guard, the forward should drive. Shoot when the guard is playing too loose within the scoring area.

Jumping

Techniques

The jumping techniques utilized for a jump ball are the focus of this section. The proper techniques are of concern to both offensive and defensive players for improving their timing and attaining an advantage over their opponents.

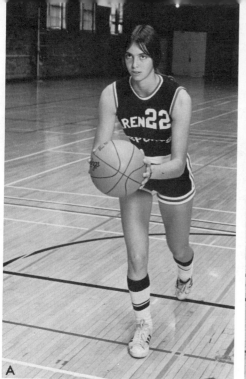

FIGURE 3–11   Rocker step.

In executing a jump from a stationary position the jumper bends the knees, focuses the head and eyes on the flight of the ball and relaxes the arms alongside the knees. The strategy of the situation determines the position of the feet and body in preparation for the jump. The jumper places one foot slightly in front of the other, initiating the upward spring from the feet. For more height the jumper executes a small step before pushing off with the toes. The player jumps, tapping the ball with the closest hand, usually the right, simultaneously lowering the other arm and raising the shoulder of the extended arm to gain an extra two or three inches in height. As the jumper taps the ball, the back is arched and the body completely extended from the toes to the tip of the fingers. If two players are equal in ability and jumping height, the ball is tapped to the rear of the player controlling the tap. The jumper who catches the ball momentarily with the fingers of the tapping hand has enough control to more accurately direct the placement of the ball.

Players should focus the eyes on the ball whether it is a jump ball, a rebound, or a high pass. To synchronize the jump to the flight of the tossed ball, start the jump just before the ball reaches its highest point. Each player should strive to tap the ball regardless of the size of an opponent.

DRILLS

1. Practice jumping from a crouched position.
2. Practice against a jumping board. Mark the height jumped. Concentrate on jumping a specific number of degrees higher each day.
3. Combine the skills of running and jumping. Jump for height—not distance.
4. Practice jumping with a partner of equal height and ability.
5. Strive to out-jump a partner who is taller.
6. Toss the ball against the wall or backboards and work on height and timing in recovering the ball.
7. Organize small groups consisting of two jumpers, a tosser, and players stationed outside the jumping circle. Rotate the players within the group until all have performed each task. Emphasis should be placed on correct timing, attaining height, and accurate placement.
8. Practice jumping on a line to prevent developing the habit of committing a violation by stepping on the line before tapping the ball.

BALL HANDLING SKILLS

Passing, receiving and dribbling are important aspects of basketball and indispensable for moving the ball into scoring territory. Although it has been said time and again that "the quickest method of moving the ball is the pass," a dribble may be necessary and effective when a pass is impractical or impossible. It is an advantage to be able to pass and dribble but it is also important to know which technique should be applied. A player should therefore acquire knowledge of the fundamentals of the pass and dribble, then progressively incorporate more advanced methods into her game.

PASSING

Basically a pass includes a step, a wrist and finger snap and a follow-through. Throughout the passing action the player maintains shoulders, hips and knees in a loose and relaxed position. Body weight shifts from the rear foot to the forward foot, while the accuracy of the pass is helped by using the small muscles of the fingers and thumbs. The player drops the hips slightly, bends the knees to insure relaxation and balance, then extends the knees as the ball is released. The force directed behind the ball by the arm and shoulder muscles controls the appropriate distance for medium and long passes. A common fault among beginners is a tendency to pass the ball using only the arms. Power is obtained through the coordinated use of shoulder muscles, elbows, wrists, fingers, thumbs, and legs.

Players should strive to catch and pass the ball with a single motion. If the force of the ball throws the player off balance, she regains control then passes. The ball is kept on the fingertips, *not in the palm;* the wrist is snapped and the player follows through by extending the arms and fingers in the direction of the pass. The wrist snap supplies additional force to the ball. Whenever possible the pass is directed between the waist and chest of the receiver, automatically placing her in a triple threat position.

Short snappy passes, the hardest passes to intercept and the easiest to control, seem to be the most effective. The adage that "the shortest distance between two points is a straight line," is also true in passing. The less time a player consumes passing the ball, the less chance there is of an interception; however, the passer constantly adjusts the intended direction of the ball with the receiver's actions. When the receiver is moving toward the player with the ball the speed of the pass must be reduced to decrease its impact. Preferably, the pass is directed ahead of a moving receiver, enabling her to run to meet the ball instead of turning around to catch it.

A common problem facing the passer is projecting the ball past the defensive player. Consequently, the defensive player's position and ability determine the pass that should be used. The following three questions help assess the guard's vulnerability.

1. Is the defensive player guarding close or loose?

2. Are the guard's feet in a parallel or front stride position?

3. Are the guard's arms up or down, or one up and one down? The closer the defensive player is to the passer the easier it is to toss the ball past her; conversely, the farther away the defensive player is from the passer, the more difficult it is to pass the ball. Players, in general, are all vulnerable in the following passing areas: (1) *over the top of the head;* (2) *over the shoulder by the ear;* and (3) *by the lower part of the leg.*

Passing practice, whether individual, partner or in a group, cannot be overemphasized. There are more fumbles in handling the ball as a result of faulty passing than there are as a result of faulty receiving.

Three abilities distinguish the highly skilled passer from the beginner: (1) She is capable of throwing the ball past a number of defenders without an interception; (2) She is adept at passing the ball from any position; and (3) She possesses the ability to pass accurately while dribbling or moving quickly. A passer relies on peripheral or split-vision (seeing beyond the direct line of focus). Peripheral vision increases by focusing on a point and observing the actions of players around that area without turning the head.

Receiving

To insure reception the receiver moves toward the pass, focusing her eyes on the ball until her fingers grab it. Although the offensive strategy determines the receiver's direction the catching movement usually places the receiver in a forward stride stance with the knees bent and relaxed and the weight on the forward foot. The receiver should continually move around the court. A stationary player in an upright position with stiff knees is a slow reacting player and a poor receiver.

The receiver holds her arms away from the body ready to receive the pass. As the ball approaches she reaches for it keeping the fingers of both hands spread and relaxed. If the ball is low the receiver points the fingers down, placing the little fingers close together and the thumbs up. If the ball is above waist level, the fingers point up with the thumbs behind the ball. As the ball contacts the receiver's fingers she grasps it firmly bending the elbows with the force of the pass. She protects the ball by pulling it close to the stomach and spreading the elbows. It is essential for a receiver who is cutting or executing a fast break to watch the ball. If the pass is fumbled or bobbled the receiver is usually at fault; however, if the ball is intercepted, the passer may be at fault. Remember, passing relies on teamwork and basketball *is* a team game.

Basic Passes

Since there are many types of passes, it is unrealistic for beginning players to attempt to master every one. Beginners should concentrate on the basic passes: the chest pass; the bounce pass; the one-hand bounce pass; the two-hand overhead pass; the baseball pass; and the underhand pass. Players may then devote additional time to practice any other passes required for offensive plays contemplated by the team.

Chest pass (two-hand)

The chest pass is considered the basic pass of basketball. It is a snappy, chest-high pass which travels for a distance of 15 to 20 feet in a plane parallel to the floor. The passer holds the ball in front of the chest with the elbows flexed and close to the sides, the fingers are spread and fully extended along the sides of the ball and the thumbs are behind it. Snapping the wrists imparts force to the ball as it is released. Players with weak wrists find it necessary to extend the arms in the direction of the pass. Discretion is necessary, however, since extending the elbows telegraphs the intended path of the ball. Weight is transferred from the rear to the front foot when the passer is in a forward stride position after releasing the ball. If the feet are parallel the passer fakes, then takes a step forward as the ball is released (Figure 4–1, page 59).

Bounce pass

The bounce pass is valuable when a direct pass is impossible. It is utilized to penetrate a zone defense, to "feed" a pivot player and to pass the ball beyond a tall defensive player or a guard whose arms are extended forward. The bounce pass resembles the basic chest pass. Started at waist level, the bounce pass has a

FIGURE 4-1   Chest pass.

more pronounced arm action and the ball is pushed to the floor with sufficient force to rebound into a teammate's hands at approximately waist level. A player ready to drive may gain the advantage of a lower ball position by stepping forward as if to drive or pass the ball. Players are often successful with a fake of the ball upward followed by a low bounce pass.

Two-hand bounce pass

The two-hand bounce pass, although expedient in game situations, has a tendency to be slow. Although a player may impart substantial force to the pass, the speed of the ball is greatly reduced the moment it contacts the floor. The slowness of the bounce pass, as well as the possibility of passing too far from the receiver, increases the chances of interception.

Players should attempt to pass without applying spin to the ball. While it is simple to impart spin to the ball, the reaction of the ball after contacting the floor makes the bounce pass difficult for the receiver to control. Players must practice applying sufficient force to rebound the ball to a teammate's waist. Balls bounced too close to the receiver will strike her knees and legs (Figure 4-2, page 60).

One-hand bounce pass

The one-hand bounce pass is a short pass primarily used when a defender is directly between the offensive player and the re-

FIGURE 4-2   Two-hand bounce pass.

ceiver. The initial position of the hands on the ball is similar to that of the chest pass. In one continuous motion, the passer steps, moves the ball to one side and turns it placing the hand on that side behind the ball and the other hand under it for support. The player then vigorously extends the elbow, *pushing* the ball down toward the floor. The ball rebounds to the receiver's waist. When passing to the right the player steps to the right with the left foot as the pivot. She rotates the ball a quarter turn to the left and brings it to the right side, placing the right hand behind and the left hand underneath the ball, then pushing the ball to the floor by extending the right elbow. Practice passing with the right and left hand.

The one-hand bounce pass may be combined with a cross-over step by crossing the left leg over and in front of the right leg, simultaneously rotating the ball to the left and placing the right hand behind the ball (Figure 4-3).

Two-hand overhead pass

If applied correctly and strategically the two-hand overhead pass is difficult to intercept. The ball is thrown directly overhead or from slightly behind the head and passed to the receiver at shoulder level. The passer grips the sides of the ball with fingers spread and thumbs behind the ball, cocks the wrists and bends the elbows slightly. The elbows are then sharply extended above the head while the passer maintains a well-balanced body position.

60

FIGURE 4–3   One-hand bounce pass.

Finally, the wrists and fingers are snapped with little follow-through of the arms. In general, two-hand overhead passes are effective for:

1. A tall player.
2. A post player, particularly when she has an opportunity to pass to a low post or to a teammate who is cutting.
3. A low post.
4. A rebounder throwing the ball to the side.
5. A player receiving a pass above her head.
6. A closely guarded short player passing the ball to a tall post. (Figure 4–4, page 62).

Baseball pass

The baseball pass is the most successful pass for initiating a fast break but a difficult pass in which to control accuracy. Most players discover it to be a natural way of throwing a medium or long range pass. The passer raises the ball to the right shoulder, level with the ear, places the right hand behind the ball, and cocks the wrist with the fingers spread and pointing upward. Simultaneously, she moves the left hand across the body to support the front of the ball and steps forward with the left leg in the direction of the pass. The elbow of the throwing arm is flexed and away from the body. For a long pass she shifts weight to the right foot, lifting the left hand as the ball is drawn behind the shoulder. The passer throws the ball by extending the elbow, snapping the wrist, following through with the fingers, and rotating the trunk so that weight is transferred to the forward foot (Figure 4–5, page 63).

Practice Hints: Accuracy is difficult to achieve, therefore, it is wise to practice initially with a stationary target. Next, a cutter is

FIGURE 4-4 Overhead pass.

added, and finally, the player rebounds the ball from the basket, turns
and passes to the cutter. If a goal is scored the player jumps out of
bounds and passes to the cutter.

Underhand (two-hand) or "shovel pass"

The underhand pass, designed for short and medium length
passes, is of particular advantage to a player who pivots or reverse turns then passes to a teammate cutting toward the basket.
If the defense interrupts a dribbling action a player may pivot and
pass to a trailing teammate. For the pass, the player spreads
and points the fingers downward on the sides of the ball, with the
palms facing and the thumbs on top of the ball pointing forward. The elbows are slightly bent, with the elbow on the side of
the pass turned outward. The weight is on the rear foot (the side
with the ball). The player shifts weight to the front foot or steps
in the direction of the pass, simultaneously swinging the arms forward and upward and extending the elbows. The ball is released
with a quick snap of the wrists at approximately waist level.
This should be a soft pass projecting the ball into the air in
such a manner that the teammate who is cutting may catch the

FIGURE 4–5   Baseball pass.

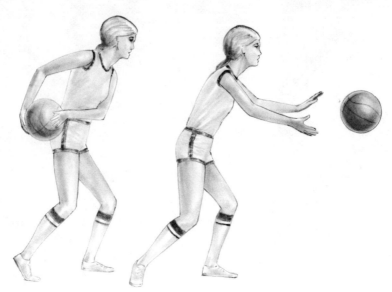

FIGURE 4-6 Two-hand underhand pass.

ball at waist level. A ball thrown from the front or side is most adequately protected when passed from the hip.

One-hand underhand pass

The one-hand underhand pass is a short pass frequently made to a teammate cutting toward the basket. Fundamentally, the one-hand underhand pass is the same as the two-hand underhand pass, except that when the ball is brought to the side of the body, the hand on that side is behind the ball and the wrist is flexed. Flexing the wrist enables the fingers to hold the ball from underneath and press it against the forearm for added support. The other hand is brought across the body and placed on top of the ball. A simple technique to increase accuracy is to step on the opposite foot as the ball is released. The passer controls the height of the pass by extending the fingers at waist level in the direction of the pass. The pass resembles a softball pitch or a bowling swing with forward motion applied as the arm extends in the direction of the pass (Figure 4-7).

Hook pass

The hook pass, perhaps the most difficult pass for women with small hands to control, is not as profitable as other passing methods.

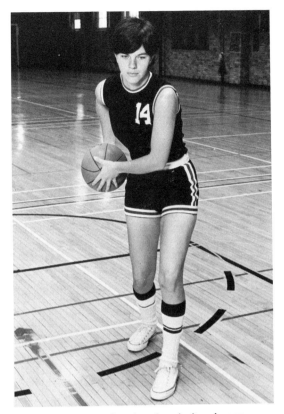

FIGURE 4-7 One-hand underhand pass.

Teams find the hook pass useful when a player facing forward desires to throw the ball sideward to a teammate, when a re-bounder attempts to pass from a position under the defensive basket to start a fast break, or when a player runs toward the sideline or endline in an attempt to return the ball to a teammate who is inbounds. The player stands with the non-throwing shoulder pointed in the direction of the pass, placing the weight of the body on the foot on the throwing arm side. The ball rests in the hand, the fingers are spread (women with small hands may place the ball against the forearm), the arm is lifted and the wrist cocked. The player swings the arm and ball upward to an overhead position, simultaneously raising the other arm to shoulder level to assist in maintaining balance. As the elbow bends and the upper arm almost touches the ear, a fingertip flick releases the pass. The player follows through with the fingertips pointed in the direction of the pass, the arm arched overhead and weight transferred to the opposite foot.

FIGURE 4–8   Hook pass.

Other passes having specific advantages in game strategy include the side hook, the lob, the two-hand shoulder pass, and the
behind-the-back pass.

PASS	USE
Side Hook	For long passes down the court; for project-ing the ball past an opponent who is over-guarding.
Lob	For a pass to an offensive center when the defensive center is playing too close to the forward; for a lead pass to carry over a defen-sive player who is playing between the passer and receiver. Use cautiously because the lob, a softly thrown high-arching pass, is always in danger of in-terception.
Two-Hand Shoulder	For short passes when the ball has been re-ceived at shoulder level. As the name implies, the two-hand shoulder pass starts from above the right or left shoulder.
Behind-the-Back	For a game situation in which a player is closely guarded and unable to execute any other pass. Danger lies in the player's inabil-ity to adequately control the direction of the pass to anyone in the circle (Diagram 4–3).

FIGURE 4–9   Side hook pass.

FIGURE 4–10   Behind-the-back pass.

DRILLS

1. *Partner Passing.* Players form two parallel lines. The distance between lines depends on the pass. (If there are not enough balls for every two people to share one ball, players use the zig-zag formation.) Partners pass the ball back and forth practicing each method of passing. The entire group may practice a pass at the same time or partners may progress as they master each pass.

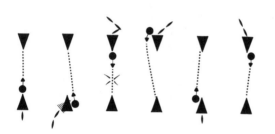

DIAGRAM 4–1 Partner passing.

2. *Circle.* Form two circles consisting of an equal number of players. At the command "GO," the leader, the player with the ball, passes in a designated fashion to the player on the right who turns and passes to the player on her right. Play continues in the same pattern around the circle until the ball returns to the starting position. The leader calls out "ONE," indicating completion of one trip around the circle; passing continues to the right until a designated total number of trips are completed. The first team to finish is the winner.

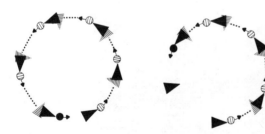

DIAGRAM 4–2 Circle passing, One.

3. *Circle Passing.* Arrange the players in circle formation with approximately seven to a circle. Using a designated pass, the players pass to anyone in the circle (Diagram 4–3).

4. *Circle Keep Away.* Divide the players into circles with one person in the center of each circle. Using any pass, players throw the ball across the circle. The center player attempts to catch or deflect the ball. If successful, the center player exchanges places with the passer. Two variations of circle keep away are: (1) players may pass to anyone except the player immediately to the right or

left; and (2) players may pass to anyone except the person from whom they received a pass or the players on the right or left.

5. *Five Players Plus One.* Separate the players into groups of five. Each group chooses its own formation then begins passing, using a variety of passes. An extra person may move into the formation as a substitute for one of the players. Constantly shifting in and out of formation should aid players in developing an awareness of all action on the court and accustom them to using peripheral vision.

6. *Two-Line Hook Passing.* Players form two lines six feet apart and facing in the same direction. The first player in the right line dribbles out 10 feet and executes a hook pass with the right hand to the second girl in the left line. Meanwhile, the first player in the left dribbles out 10 feet and performs a hook pass with the left hand to the second person in the right line. Each passer then runs to the end of the opposite line (Diagram 4-4).

DIAGRAM 4-3   Circle passing.

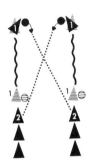

DIAGRAM 4-4   Two-line hook passing.

7. *Shuttle Passing.* Arrange the players in two lines stationed on opposite sides of the court. Player 1 has the ball. Player 2 runs toward player 1 who passes the ball to player 2. The second person in line, player 3, runs to meet the pass from player 2. Players pass the left shoulder of the approaching person, then run to the end of the opposite line. Play continues in the same formation as long as desired. For interest and developing a response to rapidly changing patterns, the type and length of passes may be varied. Emphasis should be placed on passing the ball while running and without traveling.

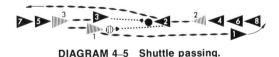

DIAGRAM 4-5   Shuttle passing.

8. *Two-Line Drill.* Form two lines facing each other with 10 feet separating the first players in each line. Player 2 stands in the middle between the two lines and faces 1, the player with

the ball. Player 1 attempts to pass the ball beyond the middle player to the first player in the opposite line. Whether the pass is successful or not, player 1 takes the position between the two lines. The middle player then runs to the end of the line left by player 1 while player 3 attempts to throw the ball past the new middle player. The two-line drill offers a more difficult position from which to pass the ball and resembles a game situation with a defensive player directly facing an offensive player (Diagram 4–6).

DIAGRAM 4–6   Two-line drill.   DIAGRAM 4–7   Pass-and-run drill.

9. *Pass-and-Run Drill.* Arrange the players in a circle. The player starting the drill passes to any player in the circle, then follows the path of the ball and takes the pass receiver's position. The receiver catches the ball and repeats the procedure. Objectives are to condition players to pass and move, and to observe the direction of the pass in order to avoid hitting a teammate running toward the passer (Diagram 4–7).

10. *Pass-and-Follow Drill.* Divide the class into four groups facing toward the center of the half court with one group stationed at each corner of the court. The ball is passed from the first player in line one to the first player in lines two, three, and four. Each passer follows the ball and takes a position at the end of the line to which the ball was passed (Diagram 4–8).

11. *Run the Gauntlet.* Players 1, 2 and 3 stand approximately 15 feet apart in a zig-zag formation. The remainder of the group forms a column facing the middle of the three stationary players. The first person in the column, player 4, passes the ball to player 1, continues running forward to receive the ball from player 1, and then passes to player 2 without traveling. Player 2 returns the ball to player 1 who continues down the line and executes the same movements with player 3. Player 4 turns around, repeats the pattern back through the zig-zag line, and passes to player 5 who follows the same procedure. Player 4 takes a position at the end of

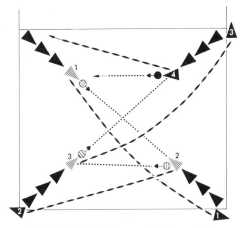

DIAGRAM 4–8   Pass-and-follow drill.

the column. The Run the Gauntlet drill provides practice in leading the runner and in controlling the ball while on the move (Diagram 4–9).

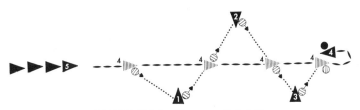

DIAGRAM 4–9   The gauntlet drill.

12. *Lateral Pass Drill.* Form two lines at one end of the floor. The first players in each line move out together and pass back and forth while progressing to the other end of the court. As soon as the two players have cleared the half court, the next players in each column perform the same action. Players concentrate on passing without dribbling and without traveling. The Lateral Pass drill develops a player's ability to toss the ball laterally to a receiver when she and the receiver are both moving (Diagram 4–10).

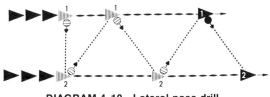

DIAGRAM 4–10   Lateral pass drill.

13. *Lateral Pass Drill for Three.* Form three lines and execute the lateral pass drill with three players. Return the ball to the center following each pass.

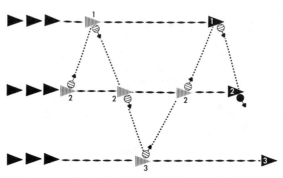

DIAGRAM 4-11   Lateral pass drill for three.

14. *Two Ball Split Vision Drill.* Have the students form a straight line with player 1, the leader, facing the group. Player 1 and one member of the line have balls. While player 1 passes the ball to any one on the line, the other ball is passed to player 1. The two balls move continuously from the line to player 1. Twenty to 30 seconds "out in front" are sufficient for each person. All participants should be given an opportunity to be leader (Diagram 4–12).

15. *Circle Passing Drill.* Form circles of six players with one person, player 1, in the center of the circle. Players are numbered from 2 to 5 clockwise around the circle. Players 1 and 5 are each given a ball. Number 1 passes the ball to 2 as 5 passes to 1. Again, timing is essential. Number 2 passes back to 1 as 1 passes to 6 and so on around the circle. Objectives of the drill are to develop peripheral vision and accurate passing.

DIAGRAM 4–12   Split vision drill.   DIAGRAM 4–13   Circle passing.

DRIBBLING

Designed to move the ball down the court, the dribble is offensively advantageous in setting up teammates for scoring opportunities, in making a fast break and in stalling tactics; defensively, it is beneficial in moving the ball from the scoring area of the opponents.

Dribbling techniques are classified with car terminology— "speed" and "traffic." A speed dribbler is one who singlehandedly controls the ball in front of the defense. The traffic dribbler refers to a player who has teammates and defensive players who are between the dribbler and the basket.

To dribble the ball the player bends the knees, inclines the trunk slightly forward and elevates the head. The dribbler strikes the top of the ball with the fingers pushing down in front and slightly to the side of the body with sufficient force to rebound the ball back to the hand. She shields the ball by pulling the opposite leg and arm forward with the elbow bent and the lower arm parallel to the floor. During the dribble the player (1) watches the position of teammates to determine the feasibility of a pass; (2) controls the dribble with finger and wrist motion; (3) avoids a

FIGURE 4-11 Dribbling. Protecting the ball.

batting action with the hand; (4) touches the ball before the height of the bounce is reached; and (5) bounces the ball approximately knee high.

The player who has learned to dribble effectively with either hand is ready to become more elusive by acquiring advanced dribbling techniques. There is a notable carry-over from body control skills to the more difficult dribbling skills. Thus, the individual who has been perfecting body control skills will easily acquire the advanced dribbling techniques.

Dribbling Techniques

Change of pace

In the change of pace the dribbler alternates between slowing down and accelerating her speed while continuing to dribble the ball at the same tempo. A similar effect is created by a dribbler who runs at a steady pace but varies the tempo of the dribble. The change of pace techniques are useful when the dribbler strives to elude a defensive player.

Drag

The drag is used by an offensive center who has her back toward the basket and the defensive player. The objective is to gain a more strategic position near the basket by constantly changing the dribbling hand and shifting weight from one foot to the other.

Cross-over

In the cross-over a player shifts the ball from one hand to the other while using the "change of direction" strategy. The dribbler plants the right foot hard, pushes off quickly to the left foot and simultaneously bounces the ball with the right hand at an angle toward the left that rebounds the ball in position for the left hand to continue the dribble (Figure 4-12).

Reverse

Occasionally, to protect the ball, a player applies a technique known as the reverse dribble. The play may be executed, for example, by the player dribbling to the right, stepping on the left foot (the outside pivot foot), and turning her back on the defensive player. She then deflects the dribble from the right hand to the left and continues dribbling with the left hand (Figure 4-13).

FIGURE 4–12   Cross-over dribble.

FIGURE 4–13   Reverse dribble.

Behind-the-back

The behind-the-back dribble is an advanced skill practiced after the other dribbling techniques are mastered. It is beneficial at certain times but of no advantage when players use the dribble to show off. The dribbler pushes the ball to the floor behind the back at such an angle that the rebound enables her to pivot and continue dribbling with the opposite hand (Figure 4–14).

Hints for The Dribbler

1. A pass moves faster than a dribble; therefore, avoid assisting the offense by over-dribbling.

2. A good dribbler reacts according to the actions of the defense.

3. A dribbler guarded by a defensive player with arms extended low should drop the ball over the guard's arms as the dribble is started.

4. A dribbler who has a guard with arms extended high should push the ball low and around to the side of the guard as the dribble is started.

5. A closely guarded dribbler places one shoulder past the defensive player then dribbles to the basket.

FIGURE 4–14   Behind-the-back dribble.

6. A drive involves dribbling fast and hard toward the basket after passing the defensive player.

7. A dribbler who is loosely guarded dribbles toward the defensive player or toward the section of the court where she may gain an advantage.

8. An alert dribbler observes the feet, body weight and reaction of the defensive player.

9. An effective dribbler immediately reacts to the guard's movements.

DRILLS

1. *Dribbling While Kneeling.* Position students at random on the court. Beginners kneel with the head up and eyes closed, dribbling the ball using specified methods. Students should repeat the drill in the same position but alternate hands with each bounce of the ball.

2. *Beginner's Low Dribble.* Divide the class into columns which are stationed at each endline. Player 1, the first player in each column, dribbles at the starting position with the left knee on the floor, the right hand on top of the ball and the left hand supporting the ball from underneath. Players dribble to the center of the floor, stand, turn around, dribble back, and pass to player 2, the second girl in each column, who repeats the action. After the students successfully dribble with the right hand, they repeat the drill using the left hand and eventually alternate hands. A change of pace is incorporated into the drill along with the cross-over dribble. The low starting position assists in reinforcing the low body position essential for proper dribbling.

3. *Length of Court.* Form columns at the endline. Each student dribbles the length of the court with the right hand, returns dribbling with the left hand and passes to the second person in the column who repeats the drill.

4. *Stops and Starts.* Form columns at the endline. Player 1, the first person in the column, dribbles down the court with the right hand and performs a stop and start at each foul line and at the center line. She returns to the starting position dribbling with the left hand and repeating the stops and starts. To control the ball, during a stop the player moves three or four steps backward and then continues dribbling forward. At the end of the drill, player 1 passes the ball to the next person in line who repeats the procedure (Diagram 4–14).

5. *Stop and Go.* Form groups of eight to 10, each with a basketball and stationed behind the endline. Confine the dribbling area to a quarter of the basketball court. On the verbal signal "GO," everyone with a ball dribbles anywhere in the specified area. On the first whistle, players "STOP" both feet but continue dribbling. On the next whistle players move again. Players dribble the ball continuously although the feet should "STOP" or "GO" with

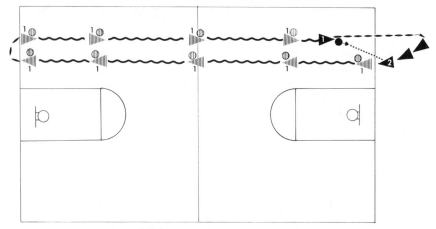

DIAGRAM 4–14   Stop and go.

alternate whistles. For variation the dribbler may shift hands at
each signal. Concentrate on the use of each hand for dribbling, moving in and out of traffic, stopping, and alternating hands.

6. *Go Get Lost.* Distribute basketballs to each player. At a
signal, all players go on the court and practice any ball handling
skill, except shooting. Dribbling, faking, changing direction, change
of pace, and pivoting are a few of the techniques players may
practice. Allow the students to rely on individual ingenuity.

7. *Individual Practice.* Give each player a basketball. On a command, each player dribbles the ball with the right hand while
standing, on one knee, on both knees, sitting, lying down, and in a
side-leaning position. Players dribble in a circle around their bodies
while kneeling on one knee, standing, in stride stance, and through
the legs. Players stop dribbling and circle the ball around the
ankles, thighs, hips, waist, knees and shoulders. The drill is repeated
using the left hand.

8. *Follow the Leader.* Players are positioned in a straight line
behind a leader. The leader faces the group and gives an arm
signal indicating the direction in which everyone is to dribble.
Emphasis is on training players to hold their heads up.

9. *Progressive Dribble.* Arrange the players in columns at one
end of the court. Each player dribbles to the free-throw line, reverse turns, and dribbles back to the starting line. The same person repeats the dribble to the center line, the three-fourths line,
and the endline. Players alternate hands on each turn as they return to the starting line after each progressive dribble. The progressive dribble perfects dribbling skills as well as assisting in
overall conditioning of the students (Diagram 4–15).

10. *Human Obstacle.* Separate the group into lines. The first
three people in each line move down the floor, spacing them-
selves 10 feet apart and facing the rest of the line. The next player
in line dribbles in and out of the three human obstacles, changing

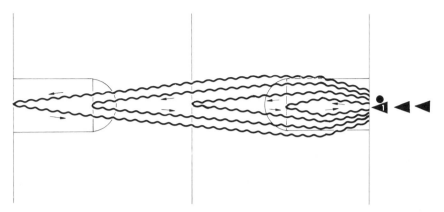

DIAGRAM 4-15   Progressive dribble.

hands frequently and keeping her body between the ball and the obstacles. The dribbler avoids the human obstacle without stopping or losing control of the ball. Each player in line repeats the pattern.

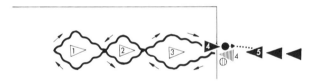

DIAGRAM 4-16   Human obstacle drill.

Variation: The players who are obstacles are permitted one step forward to attempt striking the ball as the dribbler approaches. When the students become more proficient, the human obstacles may attempt stealing the ball.

11. *One-on-One*. Station the students in columns at one end of the gymnasium. Player 1, the first person in the column, attempts to dribble the ball to the center line while the second person in the column, player 2, strives to deflect the dribble using legal guarding procedures. When player 1 reaches the center line, the students exchange positions. If player 2 intercepts the ball, return the ball to player 1 who continues the pattern by dribbling to the center line.

12. *Dribble and Pivot*. Divide the students into equal columns at one end of the gymnasium. Player 1, the first person in the column, dribbles down the court using the right hand, and executes a complete pivot at each foul line and at the center line. Player 1 returns dribbling with the left hand and performs the same pivots, then passes to player 2, the second person in the column.

To pivot, the dribbler comes to a momentary stop on the left foot, the pivot foot, and pivots in a counter-clockwise motion hold-

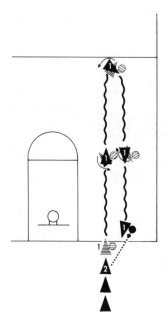

DIAGRAM 4-17   Dribble and pivot.

ing the ball close to the body. When dribbling with the left hand on the return trip, pivot clockwise with the right foot.

13. *Dribble Tag.* Give a basketball to each player. One player is designated as "IT." Playing on half of the court, "IT" dribbles continuously in an effort to catch one of the other players. Players

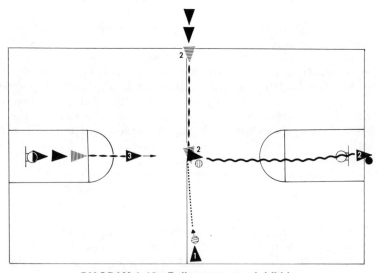

DIAGRAM 4-18   Ball recovery and dribble.

may change positions only by dribbling the ball. Any player tagged by "IT" becomes the new "IT."

14. *Loose Ball Recovery and Dribble.* Divide the students into two columns with one column stationed along a sideline and the other located behind the free-throw line. The leader stands approximately mid-court on the opposite sideline and rolls the ball toward the center line while the players in the columns take turns cutting for the ball, gaining possession of it and dribbling to the endline. Players obtain practice in picking up free balls, regaining body control and dribbling rapidly to the endline (Diagram 4–18).

15. *Pressure Dribbling.* Position players with a partner at the endline. One player has a basketball and attempts to dribble the full length of the court. The partner starts from a line even with and facing in the same direction as the dribbler. The partner's objectives are to stay in front of the dribbler and to force her to the sideline without fouling.

SHOOTING

Although individuals acquire various methods of shooting suited for specific positions, each player must first obtain proficiency in the three basic shots, the lay-up, the set, and the jump shot. Regardless of the shot, the following basic fundamentals are essential: (1) contacting the ball and relaxing the body; (2) ability to concentrate; (3) ability to aim at a specific target; (4) positioning the ball; (5) releasing the ball; (6) follow through; and (7) predetermining the flight of the ball. One of the phenomena of shooting ability is the fact that a player shooting alone may have a high percentage of accuracy, yet the moment other players begin shooting at the same basket or defensive players enter the scene, accuracy diminishes. The rapid change in accuracy seems to be a direct result of tensing the body, rushing the shot or shooting off balance. To counteract the change in proficiency, coaches should simulate game situations during practice sessions.

Basic Techniques

Maintaining proper balance while shooting is dependent upon a player's ability to shift the center of gravity. A high center of gravity places the player in a top-heavy and awkward position while a low center of gravity results in a cramped and confined position. Body balance is also controlled by the position of the feet and knees. The feet are shoulder-width apart in either a front stride or a side stride stance with a deeper bend in the knees as more power is needed. The ball is held in the fingers approximately chest high, then raised toward the basket in preparation for the shot. If additional power is desired, start the ball from a lower position. The shooter must concentrate on the actions of the defensive players, offensive patterns, and the basket, taking advantage of any opening that occurs. Whenever possible while positioning for a shot at the basket, players retain the triple threat position.

Point of Aim

While there are several controversial theories concerning the exact spot a player focuses the eyes during an attempted goal, authorities tend to agree on the "point of aim" method for lay-ups or short shots. Essentially, players look at a spot on the backboard where a ball can contact and result in a rebound into the basket. As the distance from the basket increases, the shooter alters the focus spot on the backboard to allow for the additional fall of the ball. For a particularly long banked shot, backspin is placed on the ball to lessen its speed after contacting the backboard and to force it to drop more sharply toward the basket.

The theory of aiming over the front part of rim closest to the shooter has been popular with both instructors and students. An advantage is that the point of aim is not changed as distance from the goal varies. Two disadvantages are that fatigued players tend to shoot short, and players exerting additional force behind the ball in order to reach the goal have a tendency to lose body balance. Glass backboards, while attractive, provide an unsatisfactory background for aiming at the rim, particularly if spectators are seated directly behind them.

Advantages of Aiming toward the Middle of the Back Portion of Rim

1. A ball with a diameter of 9 inches, aimed toward a rim with a diameter of 18 inches, has 9 inches of space to allow for possible error.

2. A ball that strikes the back edge of the rim and has backspin may still rebound into the basket.

3. A ball that falls short of the target, yet remains in the center of the rim, has a 9 inch margin of error.

4. A ball shot beyond the target may still rebound off the backboard into the basket.

A key to accurate and consistent shooting is coordination and follow-through of the total body. With eyes focused on the target, the shooter flexes and relaxes the knees, points the elbow toward the basket, cocks the wrist, and spreads the fingers, holding the ball between the shoulders and eyes. The shooter starts the ball upward toward the basket, imparting backspin by rolling the ball off the pads of the fingers in a backward motion and uncocking the wrists. The fingers extend downward and outward in the follow through. For additional power extend the entire body, from the toes to the finger tips, on the follow through. Return to the floor in a balanced position with the eyes on the ball and the knees flexed in preparation for a possible rebound.

The amount of force behind the ball and the direction in which it is applied determines the arc of the ball toward the basket. Studies have indicated that "the lower the angle of flight of the ball, the greater the accuracy of the direction must be." In other words the higher the arc, the more accurate the shot; however, high arc also requires more strength than a low arc. The amount of extra strength required varies according to the strength of the player, the distance from the basket, and the distance between the guard and forward. To determine the distance from the basket, use a constant factor such as the free-throw lane as a guide, not the side boundaries which may vary. When a defensive player is close, the arc must be high to clear the guard's arms. Players practice aiming the ball from a position close to the basket, gradually moving back as proficiency is attained.

Lay-up

The term "lay-up," derived from the techniques involved in the shot, describes one of the most basic and perhaps one of the most difficult shots. Frequently, a lay-up gives the forward a three point gain. As the goal is scored the guard inadvertently fouls the forward, thus placing the offensive player in a position to score an extra point. Players develop the lay-up shot through a series of practice sessions and steps.

Step One: For a righthand lay up shot, the player faces the right side of the basket at a 45 degree angle and at arm's length from the backboard. The ball is held in the pads of the fingers, balanced between the thumb and fingers of the right hand, with the elbows turned toward the basket. The player positions the ball at a level between the shoulder and eyes, and applies additional support by placing the fingers of the left hand on the underside of the ball. The eyes focus on the backboard about 8 inches above and just to the right of the rim (the point of aim). The right foot is slightly ahead of the left foot, and the knees are bent. The shooter then completely extends the body, reaching toward the point of aim with the ball and pushing it straight up, not forward. Players practice lay-up shooting with the left hand on the left side of the basket, and with the right hand on the right side of the basket (Figure 4–15).

Step Two: The forward moves one step further from the basket. To gain additional momentum and height with total body extension, the player places the left foot down then extends it, at the same time raising the right knee and reaching for the point of aim with the ball. When shooting from the left side of the basket, the initial step is taken with the right foot.

Step Three: The forward moves back another step, starting the ball at waist level. The rules state that a moving player has two steps in which to stop. If another step is to be taken, the ball must be released before the third step is made.

The forward steps first on the right foot, transfers weight to the left foot, then extends the left foot and body toward the goal while simultaneously moving the ball upward toward the basket. The left foot must be extended "up" as in a high jump, not "out" as in a long jump. At this time, practice should include passes to the forward moving toward the basket who then takes two steps and releases the ball toward the point of aim.

FIGURE 4–15 Righthand lay-up shot.

FIGURE 4–16 Lay-up following a dribble.

Step Four: Add a dribble. The forward bounces the ball with the right hand, simultaneously executing a step with the left foot, then completes the two-step lay-up shot. At first players dribble slowly, increasing the number and speed of dribbles as skill improves. For realism and extra pressure, a defensive player follows directly behind the player attempting the lay-up (Figure 4–16).

The "underhand" release, a type of lay-up shot in which the ball is laid against the backboard or just over the rim with the back of the hand facing away from the body, is performed by more advanced players. The underhand release enables a player to "ease up" on a shot and release the ball softly. The player holds the ball in the fingers of both hands, moves the shooting hand under the ball and extends the body upward, retaining a hold on the ball with the opposite hand until the shooting hand controls the shot. During the release apply adequate backspin, allowing the ball to roll off the pads of the fingers (Figure 4–18).

One-hand set shot

Popular among basketball players, the one-hand set shot is usually more accurate than shots requiring both hands. The one-hand set shot and the first step of the lay-up are similar except that the one-hand set shot is performed farther from the basket. To execute the one-hand set shot with the right hand, the player assumes a balanced position with feet shoulder-width apart, the right foot slightly ahead of the left, the knees flexed, and body weight evenly distributed on the feet. She holds the ball at approx-

FIGURE 4–17   One-hand set shot.

FIGURE 4-18   Underhand lay-up.

imately shoulder level on the pads of the fingers, cocks the wrists with the back of the right hand toward the body and the thumb and index finger forming a "V." The player places the left hand under and slightly to the left side of the ball. If necessary, she lowers the ball before starting the upward extension of the body, then moves the ball upward in front of the right eye, extending the right arm toward the target and moving the left hand for balance and protection. Backspin is applied by releasing the ball with a gentle flip of the wrist and fingers toward the target. The distance from the basket and strength of the player determines whether the follow through places the shooter on the toes or in a short jump. The eyes should remain on the point of aim until the ball is well on its way toward the target.

Two-hand set shot

The two-hand set shot is effective for a player lacking sufficient strength for the one-hand set shot, and closely resembles the two-hand chest pass. The two-hand set shot may be useful for a long outside shot when a player is not closely guarded. Preparations for the shot place a player in good position to pass, shoot, or drive. The initial positions of the two-hand set shot and the chest pass are similar. The feet are in a parallel or a front stride position with the left foot slightly forward. The ball starts at about chest level, with the fingers spread and gripping the ball along the sides while the thumbs almost point toward each

FIGURE 4-19 Two-hand set shot.

other behind the ball. Initial body movements are similar to those of the one-hand set shot with the knees flexing slightly as the ball is lowered downward. The body completely extends from the feet through the legs, trunk, and arms until the ball is released. The ball rolls off the pads of the fingers with backspin applied by snapping the wrists and pointing the fingers outward on the follow through.

Jump shot

The mechanics of the jump shot, which is becoming more popular with girls and women, are almost identical to the one-hand push shot. The difference is that in the jump shot the individual must first jump, then shoot. During the jump all forces are utilized to gain maximum efficiency from the body position. Feet, knees, hips, elbows, shoulders, and head face the basket before, during and after the shot. Coordinating proper body position with correct timing and speed will be useful in insuring maximum scoring opportunities. Near the basket the jump is higher, with the ball started and raised higher than when the player is farther from the goal. When a forward is close to the basket, the defensive player will automatically be in a close guarding position; therefore, the jump must be higher and the ball must be projected higher to evade the arms of the opponent. Jump shots executed quickly and accurately are almost impossible to block; however, short shots which do not require strength are more successful than long shots.

FIGURE 4–20 Jump shot.

Standing Jump Shot

For this shot the player faces the basket with feet hip-width apart, knees slightly flexed and weight transferred to the balls of the feet. The ball is held between the shoulder and head with the right hand behind the ball and the left hand on the left side and slightly in front of the ball. The player brings the ball above the head, cocks the wrist and points the right elbow toward the basket. The amount of elbow flexion increases as the distance from the basket increases. Short shots depend mainly on a wrist snap while long shots use both the wrist and forearm. The player pushes against the floor, jumping into the air and extending the body upward, keeping the eyes on the basket from the time the feet leave the floor until contact is re-established on the follow through. The player releases the ball at the top of the jump by fully extending the right arm and snapping the wrist. The hang, a temporary suspension in the air, is accomplished by tightening the muscles of the legs at the top of the jump or flexing the knees slightly at the apex of the jump. In the follow through, the right arm moves toward the basket, and the wrist snaps down and to the right. The player returns to the floor with knees slightly flexed and feet approximately hip-width apart.

Running Jump Shot

The running jump shot incorporates the mechanics of the dribble, stop, and standing jump shot in one continuous action. After the dribble, the player pulls up quickly, stops and pivots, squaring off to the basket, and shoots. A player dribbling with the right

hand outside the free-throw lane to the right of the basket starts
the two-step stop with the left foot. The left foot turns slightly to
the left, then the right foot is placed alongside the left to form a square
position with the basket. As soon as the right foot touches the floor,
the knees flex and the jump begins. When a player dribbles with the
left hand, the footwork is reversed. For a running jump shot from a
cut, the player receives the ball head high, stops, jumps, and
proceeds as in a running jump shot.

Turn Around Jump Shot

The turn around jump shot starts from a standing position
with the back toward the basket. The forward jumps, turns around
to face the basket and shoots. Beginners often make the mistake of
shooting before they complete the turn and squarely face the basket.

Fade Away Jump Shot

The fade away jump shot, utilized by advanced players, is
executed from a standing position or dribble. The mechanics are
identical to the other jump shots except that the forward projects
the body up and back instead of straight into the air, and follows
through with the body falling back, or fading away, from the defensive player.

THREE BASIC SHOTS

If the three basic shots, the lay-up, the set and jump shot,
are practiced until a high degree of proficiency is obtained, the
offensive player is usually capable of scoring against all but the
exceptional guard. Acquiring skill in shooting does not automatically
make an offensive player a shooting threat. Offensive players
must determine not only which shot is appropriate but also the correct time to shoot. Forwards should never arbitrarily determine
whether to shoot a lay-up, set, or jump shot before assessing the
guard's position. Through one-on-one practice (one defensive player
on one offensive player), offensive players learn that a single defensive player does not prevent an offensive player from getting
a good shot at the basket.

Hints for the Forward

1. After receiving a pass, look at the basket.
2. When within shooting distance and open, shoot a set or
jump shot.
3. When an opponent is guarding close, fake, and then drive
for a lay-up shot.
4. When the guard is sagging to prevent the drive, stop quickly and perform a jump shot.

Hook shot

The hook shot, of particular value to the center or pivot players,
is not only a difficult shot to execute, but also the most difficult
shot to block or defend. The fundamentals of the hook shot are
the same as those of the hook pass. The shooter receives the ball
with the back toward the basket, the feet parallel and shoulder-
width apart, and the body well balanced. She holds the ball in

FIGURE 4–21 Hook shot.

a comfortable position at approximately waist level until the shot is initiated, when she takes one long step backward and sideward toward the basket or baseline. For a hook with the right hand, the shooter steps with the left foot, the pivot foot, then lifts the right knee and extends the arms upward, holding the right hand underneath the ball in a cupped position with the weight of the ball resting on the fingers. She brings the ball along the right hip and turns the head and left shoulder to the left, focusing the eyes on the target. The wrists snap, releasing the ball off the finger-tips with the first two fingers imparting final impetus to the ball. During the follow through she completes the rotation with the right hip. The majority of players advocating the hook shot select the back-board as the target. Since most hook shots are executed from the side of the basket, the backboard provides an easier target than the rim of the basket. Hook shots even with or slightly behind the basket are, however, more successful if the basket is the point of aim.

Two-hand overhead shot

The two-hand overhead shot is a fast shot with a high trajectory. It is ideal for shooting behind and over screens established

FIGURE 4–22 Two-hand over the head shot.

by the opponents. To interfere with the shot the defending player is forced to guard closely, thus becoming vulnerable to any quick offensive action by the forward. The shooter holds the ball slightly above the head on the pads of the fingers and thumbs and cocks the wrists, bringing the elbows in close to the body. She bends the knees, extends the legs and propels the ball toward the basket by snapping the wrists forward. Two disadvantages of the shot are that: (1) players can consume too much time in putting the ball into a dribbling position from the overhead position, allowing the defense sufficient time to react; and (2) players with strong wrists are the only members of the team capable of reaching the goal from any distance.

Tipping

Tipping involves jumping into the air and pushing a rebound into the basket using one or two hands. Good timing, coordination, and the ability to meet the ball at the peak of the jump are required for successful tipping. The most difficult aspects of tipping include developing the ability to determine the angle at which the ball will rebound and ascertaining correct body position in respect to the angle of the rebound. It is often more advantageous to use one hand because a player can reach approximately six inches higher with one hand than with two. To tip, the player jumps into the air, catches the ball momentarily, then pushes it back toward the basket. She extends the elbows, and controls the tip primarily through finger flexion and a small amount of wrist flexion. The eyes focus on the ball throughout the action.

Free-throws

The free-throw, an unguarded opportunity to score, is a phase of shooting in which each player strives for proficiency. Free-throws frequently mean the difference between winning or losing a game and are always pressure shots. Players must develop the ability to concentrate and be completely unaware of the spectators and other players on the court.

Hints for Relaxing for the Free-Throw. (One hint or a combination may be used.)

1. Use part of the 10 seconds allotted for the free-throw to relax.

2. Take one or two deep breaths.

3. Bounce the ball several times to relax tense muscles.

4. Let the arms hang limp at the sides for one or two seconds.

5. Use either the one- or two-hand set shot, depending upon which is more frequently used during regular game strategy. (This is highly recommended for beginners since they do not have to develop another new skill.)

6. Walk slowly to the free-throw line in order to catch the breath and concentrate on what has to be done after receiving the ball.

One-hand set shot

The one-hand set, the two-hand set, and the underhand shot are the three methods most commonly used for the free-throw. To execute the one-hand set shot the shooter places the feet in a stride position with the right foot forward and close to the foul line. The toes of the right foot point inward and the toes of the left foot point slightly outward. The ball is held on the fingers as in the regular one-hand set shot. The knees bend slightly, the back is straightened, the head is up and the eyes focus on the point of aim. The shooter brings the ball back and down, moving the elbow under the ball, then completely extends the ankles, knees, arm and wrist in the direction of the basket. She releases the ball with a slight backspin to help direct the rebound from the board or the back rim into the basket. The shooter must refrain from stepping over the free-throw line before the ball touches the rim or backboard (Figure 4–23).

Underhand free-throw

The underhand method of shooting enables the player to stand in a more relaxed position for the free-throw. Beginners can usually

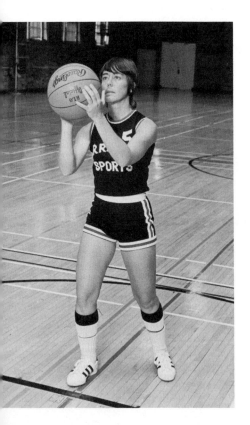

FIGURE 4–23   One-hand set shot.

FIGURE 4-24   Underhand free throw.

execute the underhand free-throw with a reasonable degree of accuracy. One disadvantage of the shot is the fact that it is solely for free-throws and has no other use in the game. For the shot the player's feet are parallel and slightly more than shoulder-width apart. With toes pointed outward, knees flexed and body weight evenly distributed over both feet, the player extends the arms downward in front of the body in a relaxed position. She holds the ball between the fingers and thumbs of both hands. The thumbs are on top of the ball and point diagonally toward each other forming a 45 degree angle. The eyes focus on the point of aim. The player starts the shot by flexing the knees, keeping the upper trunk erect, the arms straight, and slightly cocking the wrists with the thumbs and knuckles of the fingers leading. The arms swing forward and upward while the legs are straightened and the ball is released in the direction of the basket. The follow through is an upward extension of fingers, wrists and arms toward the target. Concentrate on applying equal force to the ball with both hands.

DRILLS

1. *Semi-Circle.* The class forms a semi-circle in front of the basket. Each player, in succession, shoots the designated shot and retrieves the rebound (Diagram 4–19).

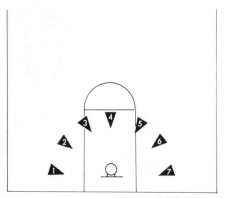
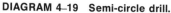

DIAGRAM 4-19 Semi-circle drill.

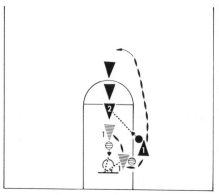

DIAGRAM 4-20 Column formation.

2. *Column Formation.* Divide the players into columns with each column located four feet in front of a free-throw line. Player 1, the first player in the column, shoots, recovers the ball and passes to player 2, who repeats the actions. Player 1 then runs to the end of the line (Diagram 4-20). Variation: (1) Position the columns to the right or left of the basket; (2) Increase the distance from the basket; (3) Have a player under the basket to retrieve the rebound, pass to the next player in line and then move to the end of the shooting line; or, (4) Divide the column into two lines, one on each side of the basket.

3. *Double Line Shooting.* The players stand in two equal columns diagonally facing the free-throw line. Player 1, the first person in column I, shoots the designated shot and runs to the end of line II. Player 2, the first player in column II, recovers the ball, passes to player 3, then goes to the end of the column I. Player 3 shoots and play continues in the same pattern as long as desired (Diagram 4-21). The same formation is useful for practicing the dribble and lay-up shot.

4. *Lay-up with a Chaser. Players are in three equal lines with* lines I and II parallel to each other and diagonally facing the left side of the basket. Line III is parallel to the endline and faces the right side of the basket. Players are designated in the following way: Line I—shooter; Line II—chaser; and Line III—rebounder-passer. When the drill is first introduced, the shooter gets a two-step lead over the chaser. The drill starts with the ball tossed toward the basket. When the rebounder-passer secures the ball, the shooter breaks toward the basket at top speed and receives a pass from her. The pass must be accurate because the chaser is close behind. The shooter attempts to score a goal while the chaser tries to intercept or deflect the ball. When the players are more skilled, the chaser moves to a position even with the shooter (Diagram 4-22).

5. *Drive and Jump Shot.* The players stand in normal offensive

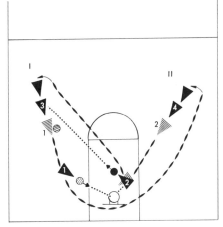

DIAGRAM 4–21 Double line shooting.

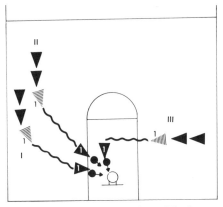

DIAGRAM 4–22 Lay-up shot with chaser.

positions. Each player has a ball and drives with one or two dribbles to the left of the basket, stopping quickly and executing a jump shot. After proficiency is acquired on the left side, players practice driving to the right.

6. *Pass, Shoot and Rebound.* Divide the players into three lines. Line I is under the basket to rebound the ball, Line II is on the opposite side of the basket facing Line III, and Line III is beyond the free-throw line diagonally facing the basket. The first person in Line II starts the drill by passing the ball to the first player in Line III. The passer throws from the top of the circle as the receiver cuts for the basket and shoots. The first person in line I recovers the ball and passes to the second person in line II. Players rotate lines (Diagram 4–23A).

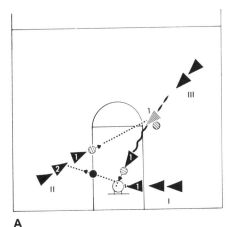

A

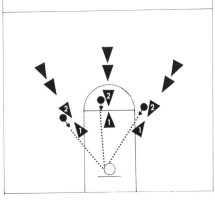

B

DIAGRAM 4–23 Pass, shoot and rebound.

7. *Hand-up Shooting Drill.* Players form three lines facing the goal. A defensive player stands in front of the first player, or forward, in each line. The object is for the forward to shoot the ball over the outstretched arms of the guard. The defensive player rebounds the ball, passes to the next forward, and runs to the end of the line. The player who shot the ball becomes the guard (Diagram 4–23B).

8. *One-on-One.* Players stand with a partner. One partner is a guard and starts in the center of the lane and one is a forward at the free-throw line. The forward uses any offensive technique to score while the guard attempts to deflect or intercept the ball. Play stops when the forward shoots or the guard is successful.

9. *High Post.* Form two lines—one on each sideline which are even with the free-throw line and face each other. Player 1, the first person in line I, passes to player 2, the first person in line II, who has moved to a high post position just beyond the free-throw line. Player 1 cuts to the outside of 2 while 2 is returning the pass. Player 1 dribbles toward the basket and shoots. Player 2 recovers the rebound (Diagram 4–24). Variations: (1) After handing off to player 1, 2 pivots, turns toward the basket to receive a return pass from 1 and shoots. Player 1 rebounds the ball. (2) Repeat the drill as in Variation (1) except that 2 passes back to 1 who executes a lay-up shot. (3) Repeat the same drill with the players starting on opposite sides of the floor.

10. *Tipping Drill.* Station the players in front of the baskets. Each player should have a ball and use half of the backboard. The object is to see who can keep the ball on the backboard for the longest period of time by tipping the ball.

11. *Circle Tipping.* Eight or nine players form a circle two or three feet from the goal. As the group begins running in a circle counter-clockwise, the first player under the goal throws the ball

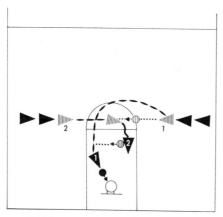

DIAGRAM 4–24 High post drill.

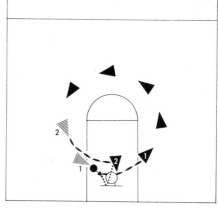

DIAGRAM 4–25 Circle tipping.

against the backboard. The next player in the circle jumps up and tips the ball back against the board. Each player tips the ball against the backboard as the circle moves around (Diagram 4–25).

12. *Reaction Shooting.* Separate the class into groups of four. Players 1 and 2 are on either side of the basket as rebounders, player 3 is even with the free-throw line but outside the circle, and player 4 constantly changes shooting positions. The drill starts with two balls; a third ball may be added later. Player 3 passes to player 4 who shoots the ball. As soon as the shot leaves the hands of player 4, player 3 passes another ball. Players 1 and 2 continually rebound and pass the balls to player 3 (Diagram 4–26).

13. *Around the World.* Mark numbers from 1 to 8 on the floor around the free-throw area. Starting at the first number, players shoot from each number consecutively until a goal is missed. Players take turns and resume shooting on the number where the previous basket was missed. The first player to complete all the numbers is the winner. Variation: A player missing the first shot from any position has the choice of taking a second shot. If the second shot misses, the player must resume shooting from the first position. A player who does not chance a second shot stays at that spot on the next turn (Diagram 4–27).

14. *Set Shooting for Speed.* Draw a line on each side of the foul line six to eight feet from the basket. Two teams play at each basket. Each team has a ball and stands behind the line. On a signal, the first player in each line attempts a field goal, recovers the ball as quickly as possible, and passes to the next player in line. The remaining players on the team continue in a similar manner until 10 baskets have been made. Each basket scores one point. Any set number of points may determine a winning team. Repeat the game after the teams change sides.

15. *H-O-R-S-E.* Select a leader who shoots a basket from any position on the court. Each player, in turn, attempts the same shot and receives the letter "H" if she misses the first basket. Players receive another letter each time a goal is missed. After a goal is

DIAGRAM 4–26   **Reaction shooting.**

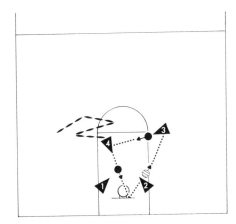

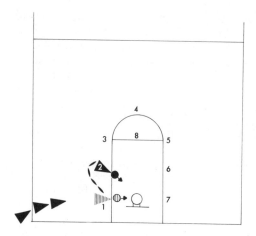

DIAGRAM 4–27   Around the world.

missed the next player in line executes any type of shot from any position on the court. The game continues until everyone, except the winner, receives all the letters of the word HORSE.

16. *Twenty-One.* Divide the players into two teams or let them compete as individuals. Each player in succession shoots a long and a short shot (follow-up shot). The long shot can be from the foul line, the edge of the circle, or any other designated spot. The player takes the long shot and whether made or missed, recovers the ball and tries for a goal from the position where the ball was recovered. No bounce, dribble, or run is permitted. Players score two points for a successful long shot and one point for a short goal. The first player or team accumulating 21 points is the winner. Variation: (1) The procedure is the same except that each player continues shooting until either the long or short shot is missed. (2) The drill is performed in the same manner except that the player who fails to make a long shot is denied a short shot.

17. *Five, Three, One.* The players stand behind the free-throw line. Each player shoots three times in succession. The first shot from the free-throw line is worth five points, the second shot, taken from wherever the ball rebounds, scores three points, and the third shot, a lay-up, is worth one point. An exception is made when the first basket is successful and the ball goes behind the backboard. The shooter may then dribble the rebound from behind the basket to a position parallel to it. The first player or team to score 50 points is the winner.

18. *Team Twenty-One.* Divide the players into groups of three or four at each goal. The game starts with one player shooting from the free-throw line and the other three players in position for a free-throw rebound. The player continues shooting free-throws until a basket is missed. All four players attempt to recover the rebound. The player who recovers the ball shoots a field goal while the other players try to block the ball. Each free-throw is worth one point, and a field goal is worth two points. The player

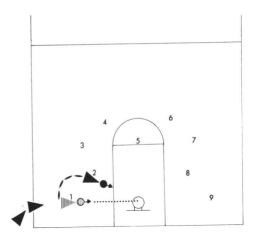

DIAGRAM 4–28 Golf.

who scores a field goal becomes the next person to shoot free-throws. The game continues until one player has scored 21 points. When there are four or more players at one goal, they may be divided into teams and compete against one another.

19. *Golf.* Draw numbers from one to nine in scattered formation on the floor. Starting at number one, each player in succession shoots the ball, remaining at each of the nine positions until the goal is made. The procedure is the same until all nine positions are completed. Establish a par score in advance. The value of a par score is that a player practicing on her own may compete against par. Individual scores or medal scores (the total number of shots necessary to complete the nine positions), may also be used (Diagram 4–28).

20. *Free Throw Contest.* The players stand at the free-throw line. Each player shoots 10 to 25 free-throws, rotating after every three shots. The player accumulating the highest total number of successful free-throws is the winner. Rebound practice may follow after a free-throw is missed.

REBOUNDING

Basic Techniques

It would be difficult to overemphasize the fact that players who control both the offensive and defensive backboards also control the game. Although the basic techniques of rebounding are similar to those of jumping, the manner in which it is performed depends upon whether the rebound is offensive or defensive. Gaining control of the ball on the rebound requires intensive practice in positioning and jumping. Positioning varies according to the following considerations: (1) the player's distance from the goal; (2) the speed of the ball; (3) the angle of the rebound; and (4) whether the rebounder is an offensive or defensive player. The angle of the rebound is identical to the angle at which the ball strikes the backboard unless the ball contacts an obstacle, such as the rim. It is most important for the rebounder to gain the inside position between the basket or anticipated angle of rebound and the opponent, and screen the assigned player out of rebound range, or impede any backward movement by an opponent trapped too far under the goal. Shots missing the basket will usually rebound to the opposite side of the basket unless the player is shooting from directly in front of the goal. A team's rebounding ambition should be a "maximum of one shot per possession of the ball for the opponents, and a minimum of one shot for a goal or repossession of the ball."

Defensive tactics

Either player-to-player or zone defense can be effective for maintaining rebounding position near the basket. In zone defense, each player assumes responsibility for a designated part of the triangle in the basket area, whereas in player-to-player defense, each player screens a specific offensive player.

When an offensive player shoots, defensive players close to the basket take a few steps backward while watching their assigned opponents. The defensive player who has just sagged off an assigned player shifts immediately to an advantageous position for blocking her. The player responsible for the pivot post who does not have an inside position moves rapidly to regain the inside position or any advantage (Figure 4–25).

FIGURE 4–25.

FIGURE 4–26   Blocking the offensive player after shot at the basket.

During the rebound, the defensive player assumes an open, side-stride position two to five feet from the basket and utilizes peripheral vision to watch the assigned player and the ball at the same time. Once proper distance from the basket has been attained the defensive player protects her position by spreading the feet, flexing the knees, raising the elbows to shoulder level, and watching the ball (Figure 4–26). A more experienced player learns to predict the offensive player's direction by sensing, or "feeling," the movement. A defensive player who neglects the ball, however, and concentrates solely on the forward's actions, often fails to judge the direction, flight or force of the ball.

Hints on Defensive Rebound Strategy

1. If the offensive player attempts to get the rebound, the defensive player pivots, stepping into the opponent's path.

2. If the offensive player moves to the inside of the defensive player, the defensive player cuts off the offensive player by executing a rear pivot and a step toward the goal.

3. If the players are close to the basket, the front pivot is frequently the most successful pivot to use in the limited space.

4. The ball is retrieved more effectively if the defensive player learns to correctly judge her distance from the basket. It should be noted, however, that the distance from the basket depends upon the height and jumping ability of the player being blocked. An offensive player who is taller than the guard must be kept farther from the goal than a player whose height is similar to the guard's.

5. If the defensive player is too far under the basket, the ball may rebound over her.

6. If the defensive player is too far from the goal, the opponent may wait until the last moment then run around her to take the inside position.

The Jump

After screening the offensive player the defensive player jumps to gain possession of the ball. The guard first determines the angle of the rebound then coordinates the jump with the flight of the ball by beginning to jump as soon as the ball strikes the rim or backboard. Ideally, the rebounder contacts the ball at the peak of the jump. Keeping the eyes on the ball, the rebounder pushes with the toes, extends the knees and ankles, thrusts the arms upward to full extension, then jumps toward the ball, placing the ball in front of the body. The body position protects the ball from any opponent behind the defensive player. To prohibit the opponent from sliding, jumping or reaching around to obtain the ball the guard lands with elbows extended and legs spread in a wide-stance position (Figure 4–27, A and B).

The guard must grasp the ball securely! Remember that everyone will be struggling for the rebound. Once a player has touched the ball, no opponent should be able to jar or dislodge it. A slight turn or twist of the ball as the rebounder returns to the floor discourages a tie ball. Although a tall player has the ability to hold

FIGURE 4–27.

the ball above the opponents' heads, a player of average height is forced to keep the ball under the chin or on the side of the body opposite the opponent. The guard dribbles the ball away from the congested area around the goal or passes to a teammate. Since passing across the front of the goal is exceptionally dangerous, the guard should pass to a teammate on the side of the court where she retrieved the ball. A rebounder anticipating a teammate's fast break locates the pass receiver while coming down from the jump then throws an outlet pass as soon as she touches the floor.

Offensive tactics

Offensive tactics for losing an opponent and acquiring the inside position for rebounding include keeping the eyes on the ball and employing a combination of feints, quickness, cunning and determination. Because the defensive player normally has the inside position, the offensive player must avoid any screens attempted by the defense and gain a position between the defensive player and the goal. When a defensive rebounder pivots too soon the offensive player has an opportunity to control the inside rebounding position.

Three options available to an offensive rebounder include tipping the ball into the basket, passing to a teammate, or dribbling away from the basket area. If at all possible the offensive rebounder shoots; however, when it is not feasible to shoot she should pass to a teammate, and as a last resort, dribble away from the crowded conditions under the basket.

Hints for Tipping the Ball into the Goal

1. Watch the flight of the ball in order to tip the ball at the apex of the jump.

2. Extend the body completely to attain maximum height.

3. Avoid spreading the legs and jackknifing the body, decreasing the height of the jump.

4. Eliminate unnecessary bouncing up and down in anticipation of the rebound.

5. Move to a more advantageous position when the ball momentarily hangs on the rim or takes a high bounce off the rim or backboard.

On a rebound, the short player can be a great asset to a team. Instead of jumping for the rebound the short player assumes a position in front of an opponent, ready to take advantage of any error. If the opponent gets the rebound and mistakenly lowers the ball, the short player ties or "pops" the ball into the air. To "pop" the ball the player strikes it with the heel of the hand in a sharp upward movement, dislodging the ball from the opponent's hands.

Free-throw rebounds

During a free-throw the defensive players in the first positions on either side of the basket have the best places for rebounding. When the ball is in the air, the defensive player raises the arms, spreading the elbows and leaning slightly toward the center of the free-throw line. The moment the ball touches either the rim or backboard she slides the foot closest to the offensive player into the free-throw lane and pivots slightly on the opposite foot, thus screening the offensive player.

Offensive players, the second players on either side of the free-throw line, try to combat the defensive players' advantage. The offensive player leans slightly forward, fakes a movement to the middle of the lane, then steps around the defensive player to the baseline. She attempts to tap the ball into the basket or back toward the shooter. Generally, it is wise to reach for the ball with two hands, although a player can often reach higher than an opponent by using only one hand.

DRILLS

1. *Jumping.* Draw two parallel lines on the floor approximately 18 inches apart. The players face the two lines. On the signal "jump" each player jumps forward and backward over the two lines. Players perform the drill as long as desired with each individual striving to jump as high as possible. Variation: Players perform the same drill but stand with the side of the body facing

the two lines. On the signal "jump," they jump sideward to the right and return to the left.

2. *Resistance Jumping.* Arrange players with a partner. While one player tries to jump as high as possible into the air, the partner stands behind and resists the shoulders of the jumper.

3. *Chest Touch.* Position the players randomly on the floor. From a standing position, each player jumps, attempting to touch the knees to the chest. Each player should acquire the skill necessary to lift the legs high in the air.

4. *Spread-Eagle Jump.* The players are in standing position with at least five feet of space between them. On a signal the players jump up, spread the legs forward in front of the body with knees slightly bent, reach out, touch the toes in the air, then land in a comfortable position with the feet together.

5. *Bouncing Drill.* Each player selects an object approximately 30 inches above her arms as they are extended overhead. Smaller players may use the bottom of the net, while taller players use the basket rim. Each player attempts to touch the object 50 times, first reaching with the right hand 10 times, then with the left 10 times and finally, with both hands 30 times. During the final 20 jumps alternate the left and right hands. Jumping is continuous with emphasis placed on acquiring greater height with each jump.

6. *Backboard Bounce.* Station one player with a ball under each basket. The player throws the ball toward the backboard, jumps, and catches the ball with both hands at the peak of the jump. Variation: The player repeats the drill, tipping the ball into the basket instead of catching it.

7. *Blocking Out.* Players form two lines on each side of the goal with line I a few inches ahead of line II. Player 1, the first person in line I, shoots the ball while the first girl in line II, player 2, blocks player 1 and tries to gain possession of the rebound. After the ball has been retrieved the players move to the end of the opposite line. Play continues until each person has practiced shooting and blocking (Diagram 4–29).

8. *Three-on-Three or Four-on-Four.* Divide the group into three defensive and three offensive players. Station a group of defensive and offensive players in front of each goal. An extra player or the coach shoots, then each defensive player tries to screen an offensive player, gain possession of the rebound and throw an outlet pass. Since defensive players are normally located on the inside rebounding position offensive players will need to use a combination of fakes and strategic movements to elude the guards and control the ball. The drill may be performed with four or five defensive and offensive players.

9. *Offensive Tipping.* Station players in two lines, one on each side of the basket. Player 1, the first person in line I, starts the drill with a jump shot. Both players 1 and 2, the first person in line II, jump and tip the rebound until the basket is made. If a player is facing the left side of the court and the ball bounces off the front of the rim she attempts the tip with the left hand. If a

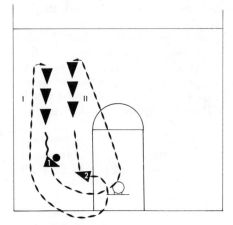

DIAGRAM 4–29   Blocking out.

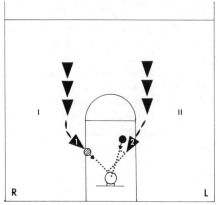

DIAGRAM 4–30   Offensive tipping.

player is facing the right side of the court she tips with the right hand (Diagram 4–30).

10. *Circle Tipping.* Players form a circle of eight or nine players approximately two or three feet from the goal. The first player under the goal throws the ball against the backboard; the next player jumps high into the air and tips the ball back against the backboard but does not attempt to place the ball in the basket. Each player in succession taps the ball against the backboard until the last player tips the ball into the basket.

OFFENSE

INTRODUCTION

To be successful a basketball team must have an offense designed to take advantage of the strengths of each player. A good offense will not be jeopardized if the defense prevents one player from playing effectively. A coach with knowledge and experience in the offensive patterns selected will not only teach more confidently, but will also be in position to answer any questions that arise and analyze mistakes that occur.

One of the most influential factors in selecting the type of offense are the various methods of defense the coach expects to encounter during the season. Naturally, if the opponents use a zone defense the offense must be able to penetrate the zone. On the other hand, when opponents have an aggressive player-to-player defense the offense must include cutting and screening techniques. In general, the best offense is one that can easily be adapted or modified to outmaneuver any type of defense.

Offensive Characteristics

1. Players must move continuously, especially teammates not directly involved in ball handling.
2. Players should possess skillful ball handling techniques, occasionally faking a pass to one player, then quickly passing to another. Players must avoid passing to the same receiver every time, forcing a pass, or passing cross-court. A successful pass must reach its target!
3. Players should move to meet a pass.
4. Players dribble only when it is necessary to change posi-

tions, drive past a defensive player, protect the ball, or create a play or score.

5. Players, except for post players, face the basket, ready to shoot or pass.

6. Rebounders on the opposing team should be drawn away from the basket.

7. Front line players drive through the middle or exchange places with other front players to determine defensive strategy. When the defense does not shift with the cutter or the exchanged players, the defense has a zone defense. The next step is to ascertain the type of zone—3-2, 2-3, 2-1-2, 1-3-1 or combination—and then set up appropriate spots for passers, shooters and rebounders.

8. Players are responsible for analyzing defensive moves and attacking areas guarded by the weak defensive players.

9. Players maintain a defensive court balance to prevent any rebound or fast break opportunities for the opponent.

10. Players must shoot accurately. They should strive to establish the 2-on-1 or the 3-on-2 situation. If possible, get in position to take a second shot at the goal but avoid forcing or rushing any shot.

11. Coaches should avoid any offensive pattern that is so intricate that players have difficulty in understanding and executing the strategy. The pattern should not be so easy, however, that the defensive team breaks the strategy in the early stages of the game. Coaches provide for individual abilities of the offensive team by creating opportunities for spontaneous moves by each player.

INDIVIDUAL OFFENSIVE TECHNIQUES

Since numerous books and articles are available on methods of offense, the following information includes only the basic techniques needed by any teacher or coach for developing an offensive pattern for players on the team.

Screens, Picks, and Rolls

The screen

The screen, pick, and roll are essential for player-to-player offense and are also effective against zone defenses. Ideally, the screen furnishes the outside forward with an opportunity to have an unguarded shot at the goal. To set the screen an offensive player moves into position in front of the defensive player guarding the teammate with the ball (Diagram 5-1).

The double screen involves three teammates handling the ball who attempt to free a high scoring player. Unlike other screening techniques the double screen may be set any place on the court. Two offensive players set the screen, while a third teammate moves in front of the screen, receives a pass and takes an unguarded shot at the goal (Diagram 5-3).

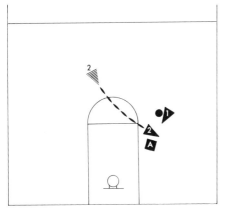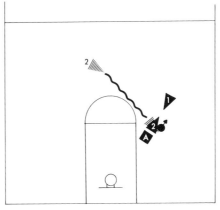

DIAGRAM 5-1   Screen.

Player 2 moves to a position between 1, who has the ball, and defensive player A. Screen should allow player adequate time to stop, "set," and shoot.

DIAGRAM 5-2   Screen set by a dribbler.

Player 2 dribbles ball in front of A, sets the screen, then passes to 1.

The moving screen, incorporated as part of play strategy, has unlimited value in offering the player for whom the screen is set a much closer shot at the basket. A team may have a variety of moving screens but one of the most common patterns involves the following movements by the two forwards.

Perhaps the most difficult screen to avoid is the *rear screen* in which the player setting the screen approaches the defensive player

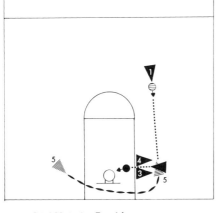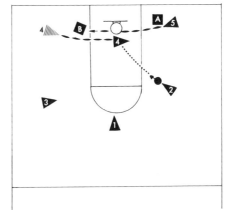

DIAGRAM 5-3   Double screen.

Players 3 and 4 set a double screen on the lane. Player 5 cuts behind the screen, receives the pass from player 1 and shoots.

DIAGRAM 5-4   Moving screen.

Players 4 and 5 cut across the lane, passing shoulder to shoulder, and screening guards A and B. Player 2 passes the ball to player 4, who attempts the shot.

from the rear. Although the player setting the screen must allow sufficient room for the defender to turn around, the element of surprise increases the effectiveness of this tactic. The rear screen, most often set by a forward or pivot player on a defensive guard, can also draw numerous fouls for the player setting the screen.

The pick

The *pick* is an offensive technique executed to momentarily free a teammate so that she may cut toward the basket to receive a pass or obtain a favorable shooting position. To set a pick an offensive player shifts to a position two or three feet to the side or behind the defensive player, spreading the legs in a wide stance to prevent the defense from moving around the pick. Any offensive player planning to take advantage of the pick begins by faking the defensive player from the desired path, then cutting as close as possible to the pick established by a teammate (Diagram 5-5).

By imaginatively executing the pick, for instance, in setting the pick on each side of the defensive player or combining it with a roll to the basket, the play becomes more difficult for the opponents to read. A pick with a roll involves two teammates in the basket area. The player initiating the pick establishes momentary contact with the defensive player or forces her to change her path, then reverse turns, cutting toward the basket in anticipation of a pass from the teammate assisting in the pick strategy. When the pick forces the defensive players to switch direction, the player who set the pick pivots in the direction of the ball, shifting toward the basket and leaving the guard behind.

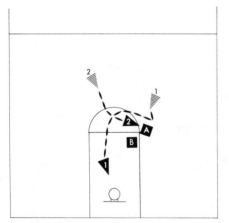
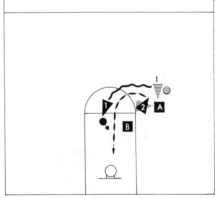

DIAGRAM 5–5   Pick.

Player 1 fakes toward the baseline as 2 sets a pick on A. Player 1 then cuts around 2 toward the goal.

DIAGRAM 5–6   Pick and roll.

Player 2 sets a pick, pivots in the direction of the ball, then cuts toward the basket. Player 1 passes the ball to 2.

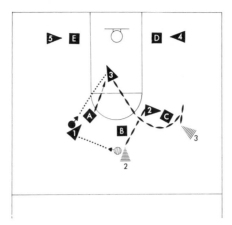

DIAGRAM 5–7   Pick "Off the ball."

Player 2 passes the ball to 1, then moves in position to set the pick for teammate 3, who fakes, cuts around the pick and receives the pass from 1.

Picks may also be set by a player without the ball in order to free a teammate—who is also without the ball—from an opponent. The teammate cuts around the pick to receive a pass from the player with the ball (Diagram 5–7).

Offensive Patterns

Single pivots

The most widely accepted offensive pattern today is the single pivot. This technique involves a player designated as the "post" who is responsible for screening defensive players, passing to teammates, scoring goals, and obtaining rebounds. The three positions of the post player include the low post, the medium high and high post (Diagram 5–8). After receiving the ball, the low post player shoots the ball without moving from her position. The low post

DIAGRAM 5–8   Post positions.

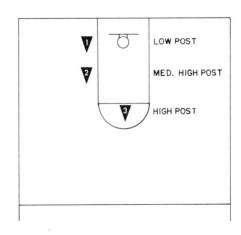

pivot player encounters more difficulty in passing to teammates who have cut toward the basket than do the other two pivot players. The medium high post offense, the most popular of the single post offenses, stands outside the free-throw lane and halfway between the free-throw line and the basket. Consequently, the post player is an offensive threat both as a scorer and as a "feeder" who passes to teammates to cut off the pivot player. The high post player is usually located along the free-throw line facing the center line, and serves more as a screener, feeder and post than as a scorer. The high post may attempt to score by turning and facing the basket or driving around the defensive player.

Post positions

There are a variety of offensive patterns that can be executed with a single pivot post. The following examples present a few of the basic formations.

Offensive Positions

The guards or "quarterbacks," generally the smaller offensive players, usually initiate plays from a balanced position behind the free-throw circle. As in football, qualities of the quarterback include the ability to run, drive, shoot, handle the ball and lead the team.

The forwards, taller and slower than the guards, may assume several positions along the sideline but are most often located at the sideline nearest the extensions of the free-throw line. The forward's task includes shooting long shots from the sides or corners, driving toward the baseline and into the free-throw area, and rebounding. The pivot player occupies one of the three post positions and is usually the tallest player on the team or the best scorer in

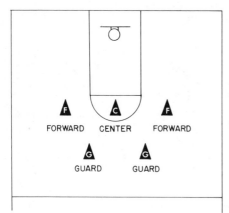

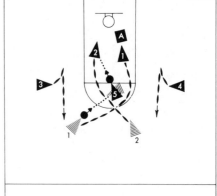

DIAGRAM 5–9   Offensive positions.

G – Quarterback, F – Forward, C – Pivot Player.   **DIAGRAM 5–10   Split the post.**

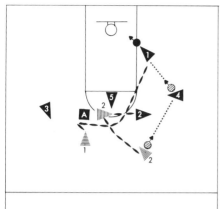 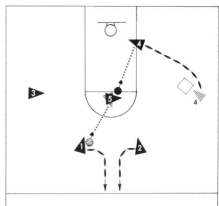

DIAGRAM 5–11   Variation of split the post.   DIAGRAM 5–12   Split the post fake.

that particular pivot area. Outside shooting ability is not necessary, but a post player who scores from outside the free-throw line forces the defense to guard closer; therefore, the taller defensive opponent is pulled away from the basket. Post players are also responsible for feeding the ball to cutters and gaining control of most of the rebounds (Diagram 5–10).

SPLIT THE POST—FROM THE HIGH POST POSITION

Player 1 passes the ball to player 5. Players 1 and 2 cut and split the post with 1 passing in front of 2 and around the opposite side of 5. Player 1 cuts before 5 feeds the ball to the open player, usually 2, who drives for the basket. Players 3 and 4 move out to cover the safety position.

VARIATION OF THE SPLIT THE POST

Player 2 passes to 4, then moves to screen from the "cutter," player 1. Player 4 passes to 1 who shoots. Following the screen, player 2 moves back toward the ball for a possible pass from 4 when 1 is covered by an opponent. Player 4 then passes to 2 (Diagram 5–11).

SPLIT THE POST FAKE

Player 1 passes to 5 then fakes a post pattern split with player 2. As the defensive player guarding 4 turns to look for the ball, player 4 cuts toward the basket and receives a pass from 5 (Diagram 5–12).

USING THE LOW POST

Player 2 passes the ball to 4, fakes a screen for 1, cuts down the middle of the key and receives the ball for a shot. If unable to receive the pass, player 2 continues through the lane and sets a screen for 5 who cuts around the screen to receive a pass from 4. The screen by player 2 is most effective when the defensive team switches guards to a player-to-player defense since the move forces a small guard to switch to the taller post player (Diagram 5–13).

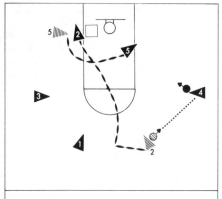

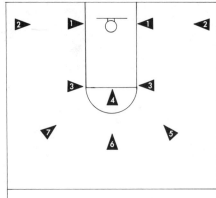

DIAGRAM 5–13 The low post.   DIAGRAM 5–14   Double post positions.

1. Pivot players playing tight.
2. Pivot players spread wide.
3. Pivot players playing high.
1 and 4. Tandem position, high and low.
5, 6, and 7. Three guards or outside players.
6. Middle guard.

Double Post

Double post offense, a strategy involving two post players, is advantageous for teams having two skilled pivot players. The players may be stationed in a low, a high or tandem (one high and one low) post position. Usually the post players rove along the free-throw foul lane, moving from the baseline to the free-throw line and changing sides only when screening for each other. Although scoring from the lane area and rebounding from the basket increase if both players are in the pivot area, driving opportunities from outside players are greatly reduced. Therefore, pivot players who can score from the corners may set up a wide post, subsequently creating driving opportunities for the guards by opening the middle of the court. Even though two players are assigned to the post position it is not always essential for both to play the position at the same time. Basically, each player is responsible for drawing a defensive player out of the way and thus opening a space for a teammate's drive toward the basket.

The outside guards, players 5, 6 and 7, should possess the same qualifications as single pivot guards. The middle guard is the "key playmaker" while the post players are scorers, rebounders and feeders for cutting teammates. If the pivot players consistently score from outside the free-throw area, a wide post strategy which pulls the taller opponents outside the lane area will increase the variety of attack patterns.

BASIC DOUBLE POST PATTERNS

Player 5 moves across the lane, sets a pick on defensive player E. Post player 4 cuts toward the basket, recieves a pass from 2, and

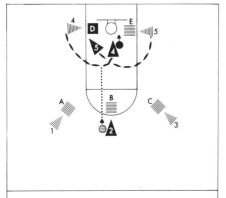 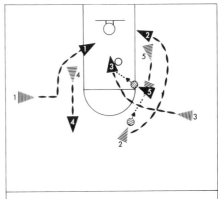

DIAGRAM 5–15   Double post patterns.   DIAGRAM 5–16   Split the high post.

shoots. The situation can be reversed with player 4 setting a pick for 5 (Diagram 5–15).

SPLIT THE HIGH POST

Player 2 passes to 5 who moves to a high post position to meet the pass. Player 2 cuts first, then player 3 cuts off post player 5. As 5, the pivot player, feeds the ball to 3, player 4 sets a back screen for 1 who cuts toward the basket. Player 3 may shoot, pass to 2 or pass to 1. Player 4 continues to move out in front for defensive safety (Diagram 5–16).

SPLIT THE MIDDLE POST

Player 2 dribbles, hands the ball to 3, then moves toward the corner. Player 3 dribbles toward the middle of the court and returns a pass to 2. As player 3 passes to 2, player 5 screens for 4 who cuts toward the ball to receive a pass from 2. Players 2 and 3 split the post (Diagram 5–17).

HIGH DOUBLE POST

Player 2 passes the ball to 1 who passes to post player 4. Player 2 moves to a position beside pivot player 5, forming a double screen for 3. Player 4 passes to 3 who has cut for the basket, or to 2 who has cut back to the free-throw line. The pass to 2 is most effective against player-to-player defense (Diagram 5–18).

Tandem Post

In the tandem position one post player is stationed at the free-throw line as the high post, and the other is at the baseline as the low post. In order to receive passes and provide screens for any middle player driving toward the basket, the high post continuously shifts from one side of the free-throw circle to the other. The baseline player stays on the side of the court opposite the ball, creating an opportunity for the wing to drive to the baseline or for the middle player to drive to the basket. Periodically, the two post players should deliberately exchange positions to disturb the guards. The following diagrams show variations of the tandem post (1-3-1 offense).

 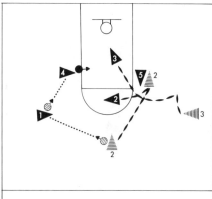

DIAGRAM 5–17   Split the middle post.   DIAGRAM 5–18   High double post.

FEEDING THE LOW POST FOR A ONE-ON-ONE PIVOT MANEUVER
    Player 1 passes the ball to 3 who passes to 5 as she cuts across
the key. When player 5 cannot shoot, 4 cuts off of 5, receives a pass
from 5 and shoots (Diagram 5–19, A).
    TANDEM POST OFFENSE
    Player 1 passes to 3, fakes to the left, cuts off of 4 forcing A to
run into 4, then receives a pass from player 3 and shoots (Diagram
5–19 B, Variation 1). If player 1 is covered and cannot receive a pass,
player 4 turns and cuts behind 1 for the pass from 3. Variation 2. If
player 1 is covered and cannot receive a pass, she runs toward the
baseline and sets a pick for the low post, player 5, who receives a
pass from 3.
    MIDDLE GUARD VARIATION
    Player 4 moves to the top of the circle, setting a pick for 1 who
dribbles taking advantage of the pick, then passes to player 5 who
has cut across the lane. Player 5 either passes to 4 who has rolled
and cut toward the basket or shoots (Diagram 5–19, C).

Figure 8 or weave

    The Figure 8, or weave offense, is a player-to-player pattern de-
signed for teams having over-all height but lacking a tall player capable of playing post. The weave requires skill in driving and in
handling the ball, but it also forces the defense to move, consequently pulling the taller opponents out on the court and into unfamiliar defensive areas.
    Personnel for the Figure 8, actually a 3-2 offense, include three
outside players and two corner players. The outside players should
not only be intelligent and alert, but also skilled in shooting, dribbling, passing, driving and cutting. One of the three outside
players, commonly referred to as the quarterback, is in charge of

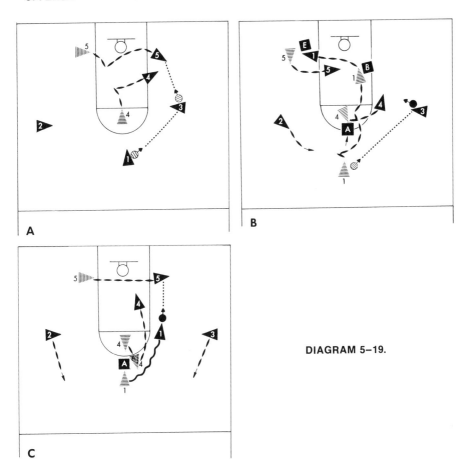

A

B

C

DIAGRAM 5–19.

offensive strategy. Corner players should have the following qualifications: (1) height; (2) accuracy in short jump shots; (3) ability to drive to the baseline; (4) ability to fake the opponents; and (5) proficiency in feeding passes to teammates cutting toward the ball or off screens.

Principles for a Successful Weave

1. The players should constantly move to obtain the ball or set screens for teammates. Moving purposefully around the court applies additional pressure on the opponents.

2. The opponents should be forced to shift with the offense to prevent sagging or blocking the middle of the court.

3. The middle of the court should be open. Cutters who do not receive the ball should continue running to the sides of the court.

4. The cutters are not restricted to receiving the ball but also (and sometimes preferably) screen for teammates.

5. The teammates of a player who passes the ball and cuts

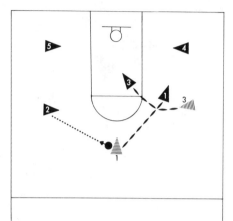

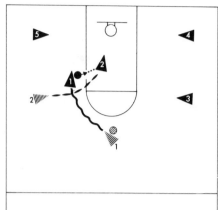

DIAGRAM 5–20 Principles of the weave. The screen.

DIAGRAM 5–21 Principles of the weave. The dribble and pass.

in the opposite direction should know that the cutter is going to screen on the weak side (Diagram 5–20).

6. The player dribbling to the "inside" expects her teammate to cut around and drive to the basket (Diagram 5–21).

7. Passes should be directed "outside" toward the receiver.

8. The responsibility for defensive balance rests with each team member. There should always be a defensive safety position.

BASIC FIGURE 8 OR WEAVE PATTERN

Player 1 dribbles a short distance, passes to 3, and continues on to the right corner to replace 4 who moves into the position vacated by 3. Player 3 dribbles to the left with the left hand, passes to 2, then moves into the position vacated by 5. Players repeat cutting from corner to corner until an opening occurs. Cutting players raise the hand opposite the ball as a target for the pass or for a possible shot at the goal. Dribblers should always be alert for an opportunity to drive toward the basket (Diagram 5–22). Variation: Instead of replacing player 3, 4 reverses and sets a screen for 1 who cuts around 4 to receive a pass from 2 and shoots (Diagram 5–23).

Shuffle offense or continuity pattern

The shuffle offense was originated by Bruce Drake at the University of Oklahoma and involves a continuity pattern in which every player is prepared to play each position. The shuffle begins with an overload to one side of the floor followed by completion of the basic options, then an overload on the opposite side of the court. For the shuffle to be successful, team members must be balanced in height and have ball handling and cutting skills. If each team member has the ability to score from outside, the defense

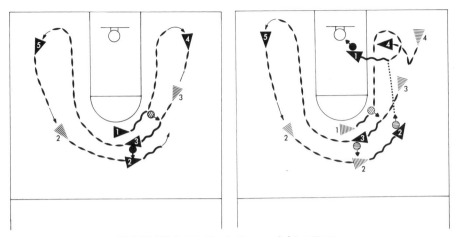

DiAGRAM 5–22   Basic figure eight pattern.

DIAGRAM 5–23   Figure eight option play.

will be unable to sag off a player and block the middle court area
To begin the shuffle pattern the best feeders are near the free-
throw lane to the right of the basket, the best cutters are to the
side of the court beyond the free-throw area, and the best scorer,
the center, is in the area extending from outside the circle to the
left of the basket near the free-throw line. The center may, however, be in the lower court position near the baseline and sideline on
the left side of the court.

PRINCIPLES OF THE SHUFFLE PATTERN

Player 1, the feeder, is stationed along the lane close to the basket
and player 2 is about three feet outside the top of the circle.

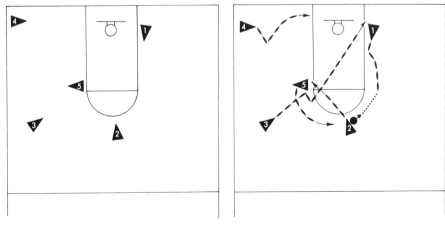

DIAGRAM 5–24   Principles of the shuffle pattern.

DIAGRAM 5–25   Basic shuffle pattern.

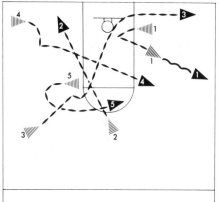

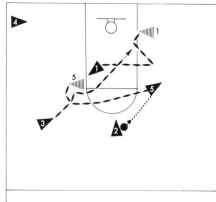

DIAGRAM 5–26   Continuity pattern.   **DIAGRAM 5–27   Variation of continuity pattern.**

Player 3, the cutter, is approximately a step ahead of 2 and about six feet from the sideline. Player 4 is near the sideline, about six feet from the baseline, and 5, the center, is at the free-throw line, outside the lane (Diagram 5–24).

THE BASIC SHUFFLE PATTERN

Variation 1. Player 2 passes the ball to 1 while 3 cuts off the screen set by 5. Variation 2. Player 4 delays until 3 cuts past 5 then 4 cuts along the baseline and into the pivot area. Variation 3. Player 2 sets a screen for 5 who cuts to the top of the circle (Diagram 5–25).

THE CONTINUITY PATTERN

The shaded areas represent the players' original positions and the darkened triangles their new positions after completing the three variations without a score (Diagram 5–26).

VARIATION OF CONTINUITY PATTERN

Since the ball must be passed to player 1 to initiate the basic offense, defensive players try to prevent 1 from receiving the ball by overplaying that position. Player 1 then cuts across the lane, sets a screen for 5 who cuts and takes the 1 position. Player 1 moves to the 5 position and sets a screen for 3, the first cutter (Diagram 5–27).

ZONE OFFENSE

In selecting a zone offense for a team the coach should examine the basic alignment and weaknesses of each type of zone defense. As the ball moves, however, and the players react to the new ball position, the original alignment and weaknesses of the zone defense are altered.

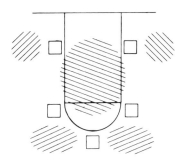

DIAGRAM 5-28   3-2 Zone.

Offense possibility = 1-3-3 or 2-3.

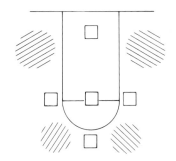

DIAGRAM 5-29   1-3-1 Zone.

Offense possibility = 1-2-2 or 2-1-2.

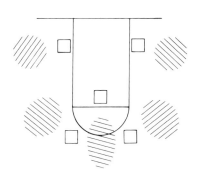

DIAGRAM 5-30   2-1-2 Zone.

Offense possibility = 1-3-1 or 1-2-2.

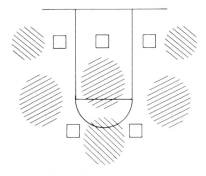

DIAGRAM 5-31   2-3 Zone.

Offense possibility = 1-3-1 or 1-2-2.

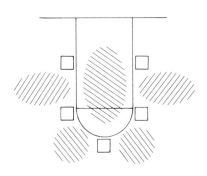

DIAGRAM 5-32   1-2-2 Zone.

Offense possibility = 1-3-1 or 2-2-1.

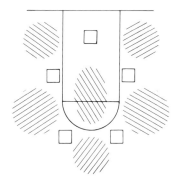

DIAGRAM 5-33   2-2-1 Zone.

Offense possibility = 1-3-1 or 1-2-2.

 = vulnerable or weak areas

Defensive Pattern Weaknesses Requiring Player Reaction as the Ball is Passed

1. The players need time to switch from an offensive to a defensive team. Whenever possible, fast break a slow team.

2. The offensive team can often pass faster than the players on defense can shift to the appropriate positions. As the ball is passed and a hole develops in the zone, players should move into the open area.

3. The offense can lessen the effectiveness of a zone by spreading across the court, forcing the defense to cover more territory. When possible, offensive players take positions between the defensive players (play the gaps).

4. The zone defensive players who sink against a cutter can often be outmaneuvered by players having accurate short set shots or jump shots. If at anytime the defense fails to cover a player cutting toward the basket, the player should attempt a lay-up shot.

5. Defensive players in a zone formation concentrate on the ball, consequently the offensive players' movements within a zone tend to confuse the defense.

6. The difficult areas to defend with a zone defense are:
   (a) the corners
   (b) the extensions of the free-throw line
   (c) the head of the key.

7. The defensive players, concentrating on the ball, are vulnerable to screens set within the area.

8. The offense frequently applies the overload principle to outnumber the defense in a particular area.

9. The offensive team may reverse play from one side of the floor to the other, forcing the defensive players to shift. If the defense is slow the forwards have an easy shot.

10. The proficient scorers play on the weak defensive side while tall players are on the side of court with short defensive players. In zone defense the coach does not have an opportunity to match each player's weaknesses and strengths with those of an opponent.

11. The offensive team with players who can score from outside the free-throw circle can force their opponents out of zone defense.

12. The team that consistently passes to the high or medium high post position will usually have success in shooting against a zone defense. The high post player is in good position to shoot at the basket or pass to a teammate who has an opportunity to score by further penetrating the zone. Players in a zone defense tend to collapse on any high post player receiving the ball.

1-3-1 Offense

The 1-3-1 is an offensive pattern having one player in the basket area, three players spread out near the free-throw line, and one player beyond the top of the circle. It is successful against most defensive patterns. The 1-3-1 offense effectively controls the 2-1-2, 2-3, 3-2, 1-2-2 and 2-2-1 zone defenses. Above all, one should remember that the simplest and most efficient method of defeating any zone defense is to score from outside the key.

Player 1 is the key ball handler and "quarterback," players 2 and 3, the wings, are proficient in side and corner shots, and players 4 and 5 excel in rebounding and jump shots from the pivot area. Player 5, also called a baseline rover, should be the best pivot scorer and possess a good shot from the baseline. In addition, the pivot player at the free-throw line has the responsibility of screening for teammates who are shooting or cutting for the basket (Diagram 5–34).

Basic 1-3-1 Offensive Pattern

To begin the 1-3-1 offense player 1 advances the ball down the center of the floor until meeting opposition, then passes to 3. As the right guard makes the defensive challenge, players 4 and 5 move toward 3. Several options are now available: Variation 1. If unguarded, player 3 shoots; players 2, 4 and 5 are responsible for the rebound, and 1 becomes the safety player. Player 3 remains in the free-throw line area to cover long rebounds or prevent defensive rebounders from making a quick pass out for a fast break (Diagram 5–35). Variation 2. Player 3 passes to either player 4 or 5. If player 3 passes to 5 at the baseline, 3 will cut through the key anticipating a return pass. Player 4 slides down the lane expecting a pass from 3 or 5. Player 3, after cutting through the lane, takes the opposite wing position. Player 1 moves into the position vacated by 3 while 2 shifts to the spot vacated by 1. Variation 3. Player 3 returns the ball to 1 who quickly passes to 2. If the passes are fast, 2 has an opportunity to shoot; otherwise, 2 has the three options that were available to player 3.

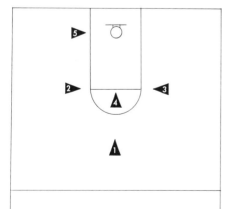

DIAGRAM 5–34 1-3-1 Offense.

DIAGRAM 5–35 1-3-1 Offense.

Variation.

Variations for Player 4

Variation 1. Player 1 passes to 3. Player 5 moves to the side of the court where the pass was made while 3 passes to 4 who moves to meet the ball. Player 4 then passes to 5 (Diagram 5–36). Variation 2. Player 1, 2 or 3 passes to 4, playing in the high post position. As the defense overplays 4, players 3 and 5 cut toward the basket. Player 4 then passes to 3 or 5, and if unable to pass to them, the pass is to 2 or back to 1 (Diagram 5–37).

2-1-2 Offense

Another basic offensive alignment, the 2-1-2, is effective against the 1-3-1, 3-2, and 1-2-2 zone defense. In 2-1-2 strategy team members should be able to score from the following positions: (1) Players 1 and 2, the guards, from outside the key area; (2) Players 3 and 4, the forwards, from their respective corners; and (3) Player 5, the center, from the pivot area near the free-throw line (Diagram 5–38).

Basic 2-1-2 Offensive Patterns

(1) Player 1 starts the attack by passing to 2 who passes to corner player 4. As 4 receives the ball, 5 cuts to the baseline and 3 moves to the medium post position. Player 4 shoots or passes to 5 or 3 who either shoots the ball or returns a pass to 2. Upon receiving the pass 2 passes to 3, or if there is no opening, 2 passes to 4, which may force an opening for 3 or 5 (Diagram 5–39). (2) If player 2 passes to 1, player 5, the center, cuts to the left corner position to receive a pass from 1. As 5 receives the pass, the forward at the free-throw line, player 3, cuts through the lane to the baseline, assuming the original duties of 5 but on the opposite side of the lane. Player 4 shifts into the position in the free-throw area vacated by 3. Player 5 passes to 3, 4, or back to 1. Players 3, 4 and 5 cover offensive rebounding while 1 and 2 stay back for safety.

DIAGRAM 5–36   1-3-1 Offense.

Option one for player 4.

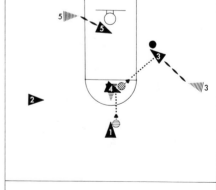

DIAGRAM 5–37   1-3-1 Offense.

Option two for player 4.

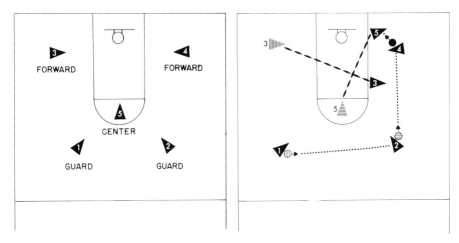

DIAGRAM 5–38   2-1-2 Offensive strategy.
DIAGRAM 5–39   Basic 2-1-2 Offensive patterns.

If the opponents have a fast breaking team and gain control of the rebound, either 1 or 2 presses the outlet pass receiver (Diagram 5–40). (3) When the defensive team is in a 3-2 zone, 1 passes to 5 to counteract the zone with an offensive 3-on-2 situation. Player 5 may shoot or pass to 3 or 4 (Diagram 5–41).

2-3 Offense

The 2-3 alignment is the standard professional style offense. It has two guards at the top of the circle and three forwards near the free-throw line and basket. For the 2-3 offense to function most ef-

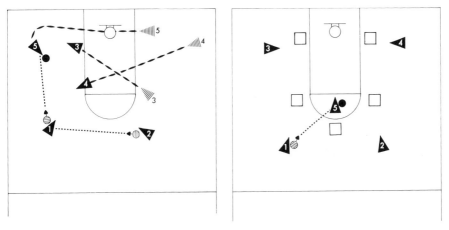

DIAGRAM 5–40   Alternative 2-1-2 pattern.
DIAGRAM 5–41   2-1-2 Pattern with a 3-2 zone defense.

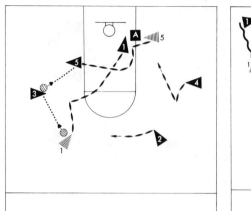
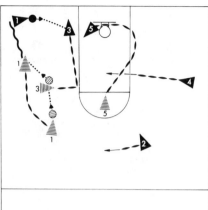

DIAGRAM 5–42   2-3 Offense.
DIAGRAM 5–43   Alternative 2-3 formation.

fectively, the coach uses at least one tall, well-coordinated player who can control the center area. Corner players are responsible for passing the ball and setting screens for tall teammates.

Basic Moves of the 2-3 Formation

(1) Quarterback 1 passes the ball to 3 and cuts toward the basket anticipating a return pass. If 1 does not receive a pass, 1 sets a screen behind the guarding of 5. Player 3 passes to 5 who has cut around the screen set by 1. Variation: Either of the guards, player 1 or 2, may initiate the pattern by passing to one of the corner players and cutting behind the receiver for a return pass. The guard 1, then passes to corner player 3, who either cuts away from the ball or toward it from the opposite side of the court (Diagram 5–42). (2) Player 1 passes to 3, follows the ball, and receives a return pass from 3. Player 3 runs toward the free-throw line as pivot player 5 moves down the right side of the lane and sets a screen near the basket. Player 3 pivots or changes direction and cuts to the basket to receive a pass from 1 who has dribbled to the corner (Diagram 5–43).

OFFENSIVE STRATEGIES AGAINST ZONE DEFENSE

Offense Against the 2-1-2 and 1-3-1 Defense

The 1-3-1 offense with one player beyond the top of the free-throw circle, three players spread across the court in line with the free-throw line and one player near the baseline, is excellent for freeing the post and side players. Since the coach frequently knows the defensive strategy opponents will use in advance, an appropriate offense can be selected before hand to combat it. The following basic 1-3-1 offensive patterns are effective against the most common zone defenses, the 2-1-2 and 1-3-1.

Offense Against a 2-1-2 Zone Defense

(1) Player 4 shifts to the side where the first pass is made, forcing the defensive player to move out, leaving 5 free to receive a pass and shoot for the goal. Player 5 may also pass to 2 who has moved toward the basket (Diagram 5–44). (2) After a pass each player shifts to the following positions: Player 2 shifts to the safety spot, 1 goes to the area vacated by 3, and player 3 moves to the area behind 5 (3 anticipates a pass from 4). Player 5, anticipating a pass from 4, moves to a low position (Diagram 5–45). (3) Player 1 passes the ball to 3, who passes to 4. As player 4 receives the ball, 3 and 5 scissors off of 4. Player 4 then passes to 3 or 5. Player 2 rebounds on the weak side while 1 remains back for safety (Diagram 5–46). (4) Player 1 passes the ball to 3. Player 4, after shifting to a side low post, receives a pass from 3. Player 5 sets a screen for 1 who breaks down the lane to receive a pass from 4. Player 2 moves to the top of the circle in the safety position (Diagram 5–47). (5) Player 5 shifts to the low post position, setting a back screen for 4. At the same time, player 1 passes to 2 and sets a screen for 3. Player 2 passes to 3 or to 4 who may cut before 3 does (Diagram 5–48).

Around-the-Horn Defense

The simplest offense is for forwards to occupy the open spaces between the defensive players. The forwards naturally pass the ball faster than the defense can shift positions; therefore, concentrate on shooting anytime an opening occurs. Although the offense frequently starts back too far to shoot, players learn to shift into any available

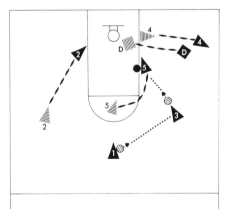
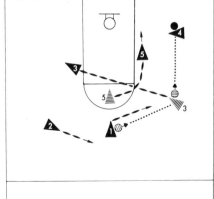

DIAGRAM 5–44   Offense against 2-1-2 zone defense.

DIAGRAM 5–45   Player positions after pass.

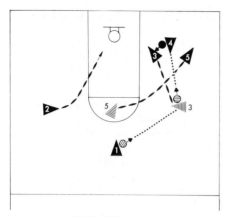

DIAGRAM 5-46

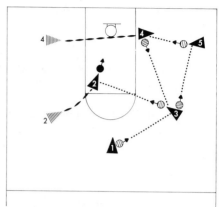

DIAGRAM 5-47

open spot. When a center defensive player moves out of the lane, the forward with the ball passes to a teammate cutting across the lane (Diagram 5–49).

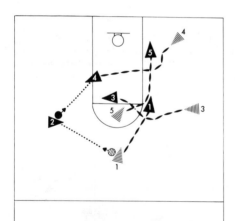

DIAGRAM 5-48

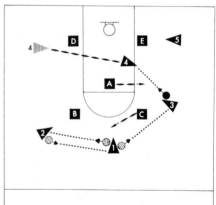

DIAGRAM 5-49 Around-the-horn defense.

Overload Principle Offense

Player 4 runs to the right side of the court, resulting in four players on the strong side of the court and one player, 2, on the weak side. The ball is passed to the overloaded side where players continue passing until an open player has an opportunity to shoot or a defensive player overshifts, creating an opening for a quick pass to 2 on the weak side and a shot at the goal (Diagram 5–50).

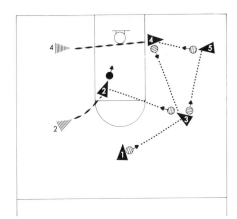

DIAGRAM 5–50   Overload offense.

Double Post Offense With Two Tall Players

The tall players stand on opposite sides of the lane. The outside forwards quickly pass the ball around the outside until a pass can be made to one of the post players. The double post provides a strong offensive rebounding strategy (Diagram 5–51).

Offense against a 1-3-1 defense

The strategies most effective against a 1-3-1 defense include the 1-2-2 and 2-1-2 offensive patterns which were explained previously as means of combating the 2-1-2 defense. In the 1-2-2 offense forwards rapidly pass the ball from one player to another, forcing the defense to shift in one direction then pass the ball to the opposite side of the zone for an open shot or drive to the goal. When the defensive wings spread too far, a direct pass to one of the forwards leads to a quick shot at the basket.

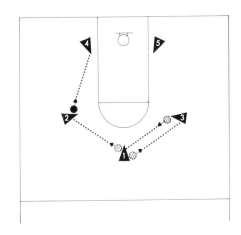

DIAGRAM 5–51 Double post offense with two tall players.

The 2-1-2 Offense Against the 1-3-1 Zone Defense

Player 1 or 2 passes the ball to 5. Player 5 passes to 3 or 4 who shoots for a basket or returns the ball to 5 who is moving down the lane. The defense shifts in anticipation of a pass to 5. Player 3 or 4 will then pass directly to the opposite forward standing in a low post position (Diagram 5–52). Player 2 passes to 4, cutting outside of 4 and moving to the baseline. Player 5 moves to the low post position as 3 moves to the high post position. Player 4 passes to 2, 3, or 5. If the path of the ball is reversed to 1, player 5 shifts across the lane, 3 goes to the side and 2 moves to a shooting position, drawing the baseline defensive player out of position (Diagram 5–53).

Screening the zone

Because they are beneficial against any zone defense, screens are set to prevent defensive players from shifting to cover offensive players in the assigned zone. When properly executed the screen changes the direction of a defensive player's movement in the zone, thus providing time for an unguarded shot at the basket. Although the possibilities for screening in the zones are unlimited, the type of zone the opponents play directly influences screening opportunities. Simple screens like those illustrated in Diagrams 5–54 to 5–58, are designed to obstruct the defense while creating an opening for a medium range jump shot, penetration of the zone or an inside pass to a teammate.

Screening Against the 2-1-2 Zone With a 1-3-1 Offense

Player 3 moves and sets a blind screen on the defensive guard, A. Player 1 dribbles around the screen and, depending upon the movement of the defense, either shoots, passes the ball to 5, who has moved to the baseline on the ball side, or passes to 3 who rolled after 1 dribbled past the screen (Diagram 5–54).

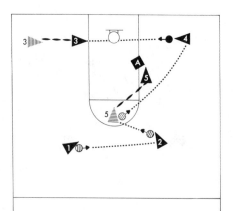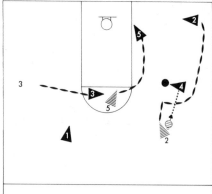

DIAGRAM 5–52   2-1-2 Offense against 1-3-1 zone defense.

DIAGRAM 5–53   Alternative play.

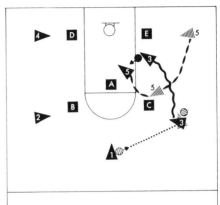

DIAGRAM 5–54   DIAGRAM 5–55

Screening Against the 2-1-2 Defense With a 1-2-2 Offense

Player 1 passes to 3 who fakes a pass back to 1 while 5 sets a pick on C. Player 3 dribbles around the pick, then shoots or passes to 5, who has rolled (Diagram 5–55).

Baseline Screen Against the 2-1-2 Zone Defense With a 1-2-2 Offense

Player 1 passes to 3. Player 5 remains in the low post position as a screen, while 4 crosses the court, receives the ball from 3 and shoots (Diagram 5–56).

Screening Against the 1-3-1 Zone Defense With a 2-1-2 Offense

Player 1 passes to 2. Player 2 dribbles around 3 who sets a pick, then either shoots, passes to 3 who rolls to the basket, or passes to

DIAGRAM 5–56

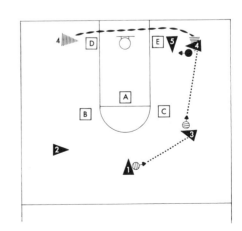

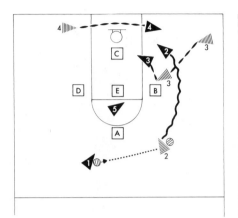

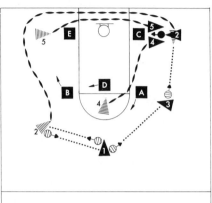

DIAGRAM 5–57   DIAGRAM 5–58

4 who cuts across to the baseline on the same side of the court as
the ball (Diagram 5–57).

**The Double Screen Preventing Defensive Players in a Zone from Shifting
Rapidly**

Player 1 passes to 3, then 3 passes to 2 who shoots from behind
the double screen (Diagram 5–58).

DRILLS

The most difficult offensive techniques to teach players are the
reactions appropriate to defensive strategy and the timing critical to
the reactions. The following list includes a few teaching suggestions
which may benefit the players.

1. Diagram the offensive position on a chalkboard. Check to
see if anyone has any questions.

2. Demonstrate the offense with seasoned players or with a
group instructed in the tactic prior to practice.

3. Practice the offense without the defense until each player
performs the strategy competently.

4. Combine the offense with a "dummy" defense. The
"dummy defense" shifts with the offensive players but does not intercept passes or block shots. Demonstrate to the offensive players
where the scoring options occur.

5. Set up a game situation with a defensive team. Allow the defense to intercept and block shots. Correct any mistakes that occur.

6. Practice drills that cover the offense less and help players
master various phases of the offense.

7. Divide the players into two teams for a full court scrimmage.

8. Discuss various parts of the offense, correct errors that occur
and answer questions during regularly scheduled skill sessions.

9. Provide opportunities for each player to practice the basic techniques. Include the one-on-one situation as well as ball handling, footwork and rebounding drills.

THE FAST BREAK

The fast break is an attempt to move the ball down the court by the fastest and most foolproof method. It is designed to outnumber the opponents in the offensive area, thus allowing a team to gain a percentage shot. While the fast break may be used sparingly or as the primary offensive pattern, incorporating it into game strategy depends on the game situation, the score, the speed of the opposition, and the skill and rebounding ability of the team. An alert team may also create a fast break situation through sheer hustle.

Offensively, players should assume a fast break will be attempted each time a teammate gains control of the ball. The highest percentage of successful fast breaks occurs after a sudden turnover such as a loose ball, stealing a ball or intercepting a pass; after a long rebound, a missed free-throw or a short rebound against a weak defensive team. Each member must be in good physical condition and well-schooled in the fundamentals of passing, dribbling and shooting.

The decision to use the fast break is usually influenced by the defense a coach intends to employ. Zone defense is more conducive to an offensive fast break because the players assume assigned positions on the court when a teammate secures a rebound. Players are then in a position to consistently execute the fast break pattern from the same lanes. Player-to-player defense tends to be more difficult for the fast break since each player must be ready to run from every possible position on the court.

Components of the Fast Break

Speed

Speed is essential to capitalize on the fast break. Starting with the first practice session all fast break drills are performed at top speed, permitting coaches to watch the players and ascertain which individuals have the ability to run at top speed, simultaneously maneuvering the ball. The player most skilled at ball handling becomes the middle player occupying the key position for the fast break.

Rebounding

Rebounding is of the utmost importance since no team can execute a fast break without the ball. A rebounder must not only clear the defensive backboard but must also initiate the fast break with an outlet pass or a dribble down court. The outlet pass, thrown to the area between midcourt and the top of the foul circle on the side of the court where the rebound was secured, must be a quick, accurate face-level pass. The receiver, or outlet player, watches the ball while shifting toward the sideline to be a target for the passer. The rebounder evaluates the positions of the outlet player and opponents to determine if the pass will be intercepted. When the outlet player is covered the rebounder searches for any other receiver occupying the middle of the court above the foul circle. Although rebounders throw the ball as soon as possible, usually before the feet have touched the floor, it may be necessary to protect the ball when landing on the floor. The rebounder then pivots on the outside foot, turns to face upcourt in position to sight the outlet players, and passes with a baseball, hook, or overhead pass to the ball-side of the court. Dribbling down the court is not the preferred method for the rebounder to initiate a fast break; however, if all outlet pass receivers are covered or if there is a long rebound, dribbling may be necessary. The less time consumed in an outlet play, the greater the chances will be to outmaneuver and outnumber the opponents at the opposite end of the court.

Advancing down court

As soon as the outlet play has been completed the ball must be advanced down court. The court is divided into three equal lanes parallel to the sidelines, with a teammate in each lane advancing down the floor for the fast break. It is the responsibility of the outlet player to get the ball to the middle position in the center lane by either passing or dribbling the ball as rapidly as possible. After receiving the ball the middle player dribbles to the foul line and stops. (Players assigned to the middle spot should practice stopping while holding the ball, faking, passing to a player in the outside lane cutting toward the basket, and shooting from the free-throw line.) As soon as the middle player stops, side players automatically cut for the basket. In a 3-on-2 situation the offensive team may be able to execute a jump shot on or inside the free-throw line. A player who cuts from the outside lane and fails to receive the ball clears out of the area by changing sides or moving back toward the corner of the lane. Although only three players move down the court for the initial fast break, all five players are expected to participate in the strategy. The fourth player is a trailer and stops at the top of the foul circle to act as a safety valve. In certain situations the middle player clears the center area and screens for the trailer who receives the ball for a shot at the basket. The fifth player, the rebounder, stops at mid-court to view the whole court and acts as a second safety valve. Using four players in the fast break leaves the team in a vulnerable position defensively. A team may hustle on a fast break, miss the shot, and find opponents retaliating with a quick reverse of the situation and a score because no player was back on defense. When the fast break opportunity is obviously lost, hold the ball and set up a regular five player offense.

DRILLS

1. *Lateral Pass Drill.* Divide the group into two lines and station them at the endline approximately 15 feet apart (Diagram 5–59). Player 1, the first person in line I, and player 2, the first person in line II, move at top speed down the floor, passing the ball back and forth until one player receives the ball near the basket and shoots. The other player retrieves the ball, and each goes to the end of the opposite line.

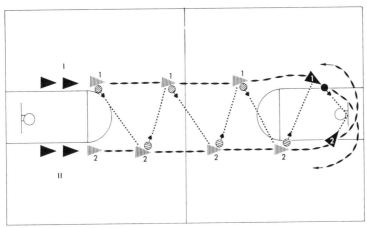

DIAGRAM 5–59   Lateral pass drill.

2. *Two-on-One.* Station team members in two lines approximately 15 feet apart in the center of the court (Diagram 5–60). A designated defensive player, A, assumes a position at the free-throw line. Player 1 the first person in line I, and player 2, the first person in line II, move down the court at maximal speed, passing the ball back and forth. The two passers work toward the goal, keeping the defensive player at an equal distance from one another. The objective is to force the guard to commit herself to one forward and then exploit the resulting opening by driving for a lay-up or dribbling toward the basket. The offense continues to shoot until a goal is scored or until the defense intercepts or rebounds the ball. The ball then goes to the next two players in line.

3. *Three-Line Passing.* Separate the group into three lines and station them at the endline (Diagram 5–61). Player 1, the first person in line II, has the ball. Players 1, 2, and 3 move down the court parallel to one another, passing the ball back and forth. After crossing the center line player 1 receives the pass, dribbles to the foul

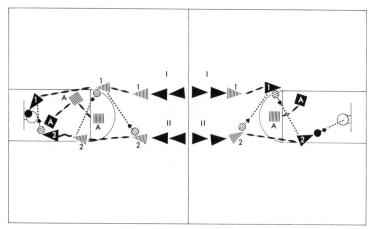

DIAGRAM 5–60   Two-on-one drill.

line, and passes either to player 2 or 3, who cuts toward the basket, stops and shoots. Player 1 returns to the end of line III, player 2 to line I and player 3 to line II.

4. *Three Player Weave.* Divide the group into three equal lines positioned at one endline (Diagram 5–62). The middle player, 2, passes to player 1, cuts behind player 1, and continues toward the basket. Player 1 passes to player 3, cuts behind 3, and continues up the court. Player 3 passes the ball to 2, cutting behind 2. The players continue passing and cutting behind the person to whom the ball is passed until one player receives the ball near the basket and shoots. Players return to the end of the line next to the starting line.

5. *Outlet Pass.* Separate the group into two columns with col-

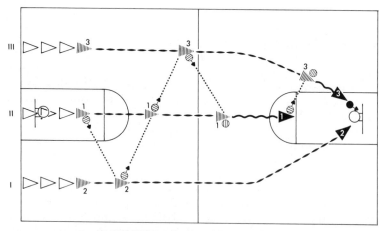

DIAGRAM 5–61   Three-line passing.

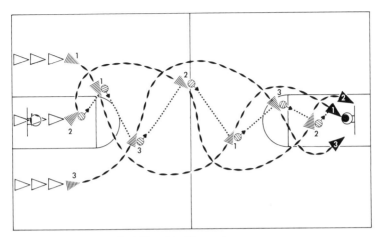

DIAGRAM 5-62   Three player weave.

umn I behind the free-throw line and column II in rebound position on the left side of the free-throw lane (Diagram 5-63). Player 1, the first person in column I, throws the ball toward the left side of the backboard then moves to the right sideline to become the outlet receiver. Player A, the first person in column II, rebounds the ball, turning in the air (if possible) and passes to 1. Players return to the end of the opposite column. Players practice the outlet pass drill on both sides of the court.

6. *Pass and Go.* Divide the players into three groups surrounding the free-throw line (Diagram 5-64). A designated player throws the ball at the backboard at an angle producing a rebound. Player 2, the first person in line II, rebounds the ball, throwing an outlet pass to player 1 or 3, called the wings or outlet pass receivers. Player 2 moves to the opposite wing position. The wing who does not receive the pass immediately runs toward the center of the

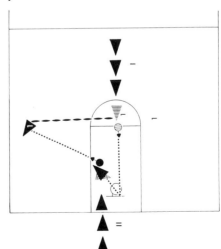

DIAGRAM 5-63   Outlet pass.

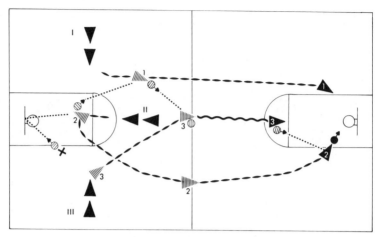

DIAGRAM 5–64   Pass-and-go.

court, receives the ball prior to reaching mid-court, and dribbles to the foul line. Player 2 and the outlet pass receiver (1) become wing players when they run down the outside lanes toward the basket. The middle player dribbles the ball to the foul line and shoots or passes to a wing. Players return to the end of the next line.

7. *Fill-the-Lanes.* Separate the players into groups of four with two guards at the free-throw line and two rebounders on either side of the free-throw lane. An extra player throws the ball so that it rebounds off the backboard. Rebounder A retrieves the ball and passes to C, the guard on the same side of the court, who shifts to the sideline, becoming the outlet player. The rebounder moves down court to the center line becoming the fast break safety valve. Guard B moves to the center of the court, receives the pass from the outlet player and assumes the position of middle player on the fast break. Player C runs down the court, filling lane I, while rebounder D occupies the third lane, sideline II. The three players complete the fast break with Guard B, dribbling to the foul line as players C and D, the two outside lane players, cut toward the basket. Players return to the end of the next line. Fill-the-lanes drills should be performed with the ball bouncing off both sides of the basket (Diagram 5–65).

8. *Three-on-Two.* The Three-on-Two drill is performed similarly to the Pass and Go drill except that two defensive players are added to protect the basket. Defensive players A and B may assume a tandem position, one behind the other, or a parallel position as in a split or zone defense. Regardless of the defense's position, the three offensive players should make the same approach to the scoring area. At the top of the circle, side players 1 and 2 cut while player 3 remains near the foul line maintaining a position for a return pass (Diagram 5–66).

Variation (1). When the defense is in tandem position at the top of the circle player 2 may be forced to pass to 2 or 3. The player

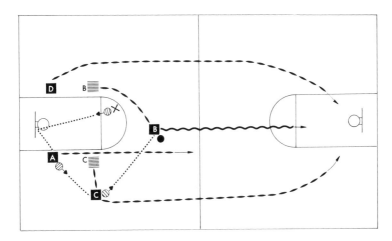

DIAGRAM 5–65   Fill-the-lanes.

should receive the ball with enough time to pass to the other cutter or, if necessary, to return the ball to player 2. A good tandem defense will often force a second pass or compel the first cutter to take a jump shot.

Variation (2). If the two defensive players are parallel, player 2 retains the ball and shifts to the foul line for a shot or passes to a cutter for a lay-up. Should one of the defensive players guard player 2 at the foul line, the cutter playing on the side where the defensive player moved should be free for a pass and a lay-up shot. In order to provide offensive players with practice in reacting to various situations, defensive players should alternate methods.

9. *Three-on-Two down, Two-on-One back.* The drill starts in

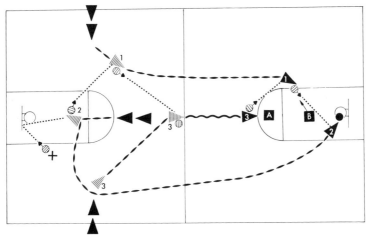

DIAGRAM 5–66   Three-on-two.

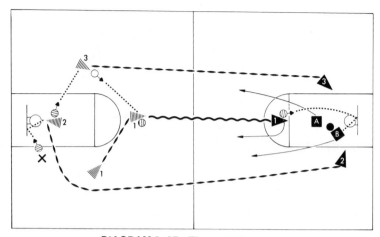

DIAGRAM 5–67   Three-on-two.

the same manner as the Three-on-Two drill. When the offense
scores, or the defense rebounds a missed shot or intercepts the ball,
the defensive players automatically become offensive players
(Diagram 5–67). The middle player in the fast break, 1, must retreat
to the opposite end of the court, forming a two (A and B) on one
situation. The two cutters (2 and 3) remaining at the original basket
become defensive players. After completion of the two-on-one
break, three more offensive players attack the new defensive
players.

10. *Five Players Run-Through.* Divide the players into groups
of five. Depending upon the defense the coach is using, the players
run through the following maneuvers for rebounding and passing to
an outlet player, and filling the three lanes. Defensive player E

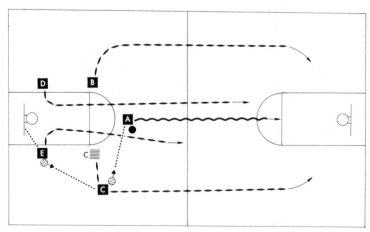

DIAGRAM 5–68   Five player run-through with 3-2 defense.

recovers the rebound and throws the ball while in the air to C, who immediately passes to A. Player A, accompanied down the sides of the court by B and C, dribbles to the offensive free-throw line (Diagram 5–68).

Fast Break from 2-1-2 Zone Defense

Fast break methods from a 2-1-2 zone are similar to those of the 2-3 formation. When all three members of the rebound triangle are under the basket, the fast break starts with a long pass to either chaser B or C. If, however, there is a long rebound to A at the free-throw line, it may be more advantageous for A to turn and dribble up the middle of the floor. In either method A normally assumes the middle position in the three lanes. If player A is detained for any reason the chaser who did not receive the outlet pass takes the middle lane. The third lane is then covered by player A or the other rebounder who did not obtain the ball (Diagram 5–69)

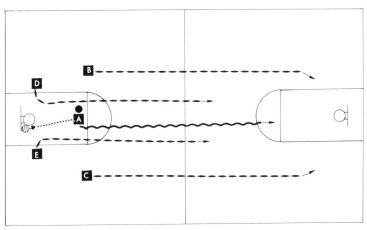

DIAGRAM 5–69   Fast break from 2-1-2 zone defense.

Fast Break from 1-3-1 Zone Defense

1. The 1-3-1 defensive positions in Diagram 5–70 illustrate what could be expected in a game situation when player 2 has the ball. Player 2 attempts a shot. Defensive players C, D, and E run in for the rebound. Player D, convinced that C will retrieve the rebound, starts up the court to participate in the fast break as players A and B break to the side lanes. Player C passes to one of the three lane-players, D, B, or A, who continues down the floor for a fast break (Diagram 5–70).

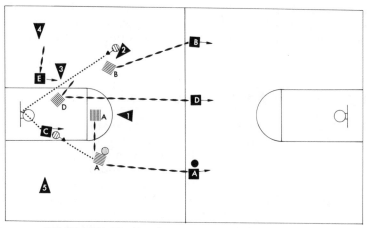

DIAGRAM 5–70   Fast break from 1-3-1 zone defense.

2. *Five-on-Two.* Two players are on offense and five players are on defense in normal guarding positions. The two offensive players shoot at the basket as the five defensive players assume rebound positions, gain possession of the ball, and execute a fast break. The two offensive players become guards and contest the outlet pass, second pass, or both passes. Variations depend upon the player rebounding the ball and the outlet player who is free. When both outlet receivers are covered the rebounder may be forced to dribble to the side and search for a cutter moving down the court behind the defense. Players not immediately involved in the fast break should practice taking trailer positions.

3. *Fast Break from the Free-Throw.* Separate the group into five lines located off the court. Three players, A, B, and C, assume normal guarding positions at the free-throw lane. Players D and E are located on the court toward the sideline. A designated player shoots at the goal. Players A and B cover the inside rebound positions while the third rebounder, player C, screens the shooter. Either player A or B, by protecting the inside rebound position, gains possession of the ball while the guard on the rebound side, E, fakes toward the center and moves to the sideline to receive the outlet pass. On the opposite side of the free-throw circle, Player D breaks diagonally to the center of the court, receives the pass from outlet player E, and becomes the middle player of the three lane fast break. Player E occupies lane I, C occupies lane III and the cut-off player is in the free-throw area. The team uses the same basic pattern after making a free-throw with the closest rebounder stepping out-of-bounds to initiate the play (Diagram 5–71).

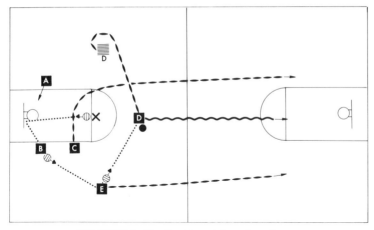

DIAGRAM 5-71   Fast break from free throw.

Summary of defensive strategy against the fast break

1. A team cannot break without the ball; therefore, offensive rebounding is crucial.

2. A team that has difficulty controlling the defensive board will have trouble initiating a fast break.

3. A single player may be assigned the task of screening the skilled defensive rebounder, or a second player may double team the rebounder with the ball.

4. A team may alter offensive shots to take advantage of the times when the most skilled rebounder is in a defensive position or is absent from the game.

5. A defensive player should also apply pressure to the outlet receiver. While the rebounder is being guarded, a guard who is not in position to stop the outlet pass should retreat to the middle of the court and attempt to prevent the second pass from going into the center of the court.

6. A team must reestablish defensive positions to stop the fast break. Rebounders not directly battling for the ball should attempt to intercept the outlet pass or cover the deep unguarded opponent.

7. A dribbler should not be allowed to bring the ball to the top of the circle. If there is no teammate near the defensive player and the opponents are breaking, the lone defender must drop back and fake, delaying the ball handler until assistance arrives.

8. A defensive strategy that includes fakes provides critical seconds for teammates to attain proper positions and stop the fast break.

9. Talking is a key to success. Teammates should constantly inform each other of the opponents' movements and strategy.

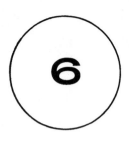

DEFENSE

INDIVIDUAL DEFENSE

In basketball, as in most sports, defensive players are vital to the success of the team. Although most players enjoy shooting the basketball, few experience the thrill of preventing a skilled opponent from scoring a goal. It is true that the public rarely acknowledges a good defensive player; however, the team confidence produced by a strong defense creates infinite self-satisfaction.

Basically, there are two types of defense: (1) Player-to-player, a method in which a player is assigned to guard a specific opponent; and (2) Zone, a system in which each defensive player protects a designated area of the court. Individual characteristics of a defensive player include footwork, balance, arm position, vision, and the ability to determine the strengths and weaknesses of the opponents.

Body Balance

Regardless of the defense selected, a guard must possess good body balance, the practice of distributing the weight equally over both feet. Exceptions to the rule of equally distributing the weight occur (1) when a forward drives toward the basket, she transfers most of the weight over the back foot; and (2) when the outside forward is unskilled in driving, she shifts additional weight toward the front foot.

Practice body balance by lowering the center of gravity. Flex the knees, keeping the back straight and spreading the feet in a comfortable stance. Since motion proceeds from the feet through the knees, any guard with tension in her knees provides the forward with at least a one-step advantage.

FIGURE 6-1 Body balance in defensive position.

Footwork

Proper footwork initiated from the boxer stance facilitates changing directions, freedom of movement in any direction, and stopping suddenly. In the boxer stance the guard places the legs shoulder-width apart in a front-back stride position with the foot closest to the center of the court placed forward as the front foot. Although the front-back stride position of the defender has a tendency to force the dribbler toward the sideline, players should continually protect the baseline since any forward eluding the guard has an unobstructed path to the basket. When the drive is forced toward the middle of the court a defensive teammate will be in position to cover the escaping offensive player. The two most successful methods of impeding the progress of the drive are: (1) If the baseline leg is forward, the defender overplays the baseline side by one-half player; and (2) If the baseline leg is back, the guard places the front leg in line with the mid-line of the forward.

The shuffle step, a technique in which the feet remain in a spread position to maintain balance, permits the guard to shift laterally, forward, and backward. Players must avoid a cross step or crossing the legs as this results in a loss of balance and reduces the ability to recover quickly. When moving laterally to the left, a player slides the left foot to the left, then places the right foot next to the left. To retreat she slides back with the rear foot, then shifts the front foot next to the rear foot. In the forward advance, the player places the front foot forward then transfers the rear foot next to the forward foot.

FIGURE 6–2 Duck walk.

When an offensive player dribbles the ball too close to the defensive player, the defensive player uses the duck walk to impede the forward's progress and obtain a more advantageous position. If the forward dribbles to the right, the defender steps back with the right foot, and laterally and back with the left foot, assuming a safe defensive position. Should the guard desire to move further back, she starts with the left foot, takes two steps back, then steps laterally and back with the left foot. When the offensive player has a driving advantage over the defensive player (dribbling even with the hip of the guard), the defender turns away from the driver, runs directly toward the basket picking up the driver as she is progressing toward the basket, and gains the step lost in the beginning.

Arms

Properly using the arms is an asset to defensive players because they are valuable for blocking passes or shots, disconcerting the offensive player, and maintaining balance. When an offensive player stops dribbling and assumes a passing or shooting position, the defender places the arms in a windmill position, one arm up and forward (usually the arm on the side of the forward foot), and the opposite arm down and out to the side. The defender concentrates on blocking shots, passes, and the view of the offensive player with the upper arm and blocking low passes with the lower arm. Before jumping to block any shot, the defender must be positive

FIGURE 6–3 Offensive player with driving advantage; defensive player turning and recovering.

that the forward is going to shoot. As soon as the forward shoots, the defender jumps, reaching for the ball with the hand closest to the ball, then taps the ball to eliminate fouls and to prevent a follow-through by the forward. Players who consistently react to the forwards force the offensive players to rush the plays and shots.

When guarding a dribbler the defender holds the arms below

FIGURE 6–4 Defensive player taking away the ball.

the waist and away from the body with the palms up. If the ball is unprotected, she taps the ball to a teammate, gains possession of the ball, or forces the ball out-of-bounds off the legs of the forward. The defender begins the tap the instant the ball is pushed to the floor as the offensive player momentarily losses contact with the ball. The arm swings forward with an upward hand motion in an attempt to strike the ball on its way down to the floor or up from its bounce.

When the forward stops dribbling, the defender steps in close, moving the arms in an effort to tie the ball, or intercept a shot or pass. As soon as the offensive player releases the ball, the defender retreats two steps into a safe defensive position.

Vision

Adequate vision is necessary for locating offensive players, other teammates in the immediate vicinity, and the ball. Peripheral vision gives a survey of the surrounding area, and alerts the player to opportunities for intercepting passes, recovering loose balls, providing defensive help for teammates, perceiving screens and covering loose offensive players near the basket.

Suggestions for Focusing the Eyes

(1) Focus the eyes on the mid-section of the forward possessing the ball.

(2) Focus the eyes on the forward without the ball but also allow the scope of vision to encompass the ball.

(3) Avoid focusing on the feet, eyes, shoulders, head, or ball. These are commonly referred to as the weapons of the fake and the guard is vulnerable to them.

(4) Avoid turning the head since an alert forward will see the advantage and drive toward the ball or basket.

(5) Focus the eyes on the forward when there is a choice between losing sight of the assigned offensive player or the ball.

(6) Retreat to the basket when the forward is lost since a drive to the goal is the offense's most common action.

Communication among defensive players creates an organized defensive unit. Teammates are informed when the player with the ball is covered, the post player or any other forward drives through the key, the forward is in position to receive a pass, the forwards are setting a screen or the guard needs assistance. While each team develops a separate type of "lingo," talking just for the sake of talking is meaningless; communicate only with teammates, do not intimidate opponents.

Alertness

Player-to-player defense requires each person to think every second of the game. During the first quarter players concentrate on assessing the strengths and weaknesses of the assigned offensive player. The defender develops the ability to sense the intentions of the offense, then challenges the player, determined not to be defeated.

Questions the Guards Should Answer

(1) Does the forward dribble effectively to both the right and left sides when closely guarded?

(2) Does the forward successfully drive for the goal?

(3) Does the forward prefer to shoot from the outside?

(4) When and in what way does the forward fake?

(5) Does the forward move without the ball?

(6) Does the passer telegraph the direction of the pass, pass in a certain direction, or hold the ball longer than necessary?

(7) Does the forward have a favorite shooting spot on the floor?

FUNDAMENTALS OF THE DEFENSE

The Basic Position

Basically, the defensive player's position on the court is directly in line with the basket, between the offensive player and the goal.

FIGURE 6-5   Basic defensive position.

FIGURE 6-6 Players demonstrating defensive positioning.

Although exceptions occur, the player who automatically assumes the basic position is in a flexible position and may make any changes necessary.

The defensive player guarding an opponent without the ball has two responsibilities: (1) preventing a pass to the assigned player; and (2) preventing a screen between the assigned forward and the player with the ball. Under ordinary circumstances the defensive player is between the assigned forward and the player with the ball. The player bends the knees, placing the feet in a comfortable stride position. She raises the arms pointing one hand toward the ball and the opposite hand toward the assigned offensive player, then focuses the eyes on a point midway between the two hands. Distance between the guard and the assigned opponent depends upon the location of the ball, the position of each player on the court, and the speed, agility and maneuverability of both players. Proper distance from the forward is determined by gauging the space in such a way that with one step forward and extension of the arm, the defensive player can touch the forehead of the assigned player. When a forward near the center line has not dribbled, the defender stands back about six feet. During the dribble, the defender overplays the dribbler in a predetermined direction, forcing the forward to reverse, to deviate from the intended path or dribble in front of the defensive player. Altering the forward's path interrupts the offensive strategy while a reversal furnishes the defense with sufficient time to switch directions. The defender forces the player to dribble with the weak hand, toward the sideline, or in the direction of another defensive player who steals the ball or double teams the dribbler.

Guidelines for Adjusting Distance

(1) Stand back about six feet when a forward near the center line has not dribbled.

(2) Close in immediately to apply pressure defense at midcourt, or near the front court when it is deemed necessary, against a forward dribbling up the court.

(3) Shift closer to a dribbler in the front court as distance from the basket decreases.

FIGURE 6–7 Over-
playing baseline side.

(4) Loosely guard a player driving for the basket.

(5) Close in to prevent a shot when the forward is within shooting range.

(6) Shift closer to stop a drive to the baseline or to force the player to drive to the middle of the half-court when a teammate may be of assistance to the guard.

(7) Closely guard a player who is a proficient scorer from outside the circle.

(8) Close in on the offensive player approaching a favorite scoring spot.

Often, the distance between the defensive player and the assigned offensive player depends upon the location of the ball. As the space between the assigned forward and the teammate with the ball narrows, the distance between the defensive player and the assigned forward closes. The greater the distance between the player with the ball and the intended receiver, the more advisable it is for the guard to sag, shifting to a position one step away from the forward. Each defensive player between the assigned forward and the offensive player provides a better angle for assisting a teammate, guarding a ball handler, preventing a screen, defending against a roll-in, or interferring with a pass to a cutter. The guard should anticipate a cut toward the basket, overplay the angle of the cut, and arrive at the destination first. If the ball is on the opposite side of the court and the offensive center overplays that side, the guard sags to block a drive or a lob pass.

Pivot Post

As a general rule, the basic guarding position does not apply to situations where the pivot post player has the ball. The height of the post player, the scoring possibilities in the post position, and the positions occupied by a post player increase the vulnerability of the defense. Usually post players occupy: (1) the low post position, on either side of the basket just outside the free-throw lane; (2) the medium post position, located half the distance to the free-throw line; (3) the high post position, outside the free-throw

154

lane just below the free-throw line; or (4) the free-throw line position, outside the key and to the center of the free-throw line. The best defense is to intercept or deflect any ball aimed toward the post. When a post player is capable of turning and shooting with one hand, guards should overplay, preventing a shot or a turn and drive toward the basket.

Defense against the post positions

(1) **Low Post.**   The guard is between the post player and the ball, discouraging passes to the low post. Verbal communication between the guards is valuable because the guard on the low post predominately faces toward the ball. The back line defensive player is responsible for assisting the defensive post (Figure 6–8).

(2) **Medium Post.**   The defensive player is stationed in front, or to the side of the post player. In the side method, which varies according to the location of the ball, the guard straddles the post from the side, then extends an arm forward between the ball and the post players (Figure 6–9).

VARIATIONS

A. Back line player with ball—straddle the post from the baseline side with the outside foot forward.
B. Front line player with ball—straddle the post to the inside or foul line side with the inside foot forward.
C. Ball moving around court—guard switches positions by sliding over the top of the post with a continuous movement from one straddle position to another. When the post gains

FIGURE 6–8   Guarding the low post.

FIGURE 6-9 Guarding the medium post player.

FIGURE 6-10 Guarding the high post.

possession of the ball the guard shifts between the post player and basket to prevent a shot at the goal.

(3) **High Post.** The guard is in a side straddle position, but avoids playing too close to the post. As the pivot player moves from one position to another, the guard slides behind, rather than over the top of the post. Teammates of the defensive post assist by "sagging" back to the post player when the assigned players are not in a scoring area or are not skilled forwards (Figure 6-10).

Screens

A player-to-player defense is often interrupted by a screen designed to force a guard to lose contact with the assigned forward, freeing the forward for a break toward the basket. To counteract the screen the guards shift into a switching defense in which they exchange assigned forwards as the screen is enforced. Since the switch may leave players unmatched in height and ability, it is limited to instances where the forwards could gain a dangerous advantage.

The guard who first anticipates the screen gives a vocal signal for the switch, takes a side-step followed by a forward-step, then leaves the assigned player to cover the new offensive player. The blocked guard quickly obtains a position between the other forward and the basket. Guards must concentrate on the timing of the switch! Any switch occurring too early leaves a driving lane open,

156

while a switch performed too late increases the opportunity for defensive fouls. Guards watch the new forward until the defensive strategy is so impregnable that an exchange can be accomplished without danger. The defensive player guarding the forward nearest the scoring area makes the first move to regain the assigned forward. Although it is important to guard the forward farthest from scoring opportunities or critical areas, both guards must be aware of the entire area since: (1) the forward near the goal cannot be left unguarded; or (2) the most distant forward cannot be left uncovered if the ball is in her immediate vicinity.

Offensive screening strategy and defensive opposition

OFFENSE	DEFENSE
(1) Forward steps in front of the screen and executes a set shot.	(1) One of the guards shifts over the top of the screen, attempting to prevent the shot.
(2) Forward with the ball may drive to the left or right, or pass the ball to a teammate (the forward who set a screen) rolling and breaking toward the basket.	(2) The guard closest to the offensive player with the ball steps forward, holding the hand down, while the second defensive player covers the forward setting the screen.
(3) Offensive player with the ball described in situation two drives in a direction opposite the side of the defensive player who steps forward.	(3) The second guard covers the forward driving toward the basket while the defensive player who rushed the shooter falls back to guard the screener.
(4) Forward who set the screen in situation three rolls and cuts toward the basket, leaving a *slow* defensive player behind.	(4) The teammates of the guard may be of assistance by holding the hands high over the head of the forward to prevent a lob pass. As soon as possible teammates regain normal defensive position.

Sliding Through

Sliding through, a defensive tactic to avoid an offensive screen, is a primary strategy used by guards against screening maneuvers. To slide through, the guard: (1) steps closer to the offensive player, slides around the screen and continues following the assigned forward; or (2) steps behind the screen while guarding the forward with the ball. The other defensive player steps back to open the defensive path for the teammate. An exception occurs when there is a loose cut off the post player with the defensive player sliding

FIGURE 6–11 Defense over top of screen.

through the two opponents. When the post cut is tight the guard shifts behind the opposing post player. If necessary the defensive center fakes a switch, reaches toward the cutter, and attempts to delay the offensive strategy until the defensive team recovers.

Change of Strategy

Converting from an offensive to a defensive strategy occurs when the opponents gain control of a rebound or obtain the ball after a turnover. Changing from offense to defense is a reaction-time maneuver that often means the difference between a two-point score for the opponents or no score. If there is insufficient time to locate the assigned opponent, each defensive player guards

FIGURE 6–12 Sliding through.

the nearest opponent, slowing the offensive attack and interrupting the offensive strategy. To be in a less vulnerable position during the change over, the defense ties the rebound, prevents an outlet pass, prevents forwards from obtaining positions behind the defense, or assumes guarding stations rapidly with all five defensive players in position for the offensive attack. Whenever possible, guards slow down the play by applying pressure on the player with the ball. Should the offense outnumber the defense, the nearest guard hustles to the middle of the foul line, protecting the area under the basket, delaying the offense, forcing the shot from outside the close shooting area, and maintaining contact with the front offensive player.

DRILLS

1. *Mass Movement.* The group spreads over the court with each player assuming a defensive stance. A designated leader stands in front of the group and arbitrarily issues the commands "Front," "Back," "Right," or "Left." Each player executes the defensive movements indicated by the signal. For example: On the command, "Right," players slide right, with the right hand down. The leader may also indicate the movements through hand signals rather than vocal commands (Diagram 6–1).

2. *Partner Drill.* The group divides into partners with player 1 facing the leader and player A facing 1. Through hand signals the leader indicates the direction of movement—front, back, right or left. Player 1 follows the command, while A, the defensive partner, performs the slide step, attempting to maintain a position between the leader and 1.

3. *One-on-One.* Station the students in two lines at one end of the gymnasium. Player 1, the first person in line one, attempts to dribble the ball to the center line while the second person in line

DIAGRAM 6–1 Mass movement.

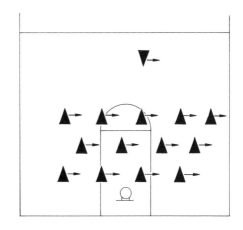

one, player A, with hands behind the back, maintains a defensive position between 1 and the center line. The defensive player concentrates on sliding the feet and moving the body rather than on reaching to stop an offensive player. When 1 reaches the center line the players exchange positions. Variation: As soon as the defensive players successfully shift the feet, they attempt to deflect the dribble.

4. *Dribble Deflection.* Divide the group into partners. Player 1 dribbles the ball in place while player A attempts to tap the ball just after 1 pushes the ball to the floor. Emphasis is on quickness, hand-eye coordination, hand and body position.

5. *Duck Walk.* Station the players in a line across the gym floor. On a signal by a leader players practice stepping back with the right foot, and back and to the left with the left foot. Players progress to executing the movement in opposition to a dribble. Eventually a player should add a turn and diagonal run to the step-back and step-over.

6. *Stop the Shooter.* Separate the group into pairs with player 1 the offensive player and player A the defensive player. Player 1 is instructed to fake, drive or shoot while A concentrates on defensive maneuvers. After five attempts players change positions. On various parts of the court players practice protecting the baseline, forcing the dribbler to the sidelines and covering the forward after all shots.

7. *Anticipation Drill.* Divide the players into groups of three. Players A and B stand 15 feet apart passing the ball back and forth while player C, halfway between the two passers and six feet from the trajectory of the ball, attempts to intercept the ball. If C has no trouble gaining possession of the ball, increase the distance between C and the flight of the ball.

8. *Three-on-Three.* Arrange the players in three lines behind the endline. Player A, the first player in each line, is a guard while player 2, the second person in each line, is an offensive player. Player 2 dribbles the ball down the court. A attempts to impede the progress of the forward. Emphasize the following: (1) Players avoid long passes; (2) A maintains a position between player B and the goal; and (3) There is no switching in early practice, thus training defensive players to slide through.

9. *One-on-One with Offensive Pivot.* Divide the players into groups of three with each group stationed at a basket. Player A, the defensive player, utilizes player-to-player defense to prevent player 1, the offensive player, from scoring. Player 1 passes the ball to player 2, the post forward, and cuts for the basket or employs the post as a screen during a drive. If necessary, A shifts over to guard the post (Diagram 6–3, A).

DIAGRAM 6–2   Anticipation drill.

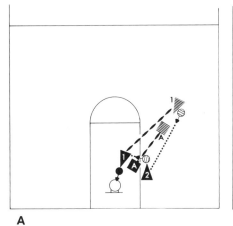
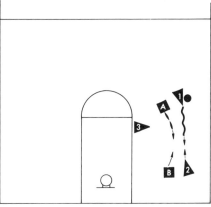

A   **B**

DIAGRAM 6–3   A. One-on-one with offensive pivot. B. Two-on-two with offensive pivot.

10. *Two-on-Two, Guard Forward Series, with Offensive Pivot.* The players are in groups of five with three offensive players— one guard, one forward and a post—and two defensive players on the guard and forward. The defensive players should slide through and as a last resort, switch. Offensive players may drive off the post at any time. Players practice player-to-player defense with little or no switching (Diagram 6–3, B).

11. *Split the Post.* Divide the players into two lines positioned behind the top of the free-throw circle. Player 1, the high pivot post, is stationed at the center of the free-throw line, while player A guards 1. Players B and C, the two guard players, guard 2 and 3 at the head of the line. Players 2 and 3 break toward the post position, passing the ball back and forth and then to 1. Players 2

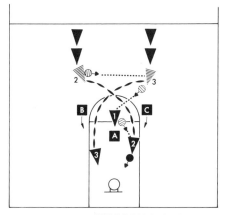
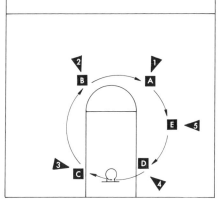

DIAGRAM 6–4   Split the post.
DIAGRAM 6–5   Five-on-five half-court rotation drill.

and 3 then cut on opposite sides of the pivot player, ready to receive a return pass. Two other defensive players may be added to increase the difficulty of the drill and give the defense practice in sliding through or switching (Diagram 6–4).

12. *Five-on-Five Half-Court Rotation Drill.* Divide the group into teams of five. The offensive team may select any method of offense while the defensive team is restricted to player-to-player defense. As soon as a defensive player gains possession of the ball twice, the defensive team rotates clockwise to new positions. The team continues rotating until the defensive players have been in each of the five positions (Diagram 6–5).

ZONE DEFENSE

Basic Strategies

The two basic defensive strategies, zone and player-to-player, are frequently employed interchangeably but discriminately according to: (1) the ability and experience of the opponents; (2) the ability and experience of the home team; (3) the knowledge and experience of the coach; (4) the length of the season; (5) the number of practice sessions; and (6) the facilities available. Although individual defensive characteristics such as watching the ball, keeping the hands up, shifting and sliding with the ball, and assigning two players to the individual with the ball, are prevalent in zone defense, the main objective of the zone is to create a mobile unit of five players dedicated to eliminating offensive scores. As the name implies, in zone defense each player is assigned a specific zone on the court and is responsible for any opponents who enter the area. Zone players are naturally interception-minded since the primary concern and point of focus is the ball. Defensive players face the player with the ball, exerting every effort to anticipate passes and intercept the ball.

To ascertain the basic defensive strategy for a team the coach considers the strengths and weaknesses of each system, as well as those of the available personnel.

Strengths of a zone defense

1. Zone defense is the best defense from which to start a fast break.

2. Tall players control the rebound positions.

3. Zone defense conceals individual weaknesses.

4. Zone defense is a team defense; therefore, when an individual is outmaneuvered in a one-on-one situation, a teammate will be in position to cover the forward.

5. Zone defense reduces the number of percentage shots.

6. Zone defense requires less scouting for the correct offensive player.

7. Double teaming is more feasible against opponents who are strong in a one-on-one situation.

8. Zone defense is effective against short shots and tactics involving cuts and passes.

9. Zone defense develops a guard's ability to watch the ball and intercept passes.

10. Zone defense has a tendency to reduce fouling as a result of the restriction on offensive driving.

11. Team members may function effectively with less effort.

12. Zone defense is advantageous against teams having a definite style of offense, a low scoring offense, or an erratic method of ball handling.

Weaknesses of a zone defense

1. An opposing team may fast break successfully against a zone.

2. A zone defense has a tendency to subconsciously induce laziness in defensive players.

3. An opponent has more opportunities to score with outside shots, particularly with the side and long shots.

4. An offense that maintains distance between teammates reduces the effectiveness of the zone defense.

5. A zone defense increases the possibility that the offense may overload one zone. Two offensive players shift into the zone covered by one defensive player.

One of a guard's primary objectives is to assume the defensive position as rapidly as possible. The guard raises both arms, bends the knees and places the feet in a wide stance (closer to the offensive player than in player-to-player defense). The guard tries to cover a large amount of space, forcing the offense to dribble in a wide arc around the defense or throw a high floating pass that is easy to intercept or deflect. It should be emphasized that it will not be too disastrous if the forward manages to drive past the guard as another defensive player is ready to assume responsibility for the ball handler. A zone defense is vulnerable when the pivot area is unprotected. Therefore, the first objective of a team is to prevent or intercept a pass into the pivot area. When the ball is passed successfully to the middle forward, the defense automatically collapses toward the ball, preventing any shot or pass.

Suggestions for Defense

1. The guards turn and run back when the offense has a fast breaking team.

2. The first defensive player back covers the dribbler while the second takes the forward who is in position to receive a pass.

3. The first guard back protects the goal when there is a potential receiver under the basket.

4. Individual defensive strategy in a zone is similar to player-to-player defense when there is no fast break.

5. The player with the ball is guarded by the defensive player responsible for that particular zone when the offense moves into the front court.

6. The defensive players must avoid fouling by becoming too concerned with intercepting the ball.

7. The guard plays close to a forward who is in the same vicinity as a teammate with the ball.

8. The defensive player covers the area where an offensive player is in position to receive a pass from a teammate located in another area.

9. The guard avoids a position directly under the basket. Any forward going behind the goal has no advantage, consequently, there is no need for the defensive player to assume a close guarding position.

10. The defensive players who are not guarding the player with the ball cover the gaps in the offense. Guards assume a stance between two offensive players in order to move in either direction or intercept a pass (Diagram 6–6, A).

Covering Offensive Gaps

Player A guards the passer from a position which enables her to take a half step toward the passer to block any pass intended. The defensive player nearest the potential receiver, 2, takes a half step in front of the receiver to intercept the pass. Players maintain body control, face the ball at all times, and move as rapidly as possible to the point of interception.

The 3-2 Zone Defense

The 3-2 zone, three players in front and two taller players under the basket, was one of the first zone defensive strategies developed. During a rebound one of the front line players assists the two back guards while the remaining two guards prepare to fast break as soon as a teammate obtains the ball. In recent years the im-

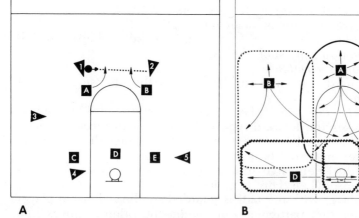

A   B

DIAGRAM 6–6 Covering offensive gaps.

provement in individual skills, particularly shooting ability, has reduced the effectiveness of the 3-2 defense.

Strengths

1. Reduces outside shooting possibilities.
2. Provides excellent fast break possibilities.
3. Valuable against a driving offense.
4. Front line players are in position to apply pressure or double team an opponent with the ball.
5. Effective defense on a wide court.

Weaknesses

1. Reduces rebounding opportunities.
2. Increases the difficulty of guarding the corners.
3. Overloads backline defensive players.
4. Reduces the protection of the foul line area. (The front line chaser should avoid advancing beyond the head of the free-throw circle.)
5. Increases the vulnerability of the baseline area.

Personnel

THE CENTER GUARD: The key player, the center guard (letter A in Diagram 6–6, B), is an aggressive, quick reacting, daring, confident and experienced leader. Although the primary defensive responsibility is the free-throw area, the center fast breaks in a straight line toward the opposite basket when a teammate gains possession of a rebound.

THE WING GUARDS: Wing guards B and C are responsible for: (1) the front-court area; (2) the sides of the court; (3) the corners, when the back guards are delayed under the basket; (4) the free-throw area; and (5) the rebounds in and around the free-throw circle. Understandably, the extent of the area to be covered demands aggressive, quick reacting players. Strategically, wing guards force the offense to pass to the sides, double team, and avoid short shots. A left handed player is often more valuable on the left side of the court in position 2.

BACK GUARDS: Both back players are strong rebounders possessing good timing, the skill to block out opponents from the basket area, the ability to pass to a teammate while in the air or as soon as the feet touch the floor, and the ability to dribble out of a congested area when closely guarded. Player 4, the best defensive player on the team, protects the left corner and the area under the basket. Player 5 covers the right corner and assists 4 in guarding the area under the basket.

Defensive Moves According to the Position of the Ball

Player 1 has the ball in the middle of the court. The center guard, A, moves to a defensive position on 1 while wing guards B and C drop back toward the free-throw line (Diagram 6–7).

Player 1 passes the ball to 4. Wing guard B immediately covers 4, A and C drop back and E moves to the left of the basket (Diagram 6–8).

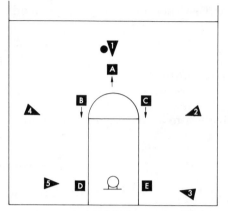
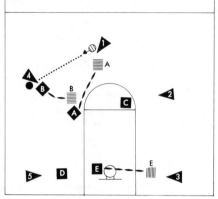

DIAGRAM 6–7   Defensive moves according to ball position.
DIAGRAM 6–8   Defensive moves according to ball position.

Player 4 passes to 5. As soon as 5 receives the ball, D assumes a close defensive position and B drops back a few steps for an anticipated pass to either 4 or 2. Player E stays in the same position to the left of the basket (Diagram 6–9).

The 2-3 Zone Defense

The 2-3 is a contemporary style of defense developed to alleviate the problem of offensive players outnumbering rebounding guards in a 3-2 defense. To shift into the 2-3 strategy from the 3-2, the center front line player drops back to a position directly in front of the basket and approximately 10 feet from the endline. The additional guard under the basket increases the ability of the

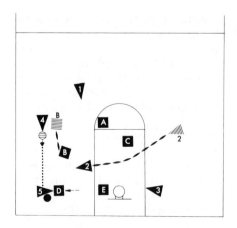

DIAGRAM   6–9 Defensive   moves according to ball position.

defense to limit offensive scoring and enhances fast break opportunities for the defense.

Strengths

1. Provides protection for the area around the basket.
2. Increases rebounding strength by providing a rebound triangle.
3. Discourages offensive maneuvers involving a low post or a short cutting pattern.
4. Protects the baseline area.
5. Enables the guards to cover the corners and side areas against opponents who are proficient in scoring from the side.
6. Complements the fast break. (The rebound triangle allows sufficient time for the guards to start toward the basket before the rebound is secured.)
7. Enhances defensive strategy on a wide court.

Weaknesses

1. Foul line is not adequately covered.
2. Post player or a center operating high may destroy the 2-3 defense.
3. Quick ball movements, such as short passes, overload the 2-3 zone.
4. Outnumbered front line players cannot cover the outside perimeter.
5. Area between the front and back defensive lines is frequently vulnerable.
6. Center player in the back line is often too close to the basket when attempting a rebound.
7. Offensive players possessing the ability to score from a long range or slide set are repeatedly successful.

Personnel

THE CENTER: Each defensive player has a designated area to guard as well as specific responsibilities to fulfill in the total defensive strategy. The center, player A in Diagram 6–10, is in position to direct teammates and unify the various zones in such a way that the team functions as a single unit. Although the area controlled by the center is the small zone in front of the basket, the position is crucial in terms of defending the goal and securing rebounds.

THE CHASERS: The chasers, players B and C, as the name implies, constantly pursue the ball, forcing the opponents to hurry passes, lose the ball on an interception, or tie the ball. Chasers are always on the alert for an opportunity to fast break toward the offensive basket, and seldom drop back further than the free-throw line.

BACK COURT GUARDS: The back guards, players D and E, are often the slowest members of the team, and protect the area around the basket from side and corner shots, block on rebounds and pass the ball into a teammate from any angle.

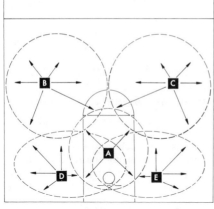

DIAGRAM 6–10

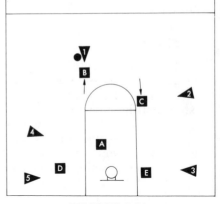

DIAGRAM 6–11

Defensive Moves According to the Position of the Ball

Player 1 has possession of the ball. Chaser B moves forward to play defense, C drops back to the circle, D, A, and E maintain positions while observing 3, 4, and 5 (Diagram 6–11).

Player 1 passes the ball to 4. Chaser B shifts with the ball or, if necessary, D covers 4. Back guards A and E move to the left, blocking the passing lanes (Diagram 6–12).

Player 5 receives the ball. D immediately assumes a close guarding position, A and E remain to the left while B drops back a few steps, covering anticipated passing lanes (Diagram 6–12).

The 2-1-2 Zone Defense

The 2-1-2 zone, the most widely accepted strategy, was conceived by coaches who believed that the conventional 2-3 zone defense inadequately protected the foul line. The 2-1-2 is a combination of the 3-2 and 2-3 zone defenses. While the 3-2 is weak under the basket, in the free-throw area and in the corners, the 2-3 defense is strong under the basket but weak on the sides, the outer half of the free-throw circle and the outside territory. Therefore, coaches shifted the center to the free-throw line, providing additional protection in the foul area and in side-court areas.

Strengths

1. The 2-1-2 zone defense is advantageous against opponents having a strong pivot or pivot attack. With two rebound players under the basket and a third at the free-throw line, the post or pivot player has difficulty obtaining a clear shot at the goal.

2. The defensive rebounding positions are excellent.

3. Fast break opportunities are increased.

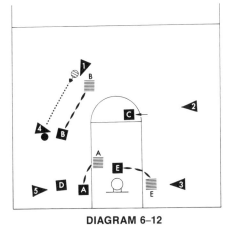

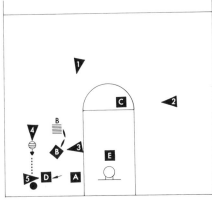

DIAGRAM 6–12   DIAGRAM 6–13

4. The defense is strengthened against an inside shooting or cutting team.

5. The effectiveness of the 2-1-2 is increased on a narrow court.

Weaknesses

1. The defense is often ineffective against a good outside shooting team.

2. The defense is vulnerable in the corners and on top of the circle.

3. The zone is weak along the baseline on the ball side when the offense sets up a triangle with one player by the foul line, one player under the basket, and one player at the forward position (Diagram 6–14).

4. The position of the defense clears an opening for baseline shots.

5. The defense is inadequate against under-the-basket sleepers.

Personnel

THE CENTER: The defensive quarterback (Letter A—Diagram 6–15), is responsible for the free-throw area, the side court areas, and completing the rebound triangle after a shot. Since player A is a chaser as well as a rebounder, coaches often select the tallest player and best rebounder for the position.

THE CHASERS: Chasers B and C, the strongest and fastest players on the team, attempt to force the offense to rush the side or long range set shots. When two chasers differ in size the position on the right side of the court is assigned to the smaller of the two. Most offensive plays are developed toward the right side, consequently, the strongest defensive players are assigned the left defensive position and the best rebounders the right side. The rebounders, players D and E, possess sufficient speed to control the free-throw lane, the corners and rebounds.

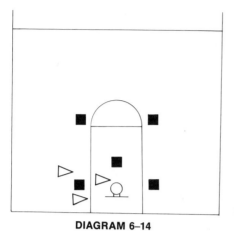

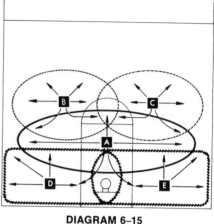

DIAGRAM 6–14   DIAGRAM 6–15

Defensive Moves According to the Position of the Ball

Player 1 has possession of the ball. To avoid double teaming 1, B and C decide who is going to move in and guard 1 (Diagram 6–16).

Player 1 passes to 2, C moves over to guard 2, players B and A shift into position to discourage a pass to the post player, and E closes in on 5 in anticipation of a pass (Diagram 6–17).

Player 2 passes to 5, and interchanges positions with 1. Player E moves closer to 5, C drops back two or three steps, remaining alert for a pass to 1, while A and D double team post player 3 (Diagram 6–18).

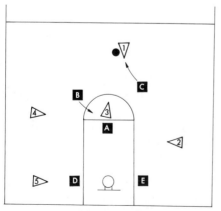

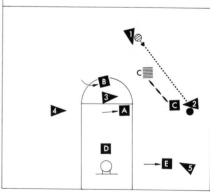

DIAGRAM 6–16 Defensive moves according to ball position.
DIAGRAM 6–17 Alternative play.

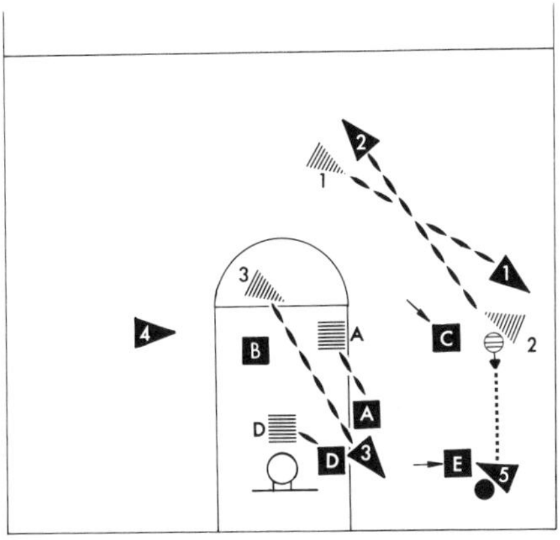

DIAGRAM 6–18 Alternative play.

The 1-3-1 Zone Defense

Dissatisfied with the standard methods of defense, Claire Bee conceived the 1-3-1 zone which provided additional protection under the goal. Any forward eluding the front line player is covered by a second line defensive player. The third guard, located behind the second line, controls the area under the basket. In the 3-2, 2-3, and 2-1-2, offensive strategy includes short shots between the defensive lines or short shots under the basket when the back line shifts forward to stop the shots between lines. The 1-3-1 defense is most effective against a team which simultaneously sets up a baseline player and a foul line player, thus overloading the middle player.

Strengths

1. The zone protects the foul line and the area under the basket. Passes under the basket or to the pivot player at the free-throw line are practically impossible. If the ball gets through, the receiver is surrounded by two or three guards.
2. Provides coverage of the baseline.
3. Tends to stall the opponents' offensive patterns.
4. Minimizes the post attack and the triangle overload offense.
5. Covers the tall offensive player in the basket area.
6. Reduces the number of close shots.
7. Places three defensive players between the ball and basket.

Weaknesses

1. Leaves the rebounding formation (triangle) incomplete.
2. Creates problems when there is an overload offense with a high post.
3. Provides openings for shots from the corners.

4. Lessens defensive effectiveness against interchanging post players.

5. Forces a one-on-one situation when the ball is passed quickly to the weak side.

6. Increases goal attempts from a few feet back and to the side of the foul circle.

7. Decreases fast break ability of the team. With every shift, however, one player is in position to become the leading fast break player. The team should avoid considering a fast break until possession of the rebound is assured.

Personnel

THE CHASER: The chaser, player A in Diagram 6–19, is not only the best defensive player on the team but also the player with leadership ability. The chaser plays the ball when it is within the area between the free-throw line and the center of the court. If two players pass the ball above the free-throw line the chaser is at a disadvantage; therefore, the wing player closest to the player with the ball shifts to the top of the circle. When the ball is passed or dribbled the chaser plays the ball on the strongest side of the floor (Diagram 6–20), while players D and E move as little as possible to maintain the 1-3-1 position. If the ball is in the corner the chaser controls the free-throw lane, attempting to force the ball toward one side of the court and preferably to the weakest shooter. Depending upon the location of the ball, the chaser has a choice of five basic guarding positions.

○ = ball
■ = five basic positions of the chaser

THE WINGS: Since the "wings," players B and C (see Diagram 6–19), require the least amount of speed, they are usually the slowest players on a team. A coach who is not afraid to gamble may have the chaser double team with the wings. A wing who is not involved

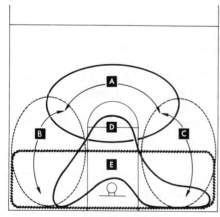

DIAGRAM 6–19

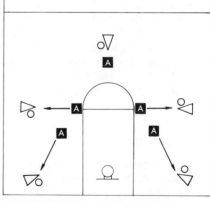

DIAGRAM 6–20 Position of chaser.

in double teaming is in position to cutoff any opponent in the passing lanes. When it is necessary, the chaser shifts back to double team with a wing. When the right defensive corner is protected by player D, B shifts to the right side of the court under the basket. Depending upon the location of the ball, there are five basic defensive positions where wing players may play (Diagram 6–21, A and B).

MIDDLE PLAYER: Because the duties of the middle player (Diagram 6–22) include rebounding and covering the largest section of the middle court, any player assigned to the position must possess both height and speed. The main concerns of the middle guard are to prevent opponents from cutting through the key and to overplay post players. Whenever a post player receives the ball, surrounding defensive players sag toward the middle of the court and the goal. The middle player also has five basic defensive guarding positions.

THE KEY REBOUNDER: The tallest player on the team, player E, is the best rebounder and the second best defensive player. Although the rebounder must shift to cover offensive players in the corners, there is seldom a need for exceptional speed. The five basic positions of the key rebounder are illustrated in Diagram 6–23.

Defensive Moves According to the Position of the Ball

The two basic methods of shifting in the 1-3-1 zone defense include: (1) the straight slide, a relatively simple method; and (2) a revolving shift, requiring considerable practice for proficiency. While any player may play chaser, in the middle or goal position in the revolving 1-3-1 defense the primary advantage comes from the speed with which openings are closed against an attacking offense. Disadvantages of the shift include the time required for the defense to master the revolving principles and the difficulty of assigning responsibility for the shift to players.

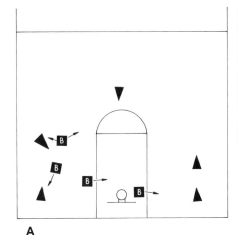 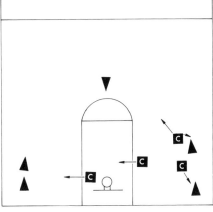

A   B

DIAGRAM 6–21 A. Player two. B. Player three.

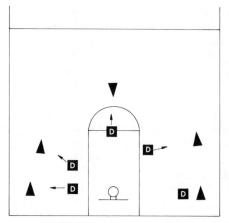

DIAGRAM 6–22   Player four.

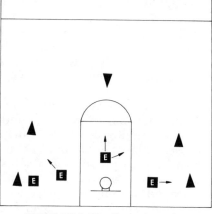

DIAGRAM 6–23   Key rebounder.

STRAIGHT SLIDES: Player 1 has the ball, player A, the chaser, covers 1, wing player B or C double teams 1 or assumes a position to intercept an anticipated pass (Diagram 6–24).

When the ball is passed to player 2, C overplays 2, D shifts toward the corner, 3 moves toward the basket and E takes one step toward the corner (Diagram 6–25).

When the right forward is defended by E, B anticipates a possible return pass to the wing; therefore, the offense attempts a high, long pass to the front. Player A, expecting the pass, is in position

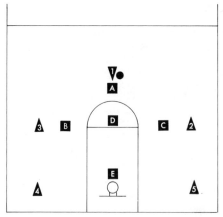

DIAGRAM 6–24   Straight slide.

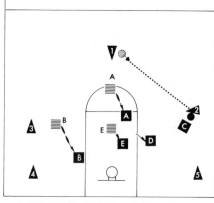

DIAGRAM 6–25   Alternative play.

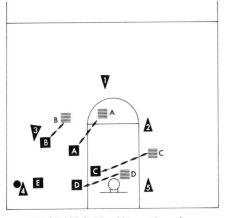

DIAGRAM 6–26 Alternative play.

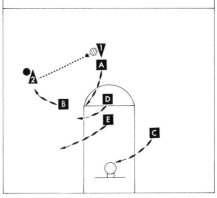

DIAGRAM 6–27 Revolving shift.

for an interception. Player D is in the second position for an interception between C, who is approximately three feet in front of the goal, and player E (Diagram 6–26).

REVOLVING SHIFT: Player 1 passes the ball to 2. Player B guards 2, D drops back a few steps to protect the free-throw area from cutting players, E moves to the corner in anticipation of a pass to the corner player and C provides additional protection near the goal (Diagram 6–27).

Player 2 throws a quick pass to 3, C, the closest guard, covers 3 while the remaining defensive players revolve accordingly (Diagram 6–28).

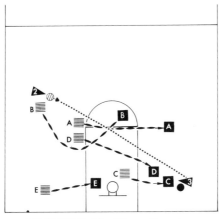

DIAGRAM 6–28 Alternative play.

The 2-2-1 Zone Defense

The 2-2-1 zone defense is frequently referred to as "the goal tending zone," because the tallest player is placed in easy "tending" position under the basket. Back court coaches rely on the 2-2-1 when the tallest player is somewhat uncoordinated and slow.

Strengths

1. Presses opponents efficient at ball handling.
2. Permits closer playing of an offense well spread across the court.
3. Prevents shots by a cutting player.
4. Lessens effectiveness of the offensive post player.
5. Increases defensive ability on a narrow court.

Weaknesses

1. Requires the two front guards to do an exceptional amount of chasing when the five offensive players score from outside the circle.
2. Lessens effectiveness of the defensive rebounding positions.
3. Leaves the baseline vulnerable.

Personnel

THE KEY PLAYER: The arrangement of the defensive positions resembles an inverted jug, with the "key" player taking a position as the "neck of the jug." The key (player A in Diagram 6–29), is the tallest player on the team and controls the defensive rebounds, protects the basket against players cutting to the goal, and places the ball in play following a goal or rebound.

THE FORWARDS: The forwards form the shoulders of the jug (players D and E). They rebound the ball as well as defend the basket, free-throw area, and sides.

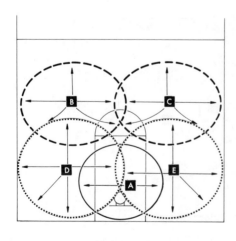

DIAGRAM 6–29

THE CHASERS: The chasers (players B and C) form the base of the jug, covering set shots from the front of the court and any type of shot from the sides of the court. Chasers are the fastest players on the squad and are responsible for leading fast breaks when not involved in defending under the basket or rebounding.

Defensive Moves According to the Position of the Ball

Player 1 has the ball. Players B and C do not move out on long shots but remain alert in case 1 dribbles toward the basket or passes the ball (Diagram 6–30).

Player 1 passes to 2 who is in scoring position, and C covers 2. The jug "moves" as though it were on an inverted pendulum (Diagram 6–31).

Player 2 passes the ball to 5. Since a shot is possible E shifts to defensive play, C drops back a few steps, remaining alert for a possible return pass to 2 (Diagram 6–32).

The 1-2-2 Zone Defense

The 1-2-2 strategy is more profitable against offensive teams having one or three players in front. In player-to-player defense the offensive attack warrants only a single guard in front. Should the offense suddenly shift two forwards to the front the defense can easily transfer to a 2-1-2 zone. Coaches with teams possessing overall height but lacking the speed necessary for player-to-player defense often select the 1-2-2 zone. Players executing the zone should be aggressive ball hawkers, rebounders and hustlers.

Strengths

1. Rushes an offensive team having a single ball handler in front or on top of the circle.

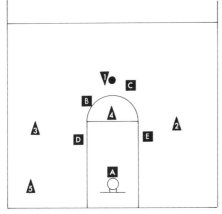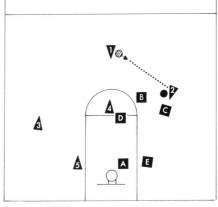

DIAGRAM 6–30   Defensive moves according to ball position.
DIAGRAM 6–31   Alternative play.

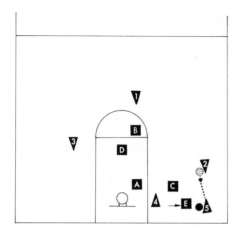

DIAGRAM 6–32   Alternative play.

2. Minimizes defensive slides.
3. Places four players between the ball and basket.
4. Discourages offensive actions under the basket.
5. Increases rebounding effectiveness.
6. Protects baseline area.
7. Outmaneuvers offense on a narrow court.

Weaknesses

1. Leaves corner shots unprotected.
2. Increases defensive vulnerability on the weaker rebounding side.
3. Provides little defense against a skilled ball handling team once the pass has been successfully projected beyond the chaser.

Personnel

To visualize the positions in the 1-2-2 zone defense, again apply the concept of a jug except that the bottle is inverted so that the neck is in front of the ball.

THE POINT: The chaser point position (player A in Diagram 6–33) requires a player possessing stamina, speed, and interception and fast break ability. The duties of the chaser include harassing the ball handler at the top of the circle, assisting teammates when the ball is thrown to the pivot, and attempting to force the player with the ball toward the weak side of the offense. Although height is not essential, a tall guard is an asset in hindering passes.

THE WINGS: The wings (players B and C) are responsible for the ball when it is on the sides of the court. The wings and point coordinate strategy to prevent a reversal of the ball or penetration deep into the court. The wings are next in height to the baseline players as they assist in gaining possession of rebounds.

BASELINE PLAYERS: Baseline players D and E, the tallest players on the team, are responsible for the pivot area and consequently defend the baseline, the corners and backboard. Stationed in such a

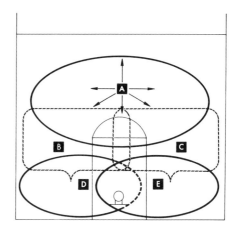

DIAGRAM 6-33   1-2-2 Zone defense.

strategic position, baseline players are usually the best rebounders on the team.

Defensive Moves According to the Position of the Ball

Player 1 has the ball. Chaser A applies pressure. Since the ball is in the middle, the two baseline players, D and E, decide who will cover the post player. Wings B and C attempt to intercept passes toward the baseline and shift to the side when a pass is initiated. (Diagram 6-34).

Player 1 passes to 3. Player B moves forward to cover 3, A drops back to assist in the post area and E covers 4. Player D slides down to the baseline in position to guard 5 and C shifts to the baseline to protect the basket area (Diagram 6-35).

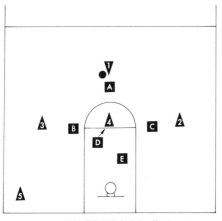
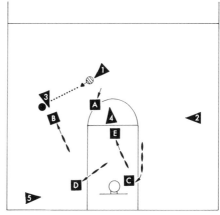

DIAGRAM 6-34   Defensive moves according to ball position.
DIAGRAM 6-35   Alternative play.

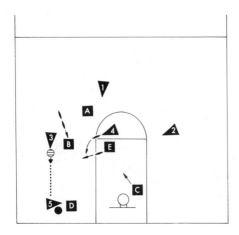

DIAGRAM 6–36   Alternative play.

Player 3 passes to 5, D guards 5 and E attempts to prevent a pass to 4 on a roll to the basket. Player B steps back toward the goal, providing additional interference in the scoring area (Diagram 6–36).

COMBINATION DEFENSES

Coaches have more recently implemented a variety of combination patterns which accent the abilities of each player and help build a solid game strategy, utilizing the best features of player-to-player and zone defense. Although the major advantage of a combination defense is the maximum use of strong defensive players, the ultimate success of any pattern depends upon how the defense executes the play, rather than upon the structure of the play.

Game Strategies

Front line zone — rear line player-to-player

Defensive strategy incorporating zone defense on the front line and player-to-player defense on the back line can be altered by varying the number of front line chasers. Strong rebound players are stationed permanently in the rebound area with the faster, more aggressive scorers on the front line.

Front line player-to-player — back line zone

As the name suggests, the front line guards use a player-to-player defense and the back line guards use a zone. The number of players assigned to the front line depends upon the personnel of the team. Whenever possible, three players are in the basket area, forming a rebound triangle. If the front line needs additional strength, one player shifts forward. In each type of strategy, the front line assists the back line when the offense cuts or when the back line is outnumbered by offensive players.

Box zone and diamond zone with a chaser

Defensive strategies that most women find easier to understand and implement are the box zone and the diamond zone with a chaser. The four player zone is similar to the box or diamond zone The difference lies in the chaser (or roamer) who covers the area or guards the opponents' "star" player with a player-to-player defense. The main task of the chaser when she is guarding is to prevent the ball from reaching the star player. If the star receives the ball the chaser attempts to force the ball or force the player and ball into a zone area where additional defensive help is available. Characteristics of a chaser include: (1) speed; (2) endurance; (3) height; (4) agility; and (5) wisdom to apply double teaming techniques. Free lance tactics are applied by a chaser who is responsible for the full court. Double teaming, cutting off passing lanes, looking for interceptions, and executing fast breaks forces the chaser to shift constantly from one position to another.

It is strategically wise to train more than one defensive player to guard the star opponent. A chaser remaining in a game too long becomes unduly fatigued and as a result of the aggressive nature of the position, fouls too frequently.

Two common methods of zone defense established behind the chaser are the box and diamond. The box has two front line players at the free-throw line and two back line players just outside of the foul lane in front of the basket. In both the box and diamond zone, one guard is in front covering the offensive player with the ball, while the remaining three guards shift into a 2-1 formation. The front guards, (players B and C, Diagram 6–37, A), sink with the ball. As one player guards the opponent with the ball, the other must drop back to prevent a pass toward the center of the zone.

The chaser A guards the "star" offensive player. Player 2 has the ball, and B moves toward 2. The logical pass receiver is 3; therefore, C drops back toward the middle to prevent a pass through the zone and to shift closer to 3, if it becomes necessary (Diagram 6–37, B).

The duties of the back guards include preventing passes to a forward breaking through the lane, detering unguarded shots in a zone, and covering the corners of the court. A pass toward the top of the free-throw circle is less critical than a pass along the endline toward the goal; therefore, the back guard overplays the forward near the baseline. A drive to the inside then forces the dribbler in the direction of the defensive players. If a guard is drawn to the corner, the other deep guard shifts to the opposite lane line, covering the space.

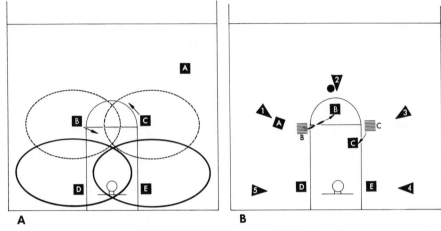

DIAGRAM 6–37   Box zone defense.

In order to have an effective box, front and back guards work as a unit. For example, if the ball is passed to the middle of the floor at the top of the free-throw circle, one of the front guards covers the player with the ball while the second front guard shifts back toward the middle. Adjusting the position of the back guards corrects any possible weakness in the zone (Diagram 6–38).

PLAY DIAGRAM OF THE BOX ZONE DEFENSE. Player 3 passes the ball to 4, and E shifts toward 4 to play close defense. Player D moves to the right side of the basket to discourage a pass to a cutter going through the lane. Player B drops back into the key, providing additional protection while the chaser continues to guard 1.

Basically, the diamond (Diagram 6–39), is designed to block

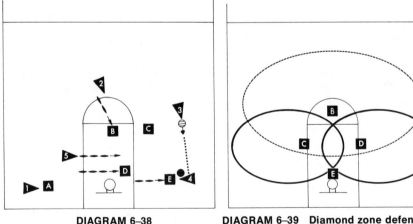

DIAGRAM 6–38   **DIAGRAM 6–39   Diamond zone defense.**

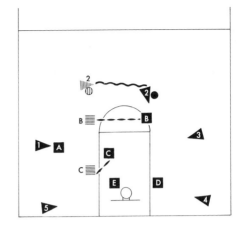

DIAGRAM 6–40   Defensive moves according to ball position.

the scoring area near the basket and restrain a high or low post when the area under the basket is weak, or there is only one defensive rebounder. The zone shifts every time the ball moves. The guard nearest the forward with the ball assumes a close guarding position.

Defensive Moves According to the Position of the Ball

When the ball is dribbled around the top of the circle the front guard covers the dribbler. The off-side guard (the guard not close to play) pulls forward slightly, increasing the difficulty of passing across the lane (Diagram 6–40).

When the ball is passed into one of the wing areas, B or C becomes the point. The 2-1 zone then forms behind the point. Player A, the chaser, maintains player-to-player defense against 1 (Diagram 6–41).

Back guard D is responsible for both corner positions. If the ball is passed to 4, D shifts toward 4, while wing guard B drops into the pivot area (Diagram 6–42).

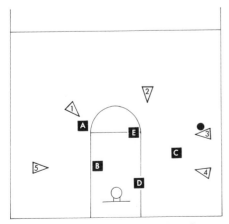

DIAGRAM 6–41   Alternative play.

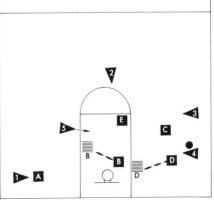

DIAGRAM 6–42   Alternative play.

DRILLS

While footwork, hand movement, and general guarding stance are basic to all systems of defense, most coaches require players to possess a reasonable amount of ability and knowledge in player-to-player defense before introducing any zone defensive techniques. The following drills help players develop the skills needed for player-to-player and zone defense.

1. *Mass Defensive Sliding Drill.* A leader stands in front of the group and calls out "right," "left," "front," or "back." The group responds by sliding to the right, left, front or back.

2. *Approach and Retreat.* The leader in front of the group verbally gives a command for the group to approach. Players shift toward the leader, raising a hand forward. When the leader calls "retreat," each person retreats in a low defensive stance.

3. *Pass and Check.* Arrange five players on the floor in the desired zone defense and five players in offensive positions around the perimeter of the zone. After the ball has been tossed to one of the forwards the guards shift to the proper guarding position. The forward holds the ball until the coach checks the stance and movement of each defensive player. The coach then signals the forward to pass the ball to a teammate. Forwards continue passing with the coach checking the defense's position after each pass.

Variation: Rearrange the offense in a different formation. Players repeat drill three, with forwards passing the ball while the coach checks the movements of each defensive player in the zone after each pass.

4. *Zone with a Post.* An assigned forward acts as a post player, cutting through the zone and attempting to pass through the zone to the pivot. The coach corrects individual positioning.

5. *Zone vs. Time.* The coach establishes a time limit for the drill. The number of passes the forwards complete through the defense's zone are counted. The drill includes passes received in the lane.

6. *Five-on-Five.* Forwards attempt to score in a five-on-five situation. A record is kept of the location from which the goals were made and the reason the forwards were successful in making the goal.

7. *Observation Drill.* The offense shoots from designated areas on the floor while defensive players observe the direction of the rebounds. Guards then cover the rebound area in each of the defensive zone positions.

PRESSURE DEFENSE

THE PRESS

Pressure defense, designed to generally disrupt offensive play, is incorporated by most coaches as a regular part of game strategy. Although half-court or full court presses have many variations, they all have one characteristic in common—the need for coordination among the five players. Fundamentally, all of the strategies of pressure defense, both team and individual, may be categorized under player-to-player or zone defense. As in any defensive or offensive technique, players must understand the methods with which presses are applied and the situations where press is used.

Strengths and uses of the press

1. *Now or Never.* The most common time for a press is late in the game when the opponents are leading. In order to score, the trailing team must gain possession of the ball.

2. *Surprise Element.* The press as a surprise tactic is successfully used at irregular intervals during a game or at the beginning of the second half. Opening a game with a full court press may also overwhelm the opponents and produce a number of scores before the team recovers.

3. *Change of Tempo.* The press, a deliberate method of changing the tempo of a game, enables a fast breaking team to increase the playing rhythm of slower opponents.

4. *Personnel Strengths.* The coach who has personnel conducive to a pressing defense may press the entire game. Such a team includes tall, agile players in excellent condition as well as two or three guards who delight in harassing the opponents.

5. *Opponent Weaknesses.* The pressing defense is effective against a team that has slow-moving, cumbersome, inexperienced,

185

physically unfit, tense or uncoordinated dribblers and ball handlers.

6. *Disrupting Set Pattern Play.* The pressure defense forces teams with set patterns to operate in unfamiliar zones, to alter the prearranged timing of each play and establish a tempo of play that is undesirable.

7. *Home Court Advantage.* The home court is an ideal situation for the press since a strange court, unfavorable spectator reaction and unfamiliar surroundings all tend to increase the tension of the players.

8. *Tension Reducer.* The pressure defense reduces tension by aggressively preparing a team mentally, thus reducing the problems encountered in contests of major importance.

Weaknesses of the press

1. *Fouls.* The nature of a pressure defense demands a more aggressive style of play, inevitably increasing the number of fouls. Young, inexperienced ball players believe that stealing the ball strengthens the effectiveness of a pressure defense; however, atempting to steal the ball is, without question, the most common means of committing a foul in the pressing game. The coach encourages front line players to harass the opponent by moving the arms, but to avoid touching the opponent in any manner.

2. *Lack of Balance.* The defensive player on the move who reaches toward the ball and temporarily loses her balance provides the greatest number of opportunities for forwards to evade the defense. Instead of lunging for the ball, the guard flicks the ball away from the forward. The guard keeps the feet ahead of the opponent while constantly moving the hands in a position to harass the opponent in an attempt to force the forward to lose the ball.

3. *Weak Front Line.* Strong defensive presses are initiated by front line defenders who are proficient in double teaming and controlling an opponent with the ball in a one-on-one situation. When the front guards are unable to control the opponents the coach may be obligated to alter the press or the overall defensive tactics.

4. *Lack of Hustle.* Defensive players must rapidly return to the defensive press position after a basket or when the press loses its effectiveness. Often the forwards will outmaneuver the press by rapidly putting the ball in play and racing up the court, or by moving the ball up the court with a long pass.

5. *Inexperience.* The amount of time necessary to learn the press produces situations in which inexperienced players are forced to execute the press. Everyone must be willing to profit by former mistakes to avoid making the same mistake twice.

Player-for-Player Pressure Defense

When a coach selects player-for-player pressure defense, each individual on the team must be well-skilled in the basic individual defensive tactics. Techniques that are necessary include:

1. The guard extends and moves the arms continuously when

guarding a player with the ball. The passer will then have difficulty in sighting receivers and will often be forced to execute a high, lob pass.

2. The guard reacts quickly with the feet. Quick retreat steps, sharp pivot steps and fast change of direction steps are necessary for maintaining balance and body control while guarding the assigned opponent.

3. A guard should assume the position in relation to the ball that is most advantageous. Players close to the ball are in a close defensive position while players away from the ball are "sagging" (ready to assist a teammate or move forward to guard a free player near the ball).

4. The defense double teams the player with the ball. Double teaming is not designed to gain possession of the ball, but to force a poor pass or a violation. Therefore, the defense can disconcert an opponent by continually moving the arms and hands and maintaining a good position with the legs and body. The defense must avoid fouling or permitting the opponent to slip between the double team. When both members of a double team are strong defensively, the players may switch on any criss-cross or double team. Forwards are forced to react with sufficient speed and agility, to anticipate the double team, and to shift into a position to possibly interrupt the play.

5. Speed and fast reaction time are necessary when a player is guarding more than one opponent. Mentally, the guard attempts to anticipate and "outmaneuver" the opponents. Ideally, each member of the team should be matched with an opponent who is similar in stature and speed or with an opponent who can be controlled.

Implementing player-for-player presses

Throughout a player-for-player press, defensive players continuously and relentlessly apply pressure on the ball as well as on the opponents. Whether or not the player throwing the ball inbounds is guarded is a matter of debate, yet the instant the ball is thrown inbounds the defensive player assigned to the person with the ball attacks, rather than waits for the ball handler. Guarding the out-of-bounds player (1) applies pressure on the offense; (2) forces a bad pass; (3) delays any attempt to throw a long pass immediately after obtaining possession of the ball; and (4) allows defensive teammates additional time to establish the press. On the other hand, the same defensive player, when not assigned to guard the out-of-bounds player, covers any potential offensive player moving toward the ball and attempts to force a bad pass or intercept the ball (Diagram 7-1).

The remaining four defensive players assume positions between the out-of-bounds player and the assigned offensive players. While guards closest to the out-of-bounds player maintain tight guarding stances, the back guards remain a few feet away from and between the designated opponent and out-of-bounds player. This slightly sagging stance enables either back line player to attempt an interception of a mid-court lob pass intended for one of

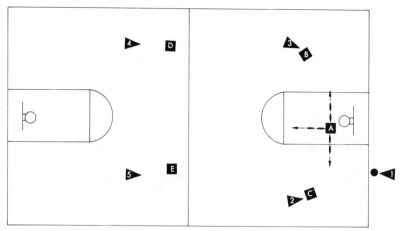

DIAGRAM 7-1   The Press.

the back court offensive players, to retreat and deflect a pass, or
to move between the opponent and the basket. Should the pass be
successfully thrown inbounds, the appointed defensive player immediately assumes a position between the player and ball, preventing a return pass.

When the opponents are on the defense there are numerous
situations where double teaming may be effective. Most frequently
double teaming occurs when opponents attempt a criss-cross or
when an opponent is so near the ball that a defensive player needs
to move only a few steps to participate in a double team situation.
Often the effectiveness of double teaming depends upon a teammate down court anticipating the play, shifting toward the opponent
whose assigned guard is already involved in the double team
strategy, and assuming responsibility for two opponents. In summary, the overall strength of the press lies in a minimum of fouls,
complete coverage of the nearest possible outlets, and the ability of
a team to efficiently double team (Diagram 7-2).

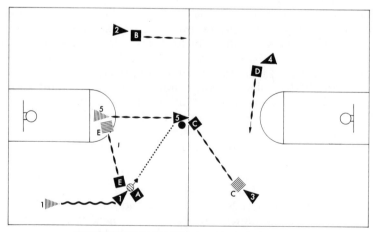

DIAGRAM 7-2   The Press in Double Teaming.

For example, in Diagram 7-2, as E runs near the ball, A and E form a double team strategy. The remaining defensive players are in position to intercept a pass to one of the four opponents. When 1 throws the ball to 5, C attempts to gain possession of the pass, D moves toward mid-court in order to guard both 3 and 4, while B runs back in case C misses the interception. If a dribbler lowers the head and starts dribbling or turns the back and starts dribbling laterally toward the sideline, a second defender moves into position to double team. The teammate on the opposite side of the court prepares for a possible interception.

Teams may effectively outmaneuver the player-for-player press by passing the ball to the best dribbler and then shifting the few remaining players down court. This play must be used with caution as the defensive team often follows the offensive pattern. In other words, three guards fall back with the offensive team while the remaining guards appear to fall back but quickly turn and double team as the opponent starts to dribble. Usually offensive players in a hurry to clear the area run too deeply into the court, eliminating any chance of receiving the ball and forcing the dribbler to retain possession of the ball until a teammate is free. As the ball moves toward the basket, players not involved with the ball are in loose guarding positions covering the assigned forwards with a minimal amount of effort and assisting other players when it is necessary.

Guidelines for a Player-for-Player Press

1. The pressure on the offensive players is continuous.

2. The most advantageous position for guarding a player without the ball is between the offensive player and ball.

3. The defensive position for guarding an opponent with the ball is between the ball handler and basket. The guard moves in position to force the dribbler to use the weak hand, to stop the dribble, or to force the dribbler to the middle of the court for a double team defense.

4. The defensive player double teams the player with the ball in the back court or the corners of the defensive court.

5. The players switch assigned opponents only under emergency situations.

6. The defensive player closest to the ball, anticipating the strategy of the opponent with the ball, covers the nearest outlet pass receiver.

7. The back line players are often responsible for two opponents and play the strong side of the ball.

8. The defense consistently strives to force violations and intercept poorly thrown passes.

9. The players avoid trying to steal the ball and committing fouls.

10. The defensive player nearest a dribbler who breaks free impedes the progress of the dribbler until the assigned defensive player recovers. In situations near the basket, with only one defensive player back, the guard delays the play and prevents the lay-up shot.

Methods of combating a press include: (1) the fast break, incorporating a long pass after a basket. It is the task of the defensive player guarding the out-of-bounds opponent to move the arms and legs, thus delaying the long pass until the press is set. (2) The use of an offensive criss-cross can put the ball inbounds or move the ball up the court. Only defensive players skilled in individual tactics have the ability to remain with an assigned offensive player. (3) The use of a screen can free a player who does not have possession of the ball. It is an advantage to have a tall, well-skilled ball handler on the team as a successful screen will enable the tall player to receive a pass, keep the ball out of the reach of the opponents, or pass to a teammate once the offense is set.

ZONE PRESSURE DEFENSE

In any of the various methods of zone defense each player follows the movement of the ball while remaining aware of any offensive players in the designated zone. To cover offensive players adequately, guards frequently interchange zones.

The zone press provides more opportunities for double teaming than the player-for-player press. The zone press allows positioning of the defensive players strategically to protect the basket area, intercept or deflect a pass, or to set up a fast break for a quick basket, and offers a team the opportunity to compensate for lack of individual ability through unified team effort. Naturally, each coach has a different theory on the advantages of a zone press. Through researching available coaching materials and conversing with leading coaches, individuals will discover the various philosophies concerning the zone press. The following zone press techniques are a compilation of ideas gathered from coaches of inter-collegiate teams for women and for men.

Trapping

As the zone press is established, individual player-for-player defense is implemented to prevent the opposition from successfully throwing the ball inbounds. If the ball is thrown inbounds the primary object of the defense is to force the player with the ball into a "trapped" (double team) situation. The farther the offensive team is from the basket, the more time the defense has to gamble and recover the press if the trap is not effective. The corners and side lines are very desirable trapping areas as the out-of-bounds line prohibits movement by the trapped player. In setting a trap, players must consider the number of possible outlet passes. Sideline trapping allows the offensive player three possible pass outlets whereas trapping in the middle of the court offers a player four outlet passes. Coaches should apply trapping tactics:

1. To press the opponents when the defensive team is behind in the game.

2. To stall a smooth-working offense.

3. To contain teams that have poor passing techniques within the basket area.

4. To take advantage of a slow-reacting team.

5. To take advantage of a team that does not use all of its players for scoring.

6. To attempt to gain possession of the ball when the opponents are visibly affected by trapping tactics.

7. To disrupt stalling tactics by the opponents.

The defensive team assumes regular defensive positions behind the safety line when:

1. The offense has effective passing techniques in the basket area.

2. The opponents have players who score from outside the basket area.

3. The offense successfully passes from one forward to another.

4. The defensive team has a small lead late in the game.

5. The offensive team has successfully attacked one side and then the other side of the defense with short, quick passes.

Trapping areas (Diagram 7-3)

1. Area 1, the best trapping area, is closest to the basket of the pressing team. The closeness of the endline and sideline affords only two passing outlets for the opponents.

2. Area 2, bordered by one sideline, has three possible outlet passes.

3. Area 3 allows four outlet passes; however, the distance from the offensive basket may force the player receiving the pass into another trap.

4. Area 4 is unsuitable since the trapped player not only has four passing outlets, but also has a chance to move toward the

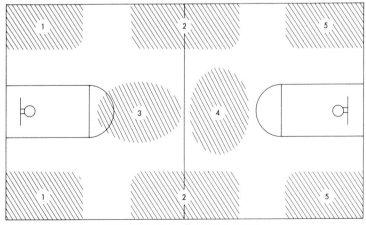

DIAGRAM 7-3 Trapping Areas.

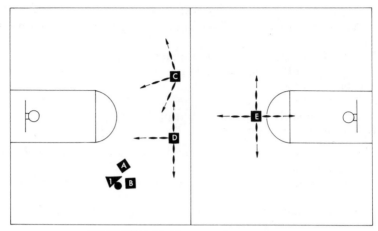

DIAGRAM 7–4   Alignment Strategy. Rule One.

basket. If a defensive player makes a mistake, the player in Area 4 becomes a scoring threat.

5. Area 5, similar to Area 1, offers two passing outlets. Players exert caution since the action is close to the basket of the offensive team.

Alignment Strategy

The development of alignments for each position has simplified a number of zone defenses. Alignment strategy enables players to recognize the positions on the floor to be filled during a trapping situation. The coach watches for necessary adjustments by observing the reactions of the players as the ball moves to various areas. The following three rules are applicable for each situation:

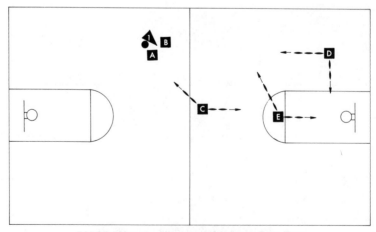

DIAGRAM 7–5   Alignment Strategy. Rule Two.

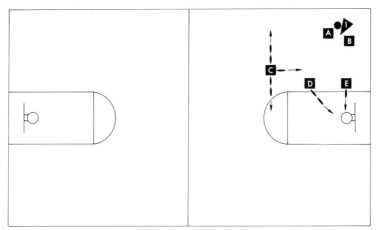

DIAGRAM 7-6 Alignment Strategy. Rule Three.

Rule One: Two on the Ball, Two Floating and One Back

Two defensive players on the ball, two floating and one back is in effect when there is no sideline situation. Player 1 is trapped by A and B; Players C and D, the floaters, attempt to intercept a pass or to force another trap if 1 passes the ball. Player E stays back in the safety position to protect the basket (Diagram 7-4).

Rule Two: Two on the Ball, One Floating, One in the Lane and One Back.

Two defensive players on the ball, one floating, one in the lane and one back is in effect whenever there is a sideline trap situation. Players A and B trap 1, who has the ball, and C forces another trap or intercepts a pass around the middle of the court. Player D, in deep court in line with 1 and the endline, is prepared to intercept a pass, move up the sideline for another trap, or retreat toward the basket for defensive protection. The safety player, E, protects the basket, attempting to make only the sure interception (Diagram 7-5).

Rule Three: Two on the Ball, One Floating and Two Back.

Two defensive players on the ball, one floating and two back is applicable for baseline corner coverage. Player 1, in possession of the ball, is trapped by A and B, in the baseline corner area, C is prepared to intercept a pass or retreat for defensive basket coverage, while D and E protect the basket (Diagram 7-6).

The 2-1-2 zone press

The 2-1-2 zone press defense is effective in the back court, in the center area, and after a delay in the game. The vulnerable areas are the sidelines, near the center line.

Personnel of the 2-1-2 Zone Press:

The chasers, players A and B, have the following responsibilities:

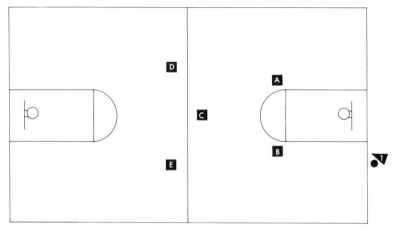

DIAGRAM 7-7   2-1-2 Zone Press.

1. To use player-to-player tactics when guarding an opponent throwing the ball into the court.

2. To guide the dribbler into a trapping situation.

3. To trap the player with the ball in the back court.

4. To trap the player with the ball at mid-court with the assistance of the middle defensive player or the wing player on the same side of the court.

5. To protect any zone left open as a result of a trap set by teammates.

6. To remain alert for possible pass deflections or interceptions.

The middle player, C, has the following responsibilities:

1. To intercept or deflect passes.

2. To set a trap with either chaser in the middle court area.

3 To set a trap at mid-court on either sideline.

4. To set a trap on the sidelines with either wing player.

5. To discourage a pass to the sidelines from mid-court.

6. To cover any defensive position left open when a player is trapping.

7. To protect the basket area whenever necessary.

The wings, players D and E, have the following responsibilities:

1. To discourage long passes, particularly along the sidelines at mid-court.

2. To intercept or deflect passes in the assigned area.

3. To set a trap on the sideline with the middle player or on the same side of the court as the chaser.

4. To force any player deep in the zone into a trap.

5. To cover defensive positions left open when a teammate traps another player.

6. To retreat to the basket area whenever necessary.

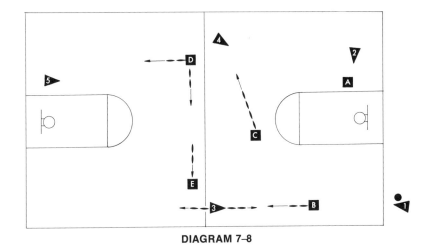

DIAGRAM 7-8

IMPLEMENTING THE ZONE PRESSURE DEFENSE

The most important part of any pressure defense is to establish the zone quickly and contest the first pass. If possible, the defense forces a pass that is easily deflected or interrupted, such as a lob or a long pass.

The offense accepted by many teams for throwing the ball into the court is illustrated in Diagram 7-8. Player A guards 2 and B watches 3, who moves toward 1, the passer. Player C covers 4, if necessary, while D intercepts any long passes and E shifts toward player 3 in case 3 decides to go deep into the court.

If the ball is successfully thrown inbounds, the defense forces the player with the ball into a trap as soon as possible. The following four diagrams depict various trapping situations.

Sideline Trap—Rule Two

(Two on the ball, one floating, one in lane and one back.) Player 1 passes to 2, A and C trap 2, and B moves toward the center to become the floater. Player D shifts up mid-court in line with the ball while E remains back in a safety position (Diagram 7-9).

Trapping Alignment—Rule One

(Two on ball, two floating and one back.) Player 1 passes to 2 and A and B set the trap. Players C and E, the floaters, protect each side of the court while D retreats toward the back position to protect the basket area (Diagram 7-10).

Trapping Alignment—Rule Two

(Two on ball, one floating, one in lane and one back.) Players B and E set the trap, A becomes the floater, D moves in line with the ball and C protects the basket area (Diagram 7-11).

Trapping Alignment—Rule Three

(Two on ball, one floating and two back.) Player 1, who has possession of the ball, is trapped along the baseline corner by A and D. The floater guarding the pivot area, B, is prepared to intercept a pass to the back court player. Players E and C are back toward the basket in position to intercept a pass to 2, 3, or 5 (Diagram 7-12).

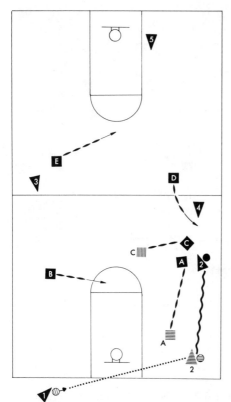

DIAGRAM 7–9 Sideline Trap. Players' positions correspond to alignment strategy of Rule Two. p. 195.

DIAGRAM 7–10 Trapping Alignment. Rule One.

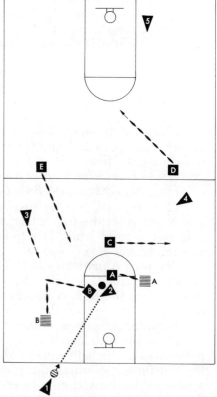

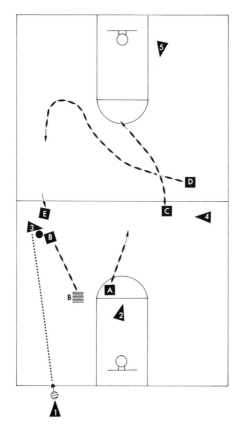

DIAGRAM 7–11   Trapping Alignment. Rule Two.

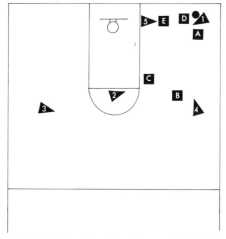

DIAGRAM 7–12   Trapping Alignment. Rule Three.

The 2-2-1 zone press

With four players in position to attack, the 2-2-1 zone press is most effective against teams challenging the sides of a press. Vulnerable passing areas—the middle of the court and deep corner areas—encourage long passes and consequently provide opportunities for interceptions. Safety players cover the back position unless a wing player drops back to protect the basket.

Personnel

THE CHASERS. The front players, A and B, are the chasers, and are skilled in the fundamentals of player-to-player defense, double teaming and forcing the opponent with the ball to dribble in the desired direction. Other responsibilities of the chasers include:

1. Preventing the throw-in with player-to-player coverage or allowing the ball to be thrown in and then encouraging a dribble. (The decision will often depend upon the philosophy of the coach.)

2. Sagging to the side of the court for the anticipated throw-in and then double teaming the dribbler.

3. Forcing the dribbler into a trap with the other chaser or the wing playing on the same side of the court.

4. Discouraging a pass and encouraging a dribble when the player with the ball looks up court to select a pass receiver.

5. Avoiding a double team near the sideline. Recovery possibilities at a point on the far end of the court are difficult and the spread position of the defense allows easier penetration.

6. Assuming the role of a floater when not involved in a double team.

7. Protecting any zone left unguarded by a teammate involved in the trap situation.

8. Deflecting or intercepting passes while floating.

9. Creating a double team situation with a wing player when the ball is in the middle of the court.

10. Dropping to the basket area to cover the nearest outlet pass possibility when the ball is passed deep into the side or baseline.

11. Sprinting back into position immediately after a long pass is thrown from out-of-bounds.

THE WING PLAYERS. The second line or "wing" players anticipate play possibilities, intercept the ball, secure the proper position in relation to the ball, and double team. Additional responsibilities include:

1. Covering the middle court when both guards are double teaming.

2. Establishing a double team with the guards when the ball is moved up the sideline or into the middle of the court.

3. Setting a double team with the safety player when the ball is deep.

4. Assuming a position to intercept or deflect a long overhead pass, yet double teaming or covering the center if necessary.

5. Assisting the guard in the center when the area is overloaded with opponents and the ball is moved up the side court.

6. Dropping back to provide protection under the basket when the ball is double teamed deep on the opposite side of the court.

7. Sprinting toward the basket when a long, full court pass is thrown.

8. Preventing lay-up shots when the forwards outnumber the guards under the basket by stalling the offense with defensive fakes.

THE SAFETY PLAYER. The safety player is a mobile person with the ability to react quickly, anticipate plays, obtain rebounds and play defense when caught in a two-on-one situation. Other duties of the safety player are:

1. Anticipating the ball handler sufficiently in order to cover the two deep players, yet knowing when to intercept or double team on the side, if necessary.

2. Preventing a quick, long pass by rapidly regaining court position.

3. Establishing a double team with the wings when the ball goes deep toward the side or baseline.

4. Guarding a player in either corner who attempts to shoot.

5. Remaining in the safety position until one of the wing players rotates to cover the safety spot.

6. Discouraging lay-up shots when outnumbered by opponents by stalling the offense until assistance is available.

7. Obtaining the rebound position after each attempt for the goal.

8. Verbally encouraging teammates.

Implementation

Player-for-Player Tactics Used to Prevent a Pass Inbounds

Player A takes a position in front of 2 and B, shifts in front of 3 who is moving into the middle area. Player C anticipates a lob pass near the center of the court while D, also near the center, dis-

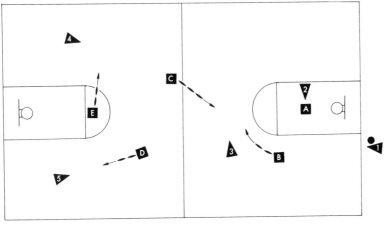

DIAGRAM 7-13

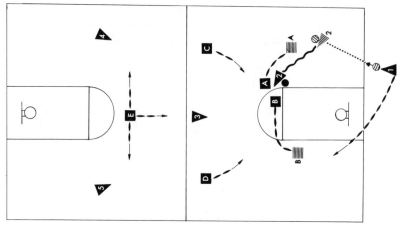

DIAGRAM 7–14

courages a pass to 5 in the corner. The safety player, E, deflects or intercepts any long pass to 4.

The following four diagrams illustrate the play possibilities and the defensive movements of the 2-2-1 zone press.

Ball Goes to the Middle–Trap Alignment One

(Two on ball, two floating, one back.) The ball is passed to 2, who is forced to dribble to the middle. Players A and B immediately set the trap, and C and D move forward to become floaters. Player E, the safety player, covers both 5 and 4 in the back court. Variation: When the ball is passed into the middle of the four defensive players, A, B, C, and D, one wing player forces the dribbler to the other wing who sets a trap in the center of the court. Players A and B shift back to become the floaters, while E retains the safety position (Diagram 7-14).

Sideline Trap—Trap Alignment Two

(Two on ball, one floating, one in lane and one back.) The ball is passed to 2 and A forces 2 to the sideline and into a trap with C. Player B becomes the floater, D moves to the safety spot and E shifts to be in line with the ball (Diagram 7-15).

Center to Sideline Trap—Trap Rule Two

(Two on ball, one floating, one in lane and one back.) The ball is released from a center trap to sideline player 3. Player B forces 3 to dribble the ball, then stops the dribbler as D runs over to assist in setting the trap. Player C becomes the floater, E the player in the lane and A the safety (Diagram 7-16).

Long Pass—Rule Three

(Two on ball, one floating, two back.) Player 5 receives the ball. Player E, favoring the baseline, moves out to guard 5. Player B runs down the court to establish a double team. Player A becomes the floater while C and D protect the basket (Diagram 7-17).

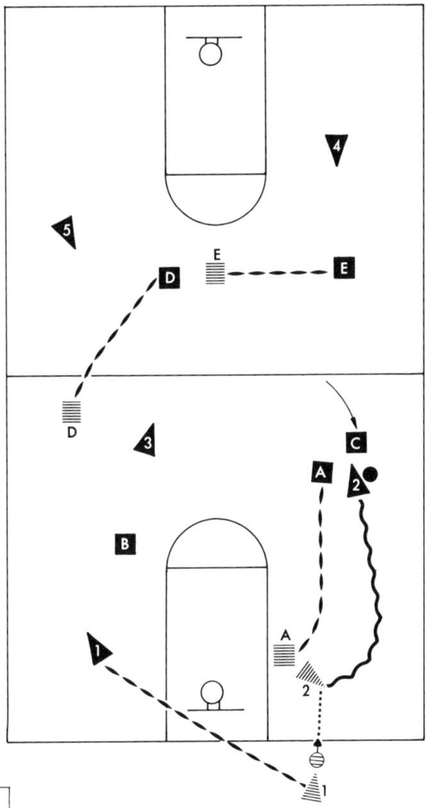

DIAGRAM 7–15

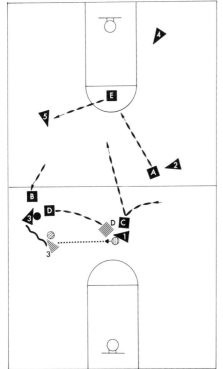

DIAGRAM 7–16

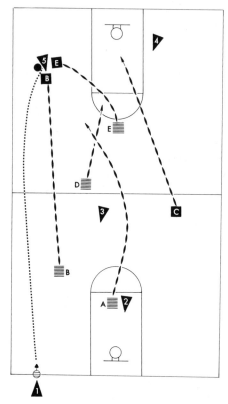

DIAGRAM 7–17

The 1-2-1-1 zone press

The 1-2-1-1 press is designed to counteract the fast break techniques a team uses immediately after a basket is scored. Occasionally, the offense has sufficient time to receive a pass inbounds and return it to the player who threw the ball into the court.

Personnel

THE CHASER.   The defensive player responsible for guarding the opponent throwing the ball inbounds is the chaser (A in Diagram 7-18). Since the arms are extended to prevent a long or a direct pass, a player with a long reach fills the chaser's position. Responsibilities of the chaser are:

1. To move toward the baseline and apply pressure vocally, and with the arms and legs, to the player attempting to pass the ball inbounds.

2. To secure a position between the ball and the player returning to the court when the ball is successfully thrown inbounds.

3. To prevent the player with the ball from moving toward the baseline.

4. To double team with either wing player.

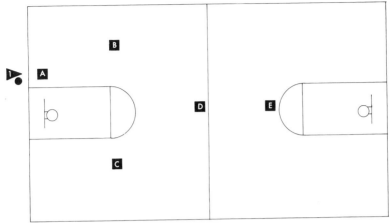

DIAGRAM 7-18   1-2-1-1 Zone Press.

5. To be a floater in any double team situation where other teammates are involved.

6. To retreat to any zone position left open.

THE WING PLAYERS. Wing players B and C are the fastest players on the court. The quicker and more alert of the two, B occupies the right side of the court while C fills the left side. The wings attempt to force the player with the ball into a double team situation. Additional responsibilities of the wing players are:

1. To discourage or intercept passes to the side of the court.

2. To assist the chaser in trapping the player with the ball.

3. To prevent the trapped player from retreating to the baseline.

4. To intercept a pass to the player who originally threw the ball inbounds from the player trapped by the opposite wing.

5. To force the dribbler into a trap situation with the middle player.

6. To assume a floating position in double team situations created by two teammates.

7. To assume a safety position when passes to the offensive baseline are successful.

THE MIDDLE PLAYER. Player D, the "middle" player, is usually the tallest guard or the fastest, most agile forward. The middle player possesses a thorough knowledge of basketball as well as an excellent ability to anticipate the opponents' intended strategy. Responsibilities of the middle player are:

1. To protect the middle area by remaining in front of any offensive player.

2. To deflect or intercept any long or cross-court passes the trapped player may attempt.

3. To double team with either wing player.

4. To double team with the safety player on long passes when the other wing player retreats to the safety position.

5. To assume a floating position when necessary and to drop back to the safety position.

THE SAFETY PLAYER. The fifth defensive position, E, is the "safety" player, usually the center forward or the tallest forward. Safety players are in a position to predict passes and defend a 2-on-1, a 3-on-1, or a 3-on-2 situation by slowing down the opponent until a teammate arrives. The safety player has the following responsibilities:

1. To discourage long passes into the back area.

2. To deflect or intercept long passes into the back area when a teammate is in position to cover the safety position or when an interception is assured.

3. To double team along the sidelines or in either corner.

4. To implement "one-player" defense against any forward who is free and attempts a close jump shot or lay-up shot.

5. To obtain the rebound after a shot at the goal.

6. To assume the role of "Court General" on the press. The safety is in position to observe the entire court and informs teammates of necessary changes in strategy.

7. To form a zone press alignment of 1-2-2 when there is no offensive player near the basket.

Implementation

The use of player-for-player principles to prevent a throw-in is a decisive factor in the 1-2-1-1 press. Immediately after losing possession of the ball, the defense initiates the 1-2-1-1 press. Whenever possible, the closest player guards the opponent throwing the ball inbounds. Teammates cover the safety position, the middle player and the wing positions.

Player A guards 1, the player with the ball, B drops back to cover 3 in the middle of the court, and C remains between the ball and 2. Player D watches 4 while E assumes responsibility for the deep player, 5 (Diagram 7-19).

BALL PASSES IN BOUNDS NEAR THE SIDELINE AND FREE THROW LINE—ALIGNMENT RULE TWO

(Two on ball, one floating, one in lane and one back.) Player 1 passes to 2. Player A extends the arms to force a lob or a bounce pass, and forces 2 to turn around and face the out-of-bounds, or prevents 2 from driving to the baseline. The floater, B, prevents a quick return pass to 1. If the ball reaches 1, A shifts over to assist B double team 1. Player D moves to the lane to intercept any pass intended for 3 and E, the safety, covers 5 (Diagram 7-20, A).

Variation: If the trapped player, 2, who is double teamed by A and B, turns and dribbles toward the baseline on the right side of the court, A moves parallel with 2 and sets a double team with B. Player C becomes the floater (Diagram 7-20, B).

SIDELINE AND CENTER LINE

(Two on ball, one floating, one in lane, and one back.) Player C primarily impedes the progress of any offensive player who attempts to dribble along the sideline. As soon as 2 receives the

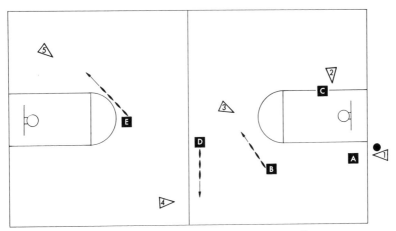

DIAGRAM 7–19   Implementing the 1–2–1–1 Press.

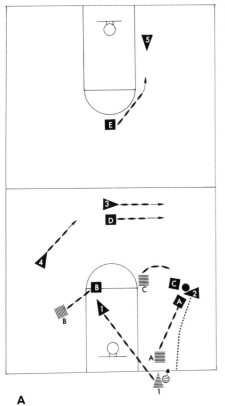

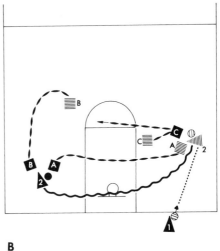

DIAGRAM 7–20   Alignment Rule Two. Ball passes inbounds near sideline and free throw line.

B

A

ball, A and C apply pressure and D discourages a pass to 3. If 2 progresses down the sideline, D shifts toward 2, while C quickly sets a double team. The floater, A, moves down the floor while E covers the lane and watches for a pass to 5. Player B has the key role in running down court and assisting in the basket area (Diagram 7-21).

MIDDLE OF THE COURT—RULE ONE

(Two on ball, two floating and one back.) If a pass is completed around mid-court, D stalls 3 until A arrives to double team 3. The floaters, B and C, intercept passes or double team when necessary. Player E remains in the safety position (Diagram 7-22).

The 1-3-1 zone press

The 1-3-1 full court zone press is similar to the 1-2-1-1 press except that in the 1-3-1, the chaser does not challenge the out-of-bounds player. Instead, the chaser forces the first receiver into a trap with one of the wings. Once the double team has been established all full court zone presses are basically alike. Teams that have a 1-3-1 zone defense and a 1-3-1 offense usually prefer the 1-3-1 zone press since team personnel occupy the same positions

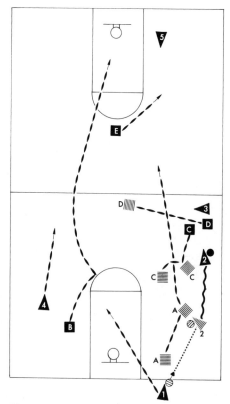

DIAGRAM 7–21 Sideline and Center Line Strategy.

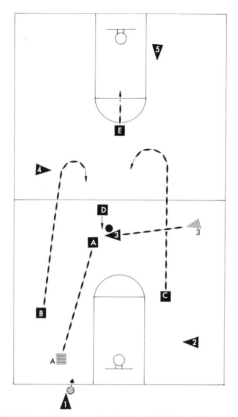

DIAGRAM 7–22   Alignment Rule One. Middle of the court play.

throughout the game. The learning process is always simplified when a player retains the same position on offense and defense.

The following two diagrams illustrate the 1-3-1 zone press in a trapping situation:

BALL AWAY FROM SIDELINE—TRAP ALIGNMENT RULE ONE

(Two on ball, two floating and one back.) The ball is passed to 2 and A guides the dribbler into a trap with B. Players C and D, the floaters, watch for possible pass interceptions while E stays back in a safety position (Diagram 7-23).

BALL PASSED TO THE OTHER SIDE OF THE COURT—TRAP ALIGNMENT RULE ONE

Player 1 passes the ball to 2 who dribbles, then passes across the court to 3. Player A, who was on the way to trap 2, reverses and sets a trap for 3 with D, Player C covers 4 while B moves to the center of the court to intercept the ball. Player E stays back as the safety player (Diagram 7-24).

The 3-1-1 half court zone press

The 3-1-1 zone press is a half-court press used against teams having poor ball handlers in the front court, or as a defensive strategy

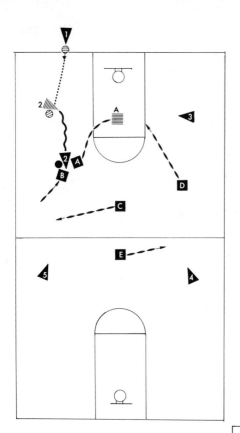

DIAGRAM 7-23

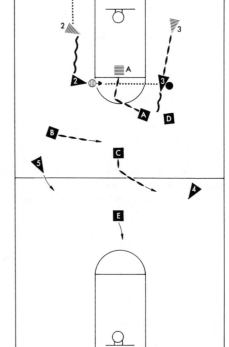

DIAGRAM 7-24

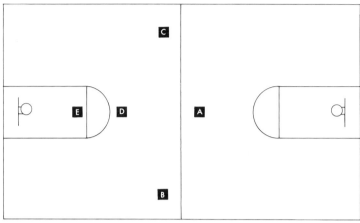

DIAGRAM 7-25   3-1-1 Half-Court Zone Press.

when the offense has no problem moving the ball against a full court press. An advantage of the 3-1-1 press is that the defense dictates the strategy by forcing the player with the ball to either one side of the court or the other (Diagram 7-25.)

Personnel

THE CHASER.   The chaser, A, a tall, aggressive player, has the responsibility of initiating an attack on the ball regardless of the position of the offensive player on the floor. When the offensive player dribbles the ball in the middle of the court, the chaser forces the player toward a sideline trap at mid-court with one of the two wing players. If the ball is passed to either corner, A retreats to cover the pivot area as a floater.

THE WINGS.   The wing players, B and C, are fast players possessing the ability to deflect a dribbled ball. The responsibilities of the wings vary according to the position of the ball: (1) If A forces the ball to the sidelines, the wings establish a double team situation; (2) If the ball moves in the opposite direction, the wings become floaters covering players in the mid-court area or in the basket area; (3) If there is a double team situation the wings turn the player with the ball back into the middle of the court by overplaying the ball to the outside; and (4) If the back safety player needs assistance, the wings drop back to the corner or double team strategy.

THE BACK SAFETY PLAYERS.   Initially the two back safety players, D and E, have different responsibilities; thereafter, the duties are identical. The front safety player, D, protects the middle of the court, covers the back safety position when E vacates it, covers the sideline area when the chaser and wing player are preparing to double team the ball, and forces a sideline dribbler toward the wing player or into a trap situation. The back safety player, E, is also the tallest player on the team. Player E protects the basket area and covers a side area when the ball moves laterally from one side of the court to the other. Both safety players block shots at the basket and try to gain possession of rebounds.

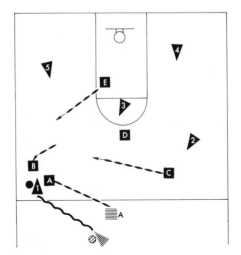

DIAGRAM 7–26 Implementing the 3–1–1 Press.

Implementation

Players A and B force the dribbler into a corner trap situation. Player D remains in front of pivot player E, C, the floater, protects the middle area while E moves out to the sideline to intercept a possible pass to 5. If 5 receives the pass, a corner trap is set with Trap Alignment Rule One (two on ball, two floating and one back, p. 200). Offensive teams attempt to elude the 3-1-1 half-court press by passing into the middle area or by a series of short quick passes from one side of the court to the other. Therefore, the defense protects the middle area while forcing the player with the ball into a possible corner trap (Diagram 7-26).

Combating the Zone Press

Although each zone press has certain weaknesses and vulnerable areas, there are a few offensive tactics effective against all pressure defenses. Under the most severe pressure, each player must maintain poise, patience and control. The offense can spread the defense over the entire court, thus avoiding the possibility of a dangerous double team situation, as in the case of a guard covering two offensive players. The offense can also lessen the effectiveness of the defense by running to receive passes, cutting to elude an opponent, and faking to receive a pass. Alert offensive teams frequently pass the ball inbounds before the defense is ready. A tall player throwing the ball inbounds has less difficulty in spotting the position of teammates and in passing the ball over the defensive player.

The zone press is designed to stop the dribbler with a well-

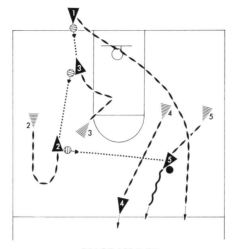

DIAGRAM 7–27

timed double team situation. If the players are sufficiently spaced to spread the zone, the ball is advanced with short quick passes from the side of the court to the center and back to the side. An excellent method of destroying the zone press is for the offense to deliberately draw the defenders into a double team situation, then pass the ball and move to an open spot on the side or in the middle of the court. Timing is essential as a pass executed too early or too late creates a pressure situation for the ball handler and fails to draw the defense out of position. The theory of overloading a zone defense is also applicable in attacking the zone press. Methods of advancing the ball to the offensive end of the court include:

Pass and pass back

Player 1 passes the ball to 2, then moves to the lane for a return pass while 4 cuts to meet the ball and 3 breaks down court. Player 1, with the option of passing the ball to 4 or 3, passes to 4 who immediately passes to 3. Player 3 dribbles down court (Diagram 7-27).

The 1-4 attack

Cutting situations vary according to the defensive zone press. Player 3 fakes to the right, then runs to the left and forward to receive a pass from 1. Player 2 starts down court to draw the defense, then button hooks back for a possible pass from 3. Player 4, anticipating a pass, cuts to the middle, pulling the defense out of the area and freeing 5 for a pass.

Variation: When 2 is unable to receive a pass from 3, 4 cuts, looking for a pass, then 5 cuts also, anticipating a pass (Diagram 7-28).

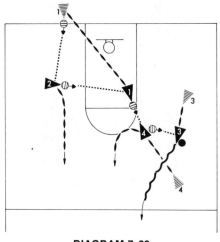

DIAGRAM 7–28

DRILLS

Drills which develop individual defense are also beneficial in developing skill for zone pressure and player-to-player pressure strategies. If the press is to be successful, each player must be in excellent condition.

1. *Throw-in Drill.* Players form two lines with line I stationed on the out-of-bounds endline even with the side of the free-throw lane, and line II positioned opposite the free-throw line but outside the circle on the same side of the floor as line I. Player 1, the first person in line I, passes the ball inbounds to 2, the first person in line II, who does a variety of offensive fakes and cuts to receive a pass. Player 2 then passes the ball to the second player in line I. Each player progresses to the end of the opposite line (Diagram 7-29).

2. *Anticipation Drill.* Repeat drill in Chapter 6, Individual Defense on page 160.

3. *Two-on-One.* Divide the class into groups of three. Starting at the endline, player 1 attempts to dribble the ball the full length of the court to score a basket. Players A and B, at the free-throw line, try to stop the dribbler, force the dribbler into a trap, or gain possession of the ball and score (Diagram 7-30).

4. *Help-out Drill.* Divide the class into four lines. Player 1 dribbles in front of the defensive basket while A and B, stationed outside the free-throw circle and behind the free-throw line, double team 1. D fakes, then shifts in position to receive an outlet pass as soon as 1 is double teamed. Rotating clockwise, the players go to the end of the next line (Diagram 7-31).

5. *Half-Court One-on-One Drill.* Divide the group into two lines with one line on either side of the center line. The first players in each line, A and B, guard 1 and 2, the second players

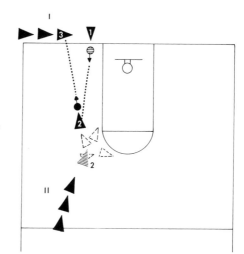

DIAGRAM 7–29   Throw-In Drill.

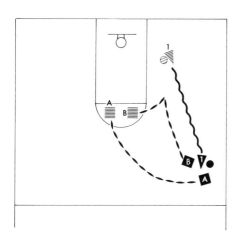

DIAGRAM 7–30   Two-on-One Drill.

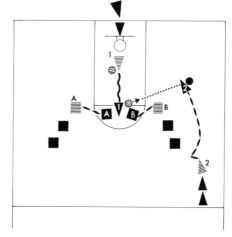

DIAGRAM 7–31   Help-Out Drill.

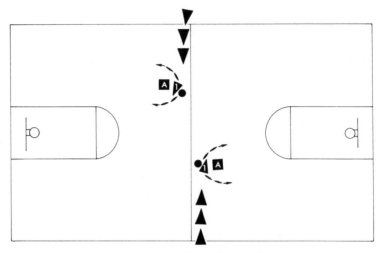

DIAGRAM 7–32   Half-Court One-on-One Drill.

in each line. Players 1 and 2 attempt to score while A and B try to force
1 and 2 to change direction. A and B do not reach toward 1 and
2, but keep the weight low, the palms up, and arrive at a spot on
the floor before the dribblers. After each player has been on defense the coach rearranges the lines, giving each person an
opportunity to guard large and small opponents (Diagram 7-32).

6. *Reaction Passing.* Divide the players into groups consisting
of seven players—four on offense and three on defense. Assign
three of the offensive players set positions. The fourth player, the
passer, is in the corner of the center court, passing the ball
alternately to the three offensive players. Two defensive players attempt to deflect or intercept the passes while the third defensive
player stands approximately five feet from the passer and distracts
the passer by moving back and forth and wagging the arms
(Diagram 7-33).

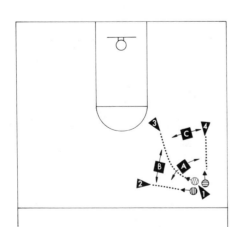

DIAGRAM 7–33   Reaction Passing.

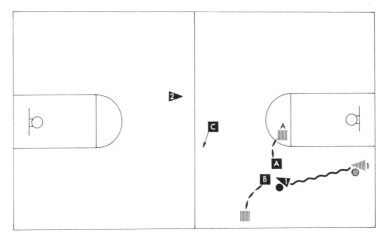

DIAGRAM 7-34 Three-on-Two.

7. *Three-on-Two*. Divide the players into groups of five with three defensive players, A, B, and C, and two offensive players, 1 and 2. Player 1 dribbles the ball and, if necessary, passes to 2. A and B attempt to trap 1 while C, the third defensive player, tries to intercept a pass to 2 (Diagram 7-34).

SPECIAL SITUATIONS
Jump Ball

Throughout each game players encounter special situations, such as out-of-bounds, free-throws and jump balls, requiring variations in team strategy. In a jump ball situation the object is to gain possession of the ball and execute a "set play" or "pattern play." As the referee tosses the ball, the jumper—as well as the rest of the team—considers the following possibilities: (1) an offensive tap, in which the jumper controls the tip; (2) a defensive tap, in which the opponent controls the tip; and (3) an even tap, in which there is a 50-50 chance of either player controlling the tip. Although jump ball situations occur at the center circle, the offensive or defensive free-throw circle, the same basic techniques are applied to obtain the ball at each position. There is a greater emphasis on defending the goal during a jump ball at the defensive circle since the opponents are in position to tap the ball into scoring territory.

Box formation

Jump ball strategies most successful for the majority of teams include the box and diamond formations. The box formation, or the 2-1-2, is particularly effective for the defense; therefore, it is recommended for jump balls at the defensive free-throw circle

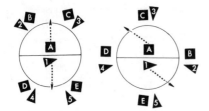

DIAGRAM 7–35 A, Box Formation
B, Diamond Formation.

(Diagram 7-35, A). The diamond formation, referred to as the 1-3-1, has excellent scoring potential, yet the position of the players naturally creates a disadvantage during jump balls at the defensive circle. The diamond is therefore limited to jump balls at the center and offensive circles, and at the defensive circle when control of the tap is assured (Diagram 7-35, B). Both formations provide each team with an "open spot," an area on the circle where two teammates are together with *no* opposing player between them, thus giving an advantage in receiving the tip. The location of the open spot depends on: (1) The dominant hand of the jumper; (2) the position of the official tossing the ball; (3) the player who will obviously control the tip; and (4) the circle where the jump takes place. It is the responsibility of the jumper to locate the open spot prior to the ball toss by the official.

During a defensive jump in the box formation, the opposing jumper has a height advantage and controls the tap (Diagram 7-36, A). In case an even tap occurs the defensive players are prepared to cut in front of an opponent to secure possession of the ball. Although the players may shift clockwise or counterclockwise, it is imperative that each has an assignment which coordinates with the jump ball strategy of the team.

In the diamond situation player E has the major defensive responsibility. E drops back for defense, C and D cut in front of the most likely receivers, and B shifts to the left or right, or guards against a back tap (Diagram 7-36, B).

Often it is beneficial to give players one specific alignment from which both offensive and defensive plays may be executed. As the ball is tossed into the air the players are alerted by a signal that a change in strategy is necessary for the jump, players then rapidly alter their individual positions. For example: In an even jump at the center circle with both teams in a box formation, one player

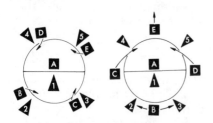

DIAGRAM 7–36 A, Box Formation
B, Diamond Formation.

DIAGRAM 7-37   Defensive Strategy. The jump ball.

possesses exceptional ability in deception, ball handling and speed. The skilled player is assigned the task of cutting into the opposing team's open spot and gaining possession of any ball tapped by the opponent.

Defensive Strategy for Jump Balls

1. The players assume defensive positions which force the opponents to establish an open spot in an area at the greatest distance from the offensive basket. The opposing jumper, 1, is guided into tapping the ball into the open spot created by 4 and 5. As the ball is tossed either D or E cuts into the open area and intercepts the ball (Diagram 7-37).

2. Station the defensive players in position to influence the direction of the tap. For example: in the box formation, D and E are close enough to 4 and 5 to discourage a tap in the open area. Jumper 1 is forced to tap to the open side, the right side of 2. On the toss, D and B move toward 2 in an effort to intercept the pass (Diagram 7-38).

Offensive and Even Jump Strategy for Jump Balls

1. The players around the circle on an offensive or an even jump prevent the opponents from cutting into the "open spot." Since the opponents are in a defensive position, the open spot is usually at the top of the circle farthest from the offensive basket and between D and E. Instead of concentrating on a quick basket, each offensive player strives for possession of the ball, simultaneously blocking the closest defensive person (Diagram 7-39).

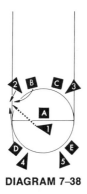

DIAGRAM 7-38

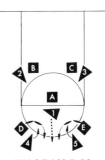

DIAGRAM 7-39

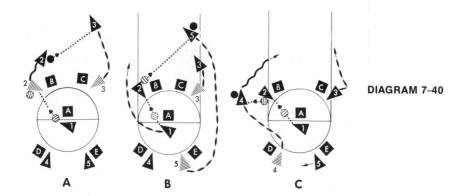

DIAGRAM 7–40

2. The two players nearest the basket area on an even jump move back and forth, covering the sides. The opposition is inclined to tip the ball to the sides rather than toward the basket; therefore, the defense exerts pressure on the side players.

After obtaining possession of the ball a team in the box formation has the following alternatives (Diagram 7-40, A, B, C):

(A) TIP-OFF PLAY FROM CENTER CIRCLE. Player 1 taps the ball to 2 while 3 breaks toward the basket for a pass from 2.

(B) JUMP BALL AT THE OFFENSIVE CIRCLE. The play is executed similarly to the tip-off except that 5 breaks toward the basket and receives the pass as 3 sets a screen for 5.

Variation: The jumper, 1, cuts around the outside of 2, gains possession of the ball by a hand-off from 2, then drives for the basket.

(C) JUMP BALL AT THE OFFENSIVE CIRCLE. Player 1 taps the ball to 2 who passes to 4. Player 4 breaks for the basket while 3 and 5 remain alert for necessary defense.

Diamond formation

The diamond formation, or the 1-3-1, is a stronger tactic than the box formation and is recommended for jump ball situations at the center circle or at the offensive free-throw circle. On an even jump

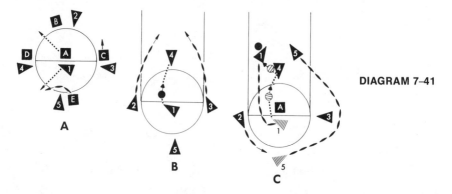

DIAGRAM 7–41

the tip is normally received by the tallest and best jumping player who creates the open spot between D and E (Diagram 7-41, A). If the jumper is unable to control the tip, the players assume defensive positions around the circle and overplay on the basket side, forcing the tip back. As a further blocking measure, the team can force the opponents' spot toward the side of the circle where the official will toss the ball.

(1) *Jumper 1 controls the tap.* Player 1 taps the ball toward the tallest player, 4, who is in the free-throw lane. As the ball is tapped, 2 and 3 break toward the basket to receive a pass from 4. The remaining player, 5, provides the defensive balance (Diagram 7-41, B).

(2) *Ball is tapped to 4.* Player 5 breaks around 3 and runs toward the basket to receive a pass from 4. To establish a defensive balance, 2 shifts to the position vacated by 5. Since teammate 4 is screened by A, the jumper, 1, gains possession of the ball or cuts for a shot (Diagram 7-41, C).

Play Following a Jump Ball

Fast break

When control of the tap is certain and the jump ball is at the center or defensive circle, there are two possible fast break patterns (Diagram 7-42, A and B).

(A) Player 5 taps the ball to 1, while 2 and 3 break down court. Player 3 receives a pass from 1, creating a 2-on-1 fast break opportunity.

(B) Player 5 taps to 1 then cuts down court as 2 shifts to the sideline at mid-court. Player 1 passes to 2, who passes to 5 for a scoring attempt. The opponent, E, jumping with 5, attempts to see where the ball is tapped, thus allowing 5 sufficient time to move down court on a fast break.

DIAGRAM 7-42

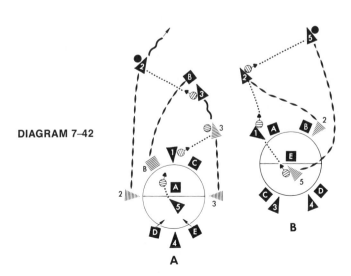

A

B

Free-throw

Defensive Team

Because women basketball players tend to have low scoring averages for the free-throw, players stationed along the free-throw lanes anticipate an unsuccessful throw and attempt to control every rebound. The defensive team is awarded the two inside rebounding positions next to the basket. As the ball touches the rim or backboard, the two inside defensive players screen the offensive players by sliding the foot next to the offensive player into the free-throw lane while pivoting slightly on the other foot. As a consequence the offensive player is screened, and the defensive player is in an advantageous rebounding position.

The final member of the rebound triangle, the third player on the free-throw line, is responsible for screening the opponent who shoots the free-throw. The third rebounder moves into the free-throw lane in front of the shooter and blocks her, then concentrates on the ball. The remaining two defensive players assume positions on each side of the court to control a long rebound, gain possession of a tip-out or recover loose balls (Diagram 7-43).

FAST BREAK FROM FREE-THROW. Players A and B are alert and in position to begin a fast break when the defensive rebounders retrieve the ball. To start the fast break after an unsuccessful free-throw, player D first obtains the rebound, then throws an outlet pass to A while B cuts across the top of the circle to receive a pass from A. Player B dribbles to the free-throw line, A and C occupy the outside lanes of the court, E follows B as a trailer and D moves down court as a safety (Diagram 7-44).

Offensive Team

Offensive players, assigned to the second positions on the lane, are at a disadvantage for obtaining possession of unsuccessful free-throws (players 4 and 5 in Diagram 7-45, A). While the team's aim is to secure as many rebounds as possible, it is often necessary to tip the ball into the goal or to a teammate. The person who took the free-throw, player 3, is usually in the best position to receive a tip. After completing the shot, 3 steps toward the back edge of the circle to assume a defensive position and provide additional space for a tip from players 4 and 5. The protective position of A and B enables defensive players 1 and 2 on the offensive team to gamble on catching a loose ball or a side tip-out.

FAST OFFENSIVE PLAYERS BLOCKING THE FIRST DEFENSIVE PLAYERS. Fast offensive player 5 successfully fakes toward the middle of the lane, then shifts in front of E, the defensive player in the first position. Occasionally the offense obtains the rebound by stepping behind and toward the baseline side of the defensive player (Diagram 7-45, B).

Out-of-bounds

Out-of-bounds plays from the *sideline* are necessary when the opponents have a player-to-player defense or press late in the game.

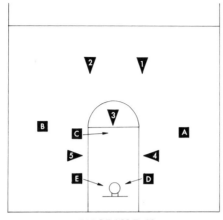

DIAGRAM 7–43

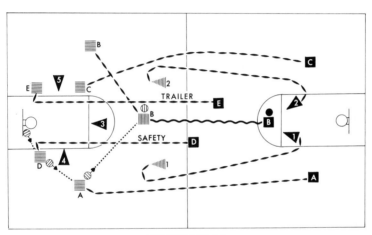

DIAGRAM 7–44

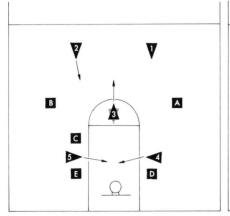 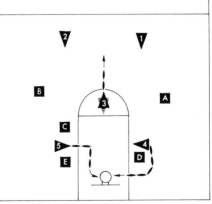

DIAGRAM 7–45

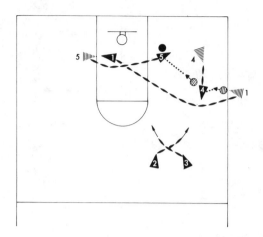

DIAGRAM 7-46 Sideline Option Against Player-to-Player Defense.

The effectiveness of the play depends upon the team creating an opportunity to use it when it is not a regular part of the offense and thereby—hopefully—startling the defense.

Selection of out-of-bounds plays is based upon the abilities of the individual players on the team. It is imperative for a player who is exceptionally skilled in passing to throw the ball inbounds because a weak pass results in an interception or an incomplete pass. If the opponents use a zone or combination defense, the player throws the ball inbounds, then proceeds with regular offensive tactics.

(1) **Sideline Option Against Player-to-Player Defense.** On a signal from 1, 4 moves and receives a pass from 1, then 1 cuts toward the basket, watching for a return pass from 4. If 4 fails to pass to 1, 1 sets a screen for 5 who is in position to cut across the middle of the court or run to the low post for a pass (Diagram 7-46).

(2) **Sideline Option Against Player-to-Player Defense.** When Player 4 is covered, 1 waits until 2 and 3 have reversed, then passes to 2. However, if 4 receives the ball (as in the previous illustration), and is unable to pass to 1 or 5, 4 starts a play by passing the ball to 2. Player 5 moves to the high post position and receives the pass from 2. Player 3 reverses positions with 2, then continues toward the basket watching for a pass from 5 and a possible shot at the basket. Player 5 has the option of passing to 4, who has cut toward the basket, to 1, who is taking advantage of a screen set by 4, or to 3 (Diagram 7-47).

(3) **Sideline Option Against a Zone Defense.** Player 1 passes to 2, then cuts for the basket while 5 moves slowly across the lane, screening for 4, who is running along the baseline. Player 1 continues moving slowly toward the baseline and also screens for 4 as player 2 dribbles to the left and passes to 4 behind the screen set by 1 (Diagram 7-48).

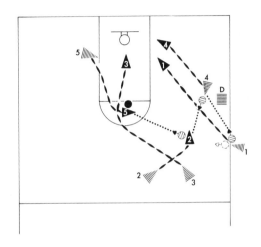

DIAGRAM 7–47 Alternative Play.

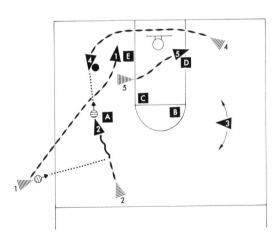

DIAGRAM 7–48 Sideline Option Against Zone Defense.

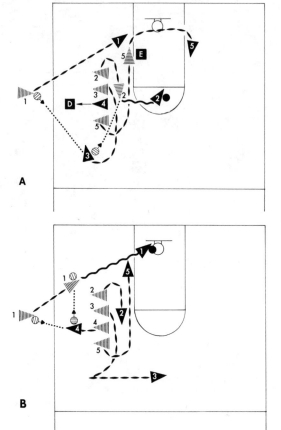

DIAGRAM 7–49 Out of Bounds Play Against Player-to-Player Defense.

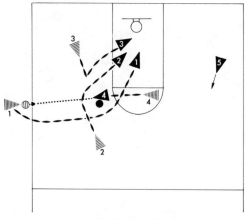

DIAGRAM 7–50

(4) **Special Out-of-Bounds Play Against a Player-to-Player Defense.**
Player 3 cuts behind 4 and 5 for a possible pass. Player 2 sets a screen
for 5 who moves toward the offensive basket as 4 shifts to the sideline.
Player 1 passes to 3, 4, or 5.

(a) If 4 and 5 are covered and 3 receives the ball, 3 passes to
2. Player 2 has the option of either dribbling to the free-throw line
and passing to 5, who has moved to the right side of the key, or
passing to 1 on the left side of the key. Player 5 could also perform
a jump shot (Diagram 7-49, A).

(b) If 4 has the ball there is an option of passing either to 2 in
the high post position or back to 1. After receiving the ball, 1
dribbles toward the basket using 5 as a screen. During all of the
options 3 remains in the defensive safety position (Diagram 7-49, B).

(5) **Out-of-Bounds Play Using the Split Post Offense.** Player 1 passes
to 4 in the high position. Player 3 fakes a screen and cuts toward the
basket looking for a pass from 4. Players 1 and 2, anticipating a pass
from 4, split the post with 1 cutting first (Diagram 7–50).

COACHING

INTRODUCTION

Contrary to popular belief, coaching is not always fun or enjoyable. It is a tense, time-consuming job requiring a considerable amount of teaching ability, determination and courage. Teaching ability is of the greatest importance since the coach is concerned with strategies, abilities and techniques. Anyone aspiring to become a coach should have a thorough understanding of the technicalities which are an integral part of a team's growth and development. Each game may be considered an examination period for the coach. A coach must have an understanding of human relations, for in all situations the decisions the coach will need to make are based upon what is best for the individual player, the team, the school and the game itself. When answering the question "Who can coach?" consider these problems: (1) What kind of coach does the person desire to be? (2) What kind of coach could the person become? and (3) What relationship is there to the nature of the position and the individual's coaching philosophy? The fact that the game is played before an audience creates an atmosphere of tension some people cannot tolerate. Decisions such as how to win, who should play, who should be excused from practice, and who should be disciplined are the responsibility of the coach. A little humor, applied with discretion, can often ease tense moments. Since opponents frequently are aware of a team's plays, new and exciting plays interspersed among the standard patterns will not only surprise the opposing team but also change the results of many games.

Although it may seem unlikely to people who are not connected with varsity athletics, counseling ability is essential for any coach. A coach should provide a guiding hand toward good sportsmanship, as well as be aware of the physical and emotional make-up of each player. Personal feelings, however, should not cloud decisions affecting individual initiative, team play or program efficiency.

The coach should show respect to the students selected for a team by congratulating each player in person and writing a short informative note to the player's parents. A letter sent at the beginning of the season may include a game schedule while a letter sent at the end of the season may list individual and team play statistics. Parents often schedule family events around practice sessions and games, thus a short note concerning team plans for the season promotes better public relations.

Assistants to the Coach

Any athletic program is more successful when the coach recognizes and cooperates with people who are willing to help. The size of the school and the importance of athletics to the school determine the number of assistants a coach must have for the season.

Assistant coach

When a school is fortunate enough to have a head coach for the varsity team and an assistant coach for the junior varsity, the coaches should develop strategies that will enable students to follow an orderly competitive transfer from the junior varsity to the varsity team. Coaches should use similar methods and work closely together since, theoretically, each is striving for the same results. In some manner the head coach should establish rapport with the assistant coach, requesting contributions and emphasizing the need for an exchange of strategies and ideas. Frequently, the assistant coach has been trained or has personal experience in a certain aspect of basketball, such as defense or offense, that offsets a weakness of the head coach. The measurement of an assistant coach's ability is the number of athletes who develop under the coach's supervision, rather than by the games won or lost.

Student manager

The student manager is selected from the students in the local school and will be of particular value to the coach. Duties of the student manager include:

1. Equipment—cleaning, getting it out and putting it away; includes such items as basketballs, pinnies, whistles, clocks, jump ropes.

2. Towels—providing towels for home and visiting teams.

3. First Aid Kit—organizing, resupplying and overseeing the first aid kit.

4. Charts—charting the team and issuing the charts to the team and coaches.

5. Officiate—referee during scrimmages, games and practice sessions.

6. Host—providing dressing space and other facilities requested by the visiting team.

7. Correspondence—writing thank you notes.

Captains

The captain of the team, a "natural" leader, is a representative of the coach as well as of the students. During game situations various types of leaders emerge. A team may have a person who leads team morale or spirit, so important in winning ball games, yet this involves no decision making. Another type of leader, usually a guard, may be selected to set up the team plays. The captain, however, is the central figure, and is usually selected by the team to regulate and direct much of the action on the court. Responsibilities of the captain include the following:

1. Arousing team spirit.
2. Creating team unity.
3. Informing the coach of any difficulties or problems.
4. Representing the team to the coach.
5. Representing the coach to the team.
6. Playing on the main team.
7. Consulting with, and thanking, the officials.
8. Receiving ground rules and relaying them to the team.
9. Presenting the line-up to the scorekeeper.
10. Leading in sportsmanship.
11. Supporting the coach.
12. Directing the pre-game warm-ups.

Custodial staff

A coach should individually establish a working relationship with the custodial staff. A detailed work sheet listing exact specifications for any job should be distributed to the custodial staff well in advance of the event. Duties of the janitors include: (1) sweeping the floor; (2) arranging the score tables and bleachers; (3) adjusting the baskets; and (4) preparing the locker rooms.

Team Selection

When a school system has a large number of students trying out for the basketball team, the coach must be concerned with selecting the team. The coach's philosophy directly determines the selection of the players, for example: (1) is the style of play determined for the season and players selected to fit that style? or, (2) are the players selected first, then the coach develops a style around their abilities?

When selecting team members the coach looks for the following characteristics:

1. Skill—body control and ball handling.
2. Potential—reaction time, willingness to improve, perseverance and intelligence.
3. Emotional stability.
4. Game experience or game sense.
5. Body build—does the individual have the strength that will be an asset to the team?
6. Cooperation—ability to play or work with others.
7. Desire and confidence.
8. Adaptability—will the player fit into the style of play?

Training Rules

Training rules and regulations may be established by the coach, by the players or by both the players and coach. In most cases, the school has standard regulations which everyone must follow. Each coach must be explicit in outlining what can and cannot be done. Listed below are some of the general regulations:

1. Eligibility—determined by the state or by each school.
2. Punctuality and attendance at practice. May a player be excused? If so, what excuse does the coach accept?
3. Dress—a code stating the type of dress for practices, games and travel.
4. Transportation—the type of vehicle, drivers, insurance, departure and arrival time and the location for loading the students.
5. Rules—policies concerning smoking, drinking, honesty, behavior, and language.
6. Attitude—includes social poise and respect for team members, opponents, waitresses, custodians, and any other personnel team members encounter.
7. Responsibility—assisting with the equipment and uniforms.

Practice sessions

Planning is important! The astute coach will take advantage of the vacant gymnasium and start practice while the boys are still outdoors finishing the football season. Thus, by the time basketball starts for boys, the girls have a headstart in conditioning and are ready to share the facilities. Some principles to be considered when planning practice sessions are:

1. The coach should eliminate all distractions, particularly people wandering around in the gym. If necessary, keep doors closed or locked.
2. The equipment should be out and ready for use.
3. The players who come to practice should know what is expected and not waste time in getting to work.
4. The short practice session increases learning.
5. The drills needed for mastering an activity should be as enjoyable as possible.

6. The coach should be on time.

7. The drills should be alternated. Demanding drills are mixed with easy drills, or physical drills with mental drills.

8. Introducing new or difficult drills should occur near the beginning of practice.

9. The coach should not plan to cover too much at any one time.

10. The practice is often initiated with warm-up drills and terminated with a scrimmage or a team drill.

11. The players should spend some time working under pressure. The coach should use game situations involving pressure plays, and stress different aspects of the game on different days.

12. Practices should be well organized. Aside from the fact that good planning produces better results, a team respects a coach who is organized.

13. Practice sessions should be interspersed with gimmicks, such as rebounding devices, weighted balls, galoshes, dark glasses, or weighted jackets.

14. Practice should be finished on a high note.

15. The way a team performs in practice is the same way it will function in a game. A team that loafs in practice will have a difficult time going all out in a contest. The coach must insist on defensive players talking to each other, letting one another know when a cutter moves through the key, when a screen is set or when a pick is in operation. On offense, the coach promotes team unity by showing appreciation for a good pass or a nice play.

16. The coach should use discretion in praising team members. Everyone needs praise, yet a problem lies in the amount and timing of the praise. Since the public seems to praise the scorer, the coach should emphasize other accomplishments in difficult phases of the game, such as rebounding, passing and defending the goal. Tactfully applied, praise before criticism can be productive in assisting team members to improve skill and strategy. One should avoid giving too many compliments to players early in the season, as players may become too content with mediocre techniques. The coach saves the best praise for the latter part of the season.

17. Practice sessions should contain an element of competition. Competition is a way of life, and basketball players thrive on it. The coach uses drills, relays and contests that force the players to vie for positions on the team.

18. The players should have a clear concept of the expectations of the coach. The players perform more competently when the purpose of a drill is explained beforehand.

Planning Events Home and Away

The details of planning home and out-of-town events vary according to the individual school situation. It is imperative for the coach to consult the principal, athletic director and department head when planning events at home or at neighboring schools.

1. Facilities — The basketball court, dressing rooms, and social areas must be clean and ready for use. The date, time and place of each match must be established well in advance of the event.

2. Invitations — Personal invitations for a match between two teams may be made by letter, phone or in person. The coach asks the opposing team to confirm the date by letter. For an away game the coach asks for directions to the gymnasium and parking facilities.

3. Officials — The home school must furnish qualified officials for any match played on its court. The coach should obtain confirmation from the officials as well as arrange to pay each official immediately after the game.

4. Custodial staff — The custodial staff should be informed of:
   a. The areas that need to be cleaned.
   b. The rooms that are to be opened.
   c. The equipment the teams desire, including a public address system.
   d. The time the building is to be cleaned and secured after the game.

5. Manager — The manager should have the equipment, uniforms, towels and first aid kit available and ready for use. A manager will often follow a checklist to insure that each routine duty is completed before the game.

6. Scorekeeper and Timer — Since the scorekeeper and timer are often students, the coach or manager may find it necessary to do some pre-game instruction to qualify the students for the positions.

7. Charters — When the coach desires a chart or record of the players' performance, someone interested in the position must be contacted and given instructions before the day of the game. If possible, the person should practice recording on a chart during practice sessions.

8. Hostess — A person is designated to officially greet and assist all visiting personnel. Each hostess should be courteous, efficient and prompt in relaying any special messages.

9. Athletic Trainer — Schedules should be provided for the athletic trainer or the school doctor. An athletic trainer generally accompanies a team while a doctor is available by phone.

10. Publicity — Contacts will have to be made with local newspapers, school newspapers and radio stations.

11. Eligibility list — Academic lists and records of medical examinations must be thoroughly checked by the coach.

12. Social get-together — A social hour should follow the game. Points to consider include: (a) the type of refreshment; (b) the place for the social event; and (c) the visitors who will be invited.

13. Team — During the warm-up, it is the coach's responsibility to have the team on the court ready to play, to record the line-up in the scorebook, and to see that all officials are present.

14. Transportation — The coach must investigate the various

methods of transportation available within the school system. Time and place of departure and arrival must be confirmed and reported to all personnel involved.

15. Number of games — The coach attempts to schedule an equal number of games at home and away.

16. Budget — Prior to arranging matches, the coach should be informed of the total amount of money budgeted for the basketball season. The total expense of the games, equipment, and uniforms should be covered by the allocated funds.

17. School calendar — A coach who checks the school calendar and plans basketball games that do not conflict with other programs in which players will be involved will have fewer problems with fellow teachers and students.

COACHING DURING A COMPETITIVE EVENT

There is an enormous amount of controversy over the amount of coaching that is permitted from the sidelines. When a coach sitting on the bench spots weaknesses in individuals or in team strategy and a time-out cannot be called, a verbal or hand signal is used to communicate with the players. For this reason, it is wise to number or name defensive and offensive patterns, so that at a signal such as "two," each player will know to change strategy. Coaches change strategy when:

1. Switching an unbalanced defensive assignment or a guard covering a weak shooter may provide defensive assistance to teammates.

2. Defensive positions may need to be changed to eliminate an out-of-bounds play or a particular play the opponents use successfully for scoring.

3. A weak defensive area can be exploited by an offensive maneuver.

4. The defensive or offensive strategy, or an unsuccessful playing tempo, needs to be altered.

5. One or two players need readjustment in order to steal a jump ball from the opponents.

Sideline strategy, time-out and half time

The coach's strategy can be of vital importance when the opponents are on the move offensively. Some of the following suggestions may be successful in halting such a rally by the forwards:

1. If the team has a time-out remaining, the coach calls time-out, then reassures the players and gives instructions in the best strategy for combating the opposing plays. As well as inspiring the players, the time-out may change the rhythm of the game, inadvertently destroying the rally.

2. If the defensive strategy is changed or a substitute is sent

into a game, the forwards' strategy will have to be altered to counteract the new players or tactics.

3. If the tempo of the game has decreased, the coach encourages players to execute a full court press and increase the speed of the game.

4. If the tempo has increased, players move the ball slowly up the court, deliberately reducing the speed of the game and attempting a more controlled shot at the goal.

5. If the team is leading and the opponents switch to a zone, players work the ball around for a good shot while forcing the opponents to move out after the ball.

6. If the score is close or tied toward the end of the first half, players hold the ball for the last shot. A team leading at the half time has a definite psychological advantage.

Substitutions

As well as changing offensive and defensive strategy, the coach should be concerned with the three strategic phases of basketball: (1) substitutions, (2) time-outs and (3) half time. Introducing a substitute into a game at an opportune moment may frequently be the deciding factor in winning the ball game. For obvious reasons, the coach must be aware of each player's emotional stability. All available knowledge should be considered in determining a player's reaction when put into or removed from a game. The coach avoids taking a player out of the game because of one mistake, yet any star player with too many fouls should be removed. Psychologically, a team will respond more positively when a leading player still has a chance to re-enter the game than when the star has fouled out. Coaches have trained substitutes with special skills that are of crucial value to a team. A clutch shooter who scores in a tight situation, a strong, fast defensive player for pressure defense, a dribbler and good ball handler who can control the ball, and a player with excellent jumping ability for control on the jump ball and on the backboards are a few of the players with special abilities who can be sent in to help a team in a difficult situation.

Time-outs

The five time-outs allocated each team can mean the difference between winning or losing the game. Legally, the coach, the captain or the players on the court may call a time-out. All should use discretion, however, for improperly used time-outs are an advantage to the opponents. Avoid taking too many time-outs early in the game. In general, time-outs are designed to allow the coach to improve strategy, provide instruction and confidence, bolster team morale, reinforce learning, or change the pace of the game.

Half time

The third vital phase of the game, the half time, should be used to the advantage of a team. While the players are resting, the coach:

(1) looks at the statistics and reveals any pertinent information to the players such as the number of fouls on each player, the weak defensive areas, and the strong points of the team, and makes general remarks which may be helpful in the second half; (2) covers the starting strategy for the second half; and, (3) builds the morale of the team and gives instructions for warming up for the last half.

Visual Aids

Player motivation may be maintained through movies, pictures, bulletin boards, charts and numerous other devices. The bulletin board is an indispensable tool for illustrating floor positions, supporting previous instruction, displaying names, and exhibiting an assortment of statistics indicating the progress or lack of improvement in the players. If the budget permits, pictures can provide an added incentive for the players. Movies taken during competition are, without question, the most accurate method of observing a team in action, studying the strategy of opponents and assessing the abilities of each player.

Charts

Shot chart
A shot chart indicates the number of field goals attempted by each player, the location of the player who made the shot and the number of

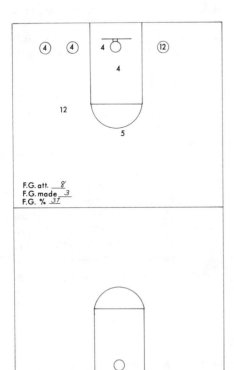

F.G. att. __8__
F.G. made __3__
F.G. % __37__

FIGURE 8-1 Shot Chart.

goals scored by each player. On the chart, place the number of the player who shoots a field goal in a position approximately where the player stood on the court. If the basket is made, the number of the player is circled. When computing the field goal percentage, field goals attempted are divided into field goals made (Figure 8–1).

Rebound Chart
The rebound chart illustrates the offensive and defensive rebounds each player obtains. Write the name of each player on the rebound chart. When a player obtains a defensive or offensive rebound, place a slash mark after the player's name under the proper rebound heading. A tally of the opponents' rebounds can be kept for comparison (Figure 8–2).

Mistake Chart
Mistake charts designate violations, fouls, bad passes, poor ball handling and the player against whom a score was made. Write the name of each player on the mistake chart. Place a slash mark under the proper category after the name of the player making a mistake. Tally the mistakes of the opponents for comparison.

Assist Chart
Another chart of value, the assist chart, includes a list of passes leading directly to a score by a teammate. Write the name of each player on the chart. Place a slash mark after the name of a player who has an assist (pass) leading directly to a basket, or who steals the ball from an opponent.

Jump Ball Chart
A chart tallying jump balls retained and lost may also indicate whether or not the team or opponents were able to score directly from the tap. The chart is divided into offensive, defensive, and center jumps, as well as first and second half and overtime periods. Place a slash mark under the appropriate jump ball and note whether the team retained the ball, lost the jump, or scored directly from the jump ball (Figure 8–5).

Rebound   Chart

Name	1st Half Def	1st Half Off	2nd Half Def	2nd Half Off	Total
Smith	III	II	II	IIII	5-6 11
Jones	II	I	I	II	3-3 6
Ashby	III	II	II	III	5-5 10
Sarno	II	IIII	II	III	4-7 11
Cupp	†††	II	I	†††	6-7 13
Total					23-28 51
Opponent	††† I	††† I	††† II	†††	13-11 24

FIGURE 8–2 Rebound Chart.

PLAYER	TRAVEL-ING	DOUBLE-ILLEGAL DRIBBLE	3-SECOND LANE	BAD PASS	LINE VIOLATION	LOST THE BALL	MISCEL-LANEOUS	MENTAL MISCUE	TOTAL
OPPONENT									

FIGURE 8–3 Mistake Chart.

PLAYER	ASSISTS	Total	STEALS	Total

FIGURE 8–4 Assists-Steal Chart.

Jump Ball Chart

Offensive	Center	Defensive
II	Retained	I
	Lost	I
I	Scored	
	1st Half	
	2nd Half	
	Retained	
	Lost	
	Scored	
	Overtime Retained	
	Lost	
	Scored	

FIGURE 8–5 Jump Ball Chart.

Good sportsmanship, a quality to be observed above all else, should be taught to players at an early stage so that each team member reacts properly in any situation. There is no excuse for poor sportsmanship. No one, including the coach, has the right to yell or glare at the opponents or officials. While it is true that players must thoroughly understand the rules to be able to participate in a competitive game, the officials are hired to referee; consequently, "Students play the game," and "Officials referee." Good sportsmanship does not diminish a competitive spirit and a desire to win. Whenever a team is on the floor, each player should possess a strong desire to win. If the team is defeated, each member of the team should congratulate the winning players and coach.

TREATMENT OF INJURIES TO ATHLETES

INTRODUCTION

First aid and treatment of injuries to athletes involve a considerable amount of technique and knowledge of anatomy, kinesiology, biology, physics and physical therapy. No longer can the athletic trainer center the world of the locker room around simple first aid, supplementary aids and bandaging. Through awareness of the American Medical Association, the American College of Sports Medicine, and the National Athletic Trainers Association, school administrators have become concerned with the need for better conditioning programs, for more inclusive and improved training procedures and for more thoroughly qualified and educated athletic trainers. A large percentage of the trainers, particularly at the high school level, are physical educators who studied heavily in the life sciences or who attended workshops and clinics on the treatment of injuries to athletes. Comparatively speaking, the position of athletic trainer is a new concept among sponsors of intercollegiate contests for women; however, the increased emphasis upon participation in athletic contests and the inauguration of state, regional and national tournaments in such sports as basketball, volleyball, golf, hockey and tennis, have forced coaches to search for assistants qualified as trainers. Currently, there is a trend toward securing personnel who have majored in biology, nursing, occupational therapy or physical therapy in undergraduate school. Ideally, a trainer should have completed all of the requirements for a degree or certificate in physical therapy in an accredited school of physical therapy. In any case, the program of study designed for

238

an athletic trainer should be centered around the following subjects:

1. Human Anatomy
2. Physics
3. Chemistry
4. Kinesiology
5. Physiology
6. Physiology of Activity
7. Psychology
8. Introduction to Physical Therapy and Medical Ethics
9. Therapeutic Exercises and Assistive Devices
10. Massage
11. Hydrotherapy
12. Electrotherapy
13. Radiation Therapy
14. Pathology
15. Neurophysiology
16. Care and Treatment of Athletic Injuries
17. Clinical Practice

Personal Qualifications of the Trainer

Regardless of employment status, a trainer must establish good rapport and a working relationship with the coach, athletes, administration, team physician, school nurse and school health services. As well as creating good public relations, the trainer must earn the respect of the coach to insure that the treatment prescribed for any athlete is accepted by the coach. The trainer and coach are frequently placed in the role of counselor or friend, and indirectly apply a major influence on the development of the student's ideas, values and philosophies. While there is a thin line dividing the responsibilities of the coach and trainer, team members and all personnel concerned function more competently when the qualifications and responsibilities of the coach and trainer are both accepted and respected by one another.

Responsibilities of the athletic trainer:

1. Cooperate with the athlete, coach and physicians in designing and enforcing a program of conditioning for athletes.
2. Administer first aid to injured athletes on the court or in the locker room.
3. Supervise, under the direction of the team physician, the reconditioning program for an injured athlete.
4. Cooperate with the physician in treating and taping injured athletes.
5. Supervise the checking of athletic equipment for proper fit and safety.

6. Assist the physician in obtaining a thorough medical examination of each athlete before approving participation in any sport.

7. Maintain skill in the application of injury preventative devices such as tapes, pads and braces.

8. Possess knowledge of the care and treatment of cuts, bruises and sprains.

9. Order and maintain detailed records of training room supplies and equipment.

10. Supervise all procedures for the training room.

11. Operate therapeutic devices such as whirlpools, ultrasonic generators, low volt generators, and steam baths.

12. Refer the athletes to a physician, dentist, health service or hospital when the injury is beyond the qualifications of a trainer.

13. Cooperate with the athletes and coach in designing diets and recommending supplementary aids for the athletes.

14. Supervise the student trainers.

15. Maintain a professional attitude at all times.

16. Retain a friendly, patient and polite manner when working with the athlete.

17. Remain calm and confident throughout the administration of first aid and treatment of injuries to athletes.

18. Develop an accident report blank indicating the sport being played, the nature and extent of the injury, cause of the injury, emergency treatment administered, disposition of the athlete, and the date, time and place of injury.

Serious Injury

Although the majority of injuries are minor, the trainer must maintain an accurate and up-to-date card file for each athlete outlining referral procedures of a major injury. Details concerning the following questions should be obtained from the parents of each athlete:

1. The physician to be called.
   a. team physician
   b. family physician
   c. health service
2. The phone number for each physician to be notified.
3. The ambulance service desired and the phone number.
4. The phone number of a person to contact in case the family cannot be located.
5. The hospital service desired and the phone number of the hospital.
6. Consent for emergency procedures.
7. An agreement is made about which physician is to be called first, and the time the family physician should take over.
8. The person who is to make the phone calls.
9. The person who is to be left in charge of first aid until the physician arrives.
10. The extent and services of insurance issued by the school and coverage by family policies.

Half Time Duties

Time-out during the half time can be very useful to the trainer as well as the coach. Taping, bandaging, equipment and the general condition of the athletes should be checked and treated and first aid provided for any slight injuries. Control dehydration by supplying the athletes with cool water or fruit juice diluted with cool water. If the game is being conducted in a particularly dry or humid climate, salt tablets may be necessary.

Post Game Duties

At the conclusion of the game, all tape and equipment should be removed and injuries carefully examined by the trainer and perhaps the physician as well. Bruises should be treated with cold packs to minimize swelling and flesh injuries should be treated immediately. At this time the physician or the trainer makes an appointment with each injured athlete for a follow-up examination of the injury on the succeeding day.

DUTIES OF STUDENT TRAINER

Student trainers may be recruited from non-athletic students or from athletes who do not qualify for the traveling team. The position requires an intelligent young woman who can accept responsibility and fulfill the following duties as student trainer:

1. Assist the trainer in routine duties.

2. Check the room temperature of the gymnasium and locker room.

3. Arrive at scheduled events ahead of time.

4. Warm cars before players enter.

5. Carry drinking water when there is some concern about the water in a new town.

6. Place towels in an accessible place for members of each team.

7. Supervise cleaning and laundering of uniforms and practice suits.

8. Study a new playing court for possible defects.

9. Keep towels, water and a first aid kit near the trainer at the players' bench.

Legal implications

The athletic trainer is placed in the dual position of treating the athlete with techniques and modalities requiring special, if not medical training, while protecting the school, the principal, the superintendent and the Board of Education by guarding against any action that could inadvertently result in a law suit. The trainer and coach are both in vulnerable positions since the school may claim immunity as a governmental agency. Extreme caution must be used in administering any type of medicine and treatment without a written prescription from the team physician. A person with a physical therapy certificate or a certificate from an auxiliary medical service is legally more qualified to use advanced techniques and modalities than a trainer who has not been accredited in any way. Legally the trainer can be prosecuted for:

1. Failing to perform a legal duty.
2. Committing an act that is unlawful.
3. Performing an act of negligence such as moving an injured athlete from the playing court.

Athletic Insurance

An athlete participating in any sport should be substantially covered by health, hospitalization and life insurance. The majority of states have classified athletics as an extramural activity, consequently excluding the intercollegiate program as a classroom activity legally covered by school insurance. Individual companies offer insurance policies to high school and college athletes to protect the athlete against the costs resulting from injuries acquired during practice sessions or game situations. In recent years the number of law suits have increased, forcing the cost of athletic insurance to soar upward. Premiums, however, are often covered by the college, schools or parents, or by a special fund or combination of these methods.

The Team Physician

The team physician is, without question, the final authority in determining whether an athlete is in condition to participate in any sport or resume competition after an injury. As in the case of all injuries, the physician's objective is to return the person to a normal routine; however, in the case of an athlete, the patient must completely recover from the injury or no longer be considered eligible for participation. The physician must have knowledge of the psychophysiological demands of the sport as well as be familiar with the intensity, duration, speed and agility that are part of any given activity. Doctors interested in becoming team physicians generally seek additional information on the type and degree of injuries occurring in various sports, and the most competent methods of treating the injury and restoring the athlete to full-time participation. Through the cooperation of coaches, athletes, athletic trainers and physicians, the number of athletic injuries has been greatly reduced and the period of disability for the athlete has been shortened.

Once the role of team physician has been accepted, policies must be established to regulate emergency care, legal liabilities, facilities, personnel relationships and duties. Team physicians should plan to be in attendance at all athletic contests conducted in the home community. For out-of-town games it is customary to rely on the services of the home team physician.

Of primary concern is early detection of the nature and degree of injury. For this reason it is ideal to have a physician in attendance at all practice sessions. The initial examination is completed by the trainer or coach and the information is relayed to the physician. In general, an early examination facilitates the diagnosis and prognosis of an injury. The diagnosis becomes increasingly difficult as pain, swelling, edema and hemorrhage increase. If the opinion of a specialist is desired, the athlete should be examined immediately by the specialist in order to have the advantage of an early diagnosis. Once a course of action is decided upon, treatment should be carried out by the person under whose supervision the treatment falls: the trainer; the team physician; or the specialist.

Duties of team physician

1. Obtain a complete medical history of each athlete.
2. Conduct physical examinations of athletes before competitive events.
3. Supervise the trainer on medical problems and in special procedures to be followed in restoring athletes to competition.
4. Respect the ambitions of the athlete.
5. Make complete recovery the goal for each injury.
6. Adopt the best method of treatment, avoiding expediency and pressure from groups desiring to have the athlete returned to the game before complete recovery is assured.
7. Attend all home games.
8. Provide prompt treatment.
9. Disqualify players from participation when it is deemed necessary for the benefit of the athlete.
10. Cooperate with the trainer, coach, health services and school administration in conditioning athletes and in maintaining a high professional standard for the treatment of athletic injuries.

Emergency First Aid

The emergency treatment administered to any injured athlete is designed to care for the injury until the services of a physician can be obtained or until it is determined that the services of a physician are not necessary. Persons giving first aid should be skilled in applying sterile bandages to a wound, splinting a fractured extremity, applying a sling, determining shock and judging when a person is so seriously injured that no movement should be attempted. Carelessness in moving or handling an injured player may easily result in an injury to the spinal cord or lungs or compound a simple fracture. It should never embarrass a player or a trainer to remove an athlete by stretcher. If there is any doubt whether or not a player should be allowed to continue in the game, "Remove the player!" A player removed from the game and treated at the first sign of trouble will be able to return to the game much earlier than one who is allowed to compound a simple injury by continued physical competition.

Procedures for "On the Court" First Aid

1. Determine the seriousness, type and extent of injury.
2. Send for the physician when the injury is beyond the scope of a trainer.

   3. Provide first aid if it is indicated.
   4. Determine removal procedures for the athlete.
      a. Should an ambulance be called?
      b. Should a medical sanction be obtained before initiating
any action?

General Rules of Injury Diagnosis

   1. Check breathing.
   2. Examine for profuse hemorrhaging.
   3. Observe whether player is conscious or unconscious.
   4. Observe position of head, trunk, limbs and immediate area
around injury.
   5. Handle injured area with care.
   6. Remain calm and self-confident.
   7. Avoid distorting the injury report or minimizing the injury.

SPECIFIC STEPS OF INJURY DIAGNOSIS

   1. Obtain a history of injury from the player if conscious, or
from teammates.
   2. Determine:
      a. Anatomical structure involved.
      b. Disability of injured area, immediate or delayed.
      c. Type of pain.
      d. Deformity of injured part, present or past.
      e. Any unusual sounds player may make.
      f. Previous history of similar injuries.
   3. Inspect the injured area carefully, determining the difference between the injured part and the corresponding part without
injury.
   4. Palpate the injured area, noting any tenderness.
   5. Manipulate the area to determine the amount of swelling
and the presence of pain.
   6. Test the mobility of the muscle or joint to detect any
amount of restriction during motion.
   Although basketball is not considered a hazardous sport, the insurance companies rank basketball second to football in the prev-
alence of injury. Officially, players are penalized for body contact;
however, the introduction of five-player rules, the fast break and the
unlimited dribble have not only increased the number but also the
seriousness of the injuries. Players may incur any number of injuries, ranging from a minor bruise to a compound fracture or even
death. Trainers for intercollegiate women's basketball teams will,
for the most part, be concerned with the diagnosis and treatment of
contusions, sprains, strains and minor infections. The remainder of
the chapter is devoted to the suggested methods of treatment, the
symptoms and definition of the most predominant injuries, and infections of the feet, ankle, lower leg, knee, thigh and hip, and the
head, shoulder, elbow, wrist, and hand.

Treatment of Injuries

Foot

Excessive Foot Perspiration
Definition. An excessive amount of sweating of the feet, increasing the probability of skin irritation.
Symptoms
    Athletic shoes and socks unusually wet
    Feet overly warm
    Redness
    Irritation resembling heat rash
    Odor
Treatment
    Coating of benzoin and talcum powder before exercise
    Cleanse feet with alcohol after practice
    Powder street shoes, socks and feet
    Loosen the shoelaces of practice shoes
    Hang practice shoes in circulating air

Calluses
Definition. An accumulation of keratin which forms a hard mass vulnerable to tears and cracks. Calluses are usually caused by friction or pressure on the foot from poorly fitted shoes.
Symptoms
    Hard mass
    Bruise in underlying tissue
    Pain
    Callus may tear or crack
Treatment
    Proper foot hygiene
    Two pairs of socks — cotton socks next to skin
    Stretch shoes at callus area
    Apply benzoin and talcum powder
    Soften callus with lanolin
    Buffer callus with an emery board
    Pad area to relieve pressure during activity

Blister
Definition. An accumulation of water or blood between separated layers of skin caused by excessive pinching or friction.
Symptoms
    Pain
    Redness
    Enlarged area containing fluid
Treatment
    Clean area with alcohol
    Puncture blister with sterilized needle or scalpel
    Press edge of blister with gauze pad to remove fluid
    Apply vaseline
    Pad the area
    Use benzoin and "tough skin" to prevent reoccurrence
    Two pairs of socks — cotton next to skin

Athlete's Foot

Definition. A form of ringworm resembling small blisters which emit a yellow fluid.

Symptoms
> Rash
> Small blisters
> Redness
> Inflamed area
> Itching
> Red, white or gray scaling of area
> Dry blisters look brown on outer skin
> Sore red fissure under brown area

Treatment
> Consult physician
> Take sample of foot scrapings to determine the best medication
> Disinfect athletic and street shoes
> Apply foot medication
> Wear white cotton socks — change several times a day

Corns

Definition. A growth, usually on top of the fourth and fifth toes or between the fourth and fifth toes, caused by pressure from incorrectly fitted athletic or street shoes.

Symptoms
> Hard or soft growth in affected area
> Redness
> Pain on pressure
> Local tenderness

Treatment
> Soften with lanolin
> Trim area
> Pad to protect from additional pressure
> Keep area dry
> Apply salicylic acid in liquid form or on cotton pad between toes
>   for increased air circulation

Metatarsal Arch Sprain

Definition. A fallen or injured metatarsal arch caused by over-stretching or overstressing one or more ligaments (Figure 9-1, A, B).

Symptoms
> Irritation
> Pain
> Redness on ball of foot
> Callus
> Toe cramping
> Burning sensation

Treatment
> Ice packs until swelling subsides
> Compression bandage
> Elevate foot
> Hydrotherapy after swelling ceases
> Analgesic pack

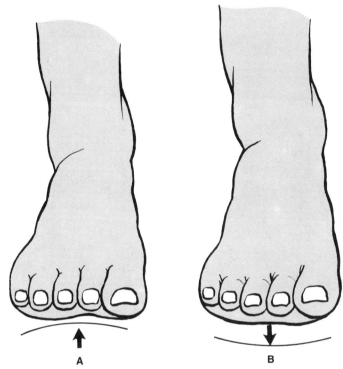

FIGURE 9–1   (Left) Normal Metatarsal Arch   (Right) Fallen Metatarsal Arch.

Metatarsal pads
Plaster splint (if severe) followed by a plaster boot
TAPING METATARSAL ARCH
Apply a metatarsal pad to the ball of the foot. Circle the foot and pad with several strips of tape, overlapping each previous strip by half the width of the tape (Figure 9–2).

Longitudinal Arch Sprain

Definition. A fallen or an injured arch caused by overstretching or overstressing one or more of the ligaments of the longitudinal arch.
Symptoms
Tiredness in arch and heel
Pain in arch and heel
Fallen arch
Swelling
Treatment
Ice packs until swelling subsides
Elevate feet
Compression bandage
Hydrotherapy two or three times a day after swelling subsides
Friction massage
Analgesic packs
Longitudinal pad
Protective taping

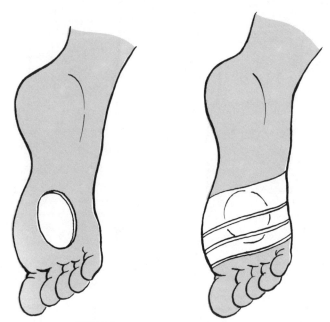

FIGURE 9–2 Taping Metatarsal Arch.

TAPING LONGITUDINAL ARCH

TO APPLY LONGITUDINAL PAD: Start at the base of the metatarsal arch, place a piece of tape on the bottom of the foot and extend
over both sides of the foot, crossing the ends on top of the foot. Repeat three or four times, overlapping the previous strip by half an
inch (Figure 9–3).

Lower leg

Shin Splints

Definition. A tear, irritation or inflammation of the tissue lying between the tibia and fibula. Pre-season shin splints usually occur
during the first two or three weeks of practice or when an athlete
plays on a different floor surface or changes the type of practice
shoe. Chronic shin splints are so severe that complete recovery is almost impossible.

Causes

   Faulty posture alignment
   Fallen arches
   Muscle fatigue
   Muscle stress
   Lack of muscle development in lower leg
   Improper warm-up
   Unusual and strenuous exercise
   Change in playing surface
   Sprained or weak longitudinal arch
   One leg shorter than the other

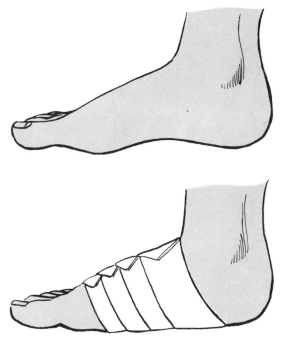

FIGURE 9-3 Taping Longitudinal Arch.

Symptoms
    Severe pain
    Irritation on front of lower leg
    Inflammation
Treatment
    Ice packs until swelling subsides
    Analgesic balm packs on leg
    Heel lift (if one leg shorter)
    Whirlpool
    Heat pack in middle of back
    Pads under sole of arch or heel
    Strap arch and shin (tape or gauze and foam rubber)
    Ultrasonic treatment
    Massage shin and surrounding area
    Caution—Contrary to some theories "running them out" does not cure shin splints but only lessens the pain through development of scar tissue and bone growth.
    TAPING SHIN SPLINTS
    Technique One
    Limit movement of the injured area by placing two felt strips approximately ¼ inch thick, ½ inch wide and 6 inches long on each side of the tibia. Criss-cross tape over the felt pads starting at the lower part of leg, opposite the injury. Circle around the back of the leg, crossing over the pad (Figure 9–4).

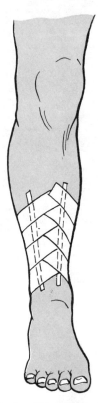

FIGURE 9–4   Taping Shin Splints. Technique One.

Technique Two

Place a strip of foam rubber lengthwise over the affected area. Cross tape over the foam. Secure the longitudinal arch by criss-crossing three strips of tape from the base of the metatarsal arch to the end of the longitudinal arch (Figure 9–5).

FIGURE 9–5   Technique Two.

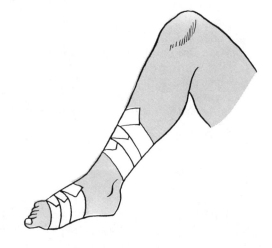

Technique Three (Figure 9–6)

Place two anchor strips of tape (A and B) on the outside of the leg, circling around the heel and covering the ankle. Tape the longitudinal arch as in the previous technique (C,1,2,3,4). Criss-cross the tape over anchor strips, starting on the front of the leg. Circle down toward the outside and behind the leg (C,5), then up in front. Reverse the procedure (D,6), circling toward the inside of the leg. Repeat the criss-crosses, circling to the outside, to the inside, and back to the outside (E,7).

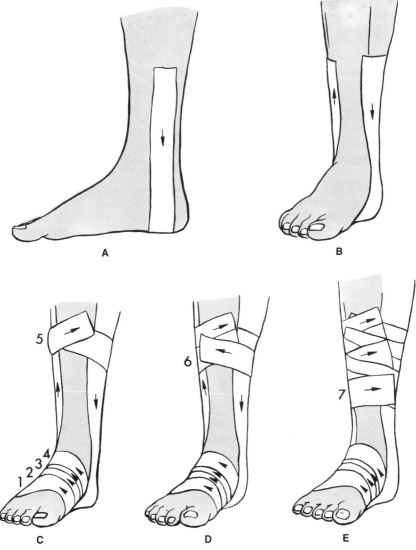

FIGURE 9–6 Technique Three.

Muscle Spasms

Definition. A clonic or tonic, sudden, violent and involuntary contraction of one or more muscles. In tonic spasm the muscle is in a continual state of contraction, whereas in clonic spasm the muscle alternately contracts and relaxes.

Symptoms

    Pain

    Hard, rigid, inflexible area

    Athlete is often fatigued

Treatment

    Deep massage until muscle relaxes

    Place muscle on stretch (forcibly stressing the muscle)

    Analgesic balm

    Salt supplements if abnormal mineral loss occurs through sweating

Ankle Sprain

Definition. An ankle sprain, one of the most common injuries in athletes, is an injury to one or more of the ligaments of the ankle joint.

Symptoms

    Tenderness over affected area

    Swelling in area throughout ankle and foot

    Tenderness over lateral side of foot and ankle

    Normal motion may be painful in more severe sprains

Treatment

    Local injection of hyaluronidase and procaine (for severe cases)

    Compression bandage and ice pack for 24 hours

    Elevate limb

    Heat for 20 minute periods several times throughout the day after swelling ceases

    Analgesic packs

    Lateral stirrup splints

    Walking cast

    Adhesive strapping

TAPING TECHNIQUE FOR SUPPORT OF THE ANKLE DURING ACTIVITY (FIGURE 9–7)

Start end of bandage on top of the foot, circling toward the inside, then wrap under the foot (A). Wrap over the top of the foot progressing toward the ankle (B). Circle the bandage in back of heel to the outside, then under the heel (C). Bandage over top of the arch, back of heel, inside the heel, outside heel, and over ankle joint (D). Alternate circling around ankle and foot until ankle is well-supported (E). Anchor with tape.

Knee Sprain

Definition. An injury to the fibers of a knee ligament ranging from slight damage to a tear in the ligament.

Classifications according to severity are:

(1) Mild—Damage to a few muscle fibers
(2) Moderate—A tear in a ligament—ligament loses strength
(3) Severe—A tear completely across a ligament with complete loss of ligament strength and function—ligament may separate

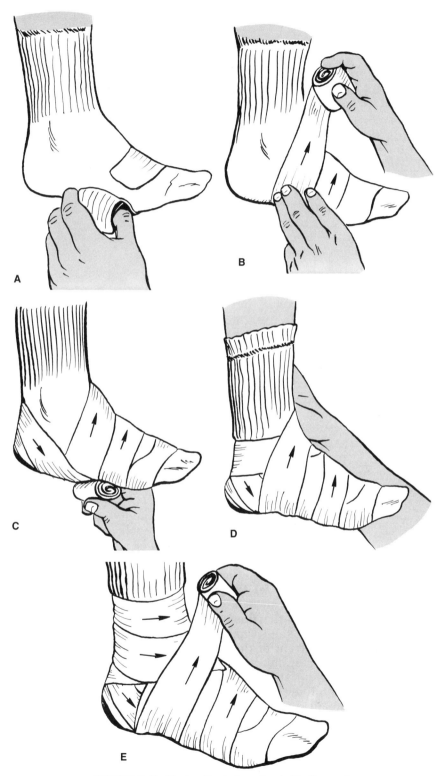

FIGURE 9–7 Taping Technique for Ankle Support.

253

Symptoms
    Tenderness at site of injury
    Pain during movement
    Swelling
    Pain on lateral or rotating motion
    Locking of knee may occur
    Blood in joint
Treatment
    Mild—Cold packs until swelling subsides (one to 24 hours)
    Elevation of leg
    Rest
    Local injection
    Compression bandage
    Heat after swelling ceases
    See physician
    Moderate—Cold packs first 36 hours
    Bed rest
    Elevate leg
    Aspiration
    Injection of anesthetic and hyaluronidase
    Severe—Whirlpool after 36 hours
    Deep heat therapy after 36 hours
    Compression bandage
    Leg cast
    Protective taping
    Rehabilitation exercises
    Surgery is usually required

TAPING LATERAL LIGAMENTS (FIGURE 9–8)

Place an anchor strip of tape above and below the knee (A). Criss-cross strips of tape alternately, extending from the outside of the lower leg over the inside of the knee to the inside of the upper anchor (B). From the inside of the lower anchor, extend tape over the inside of the knee to the outside of the upper anchor (C). Continue criss-crossing (D) and overlapping (E) each previous strip of tape until the area between the two anchor strips (F) is covered (leave knee cap free). Secure the bandage with three anchor strips around the lower leg and three anchor strips around the upper leg.

Elastic Knee Strapping for Medical or Lateral Support (Figure 9–9)

Athlete stands with knee flexed, toes straight ahead, and heel supported 2 inches off the floor. Place bandage on the outside of the leg, up over the knee cap, around the back of the leg, then down and across in front of the knee cap (A). Repeat the previous action, circling above and below the knee cap three times, overlapping each previous strip (B). If desired, apply a pressure pad on the weak side of the leg after strips four or eight.

For additional support, weave four strips around the knee following the identical line and contour of the first four strips (C). Secure the bandage by circling the leg two or three times below the knee and three or four times above the knee with adhesive tape (D).

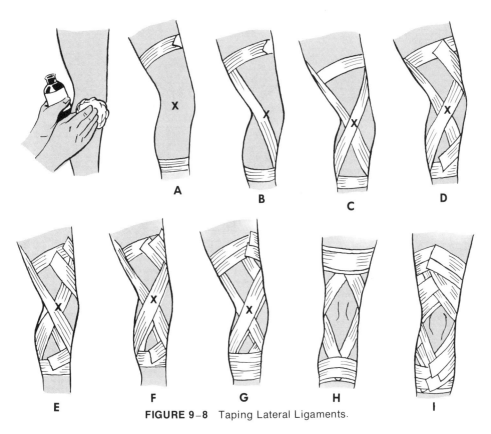

FIGURE 9-8 Taping Lateral Ligaments.

Hip and thigh

Hamstring Contusion

Definition. A bruise of one or more of the hamstring muscles caused by a fall or a blow on the thigh.

Symptoms
  Pain
  Tenderness
  Swelling
  Possible loss of function
  Possible protrusion of muscle fiber

Treatment
  Ice packs until hemorrhage ceases (possibly one to two days)
  Compression bandage
  Elevation for one or two days
  Rest for affected area for one or two days
  Heat treatments after swelling ceases
  Moist hot packs or analgesic packs
  Passive thigh stretching
  Ultrasonic therapy
  Daily treatments of whirlpool followed by analgesic
  Packs may be sufficient for mild injuries

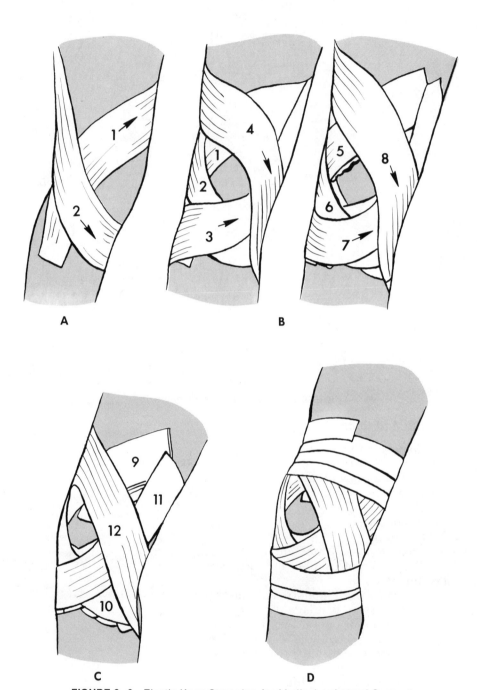

FIGURE 9–9   Elastic Knee Strapping for Medical or Lateral Support.

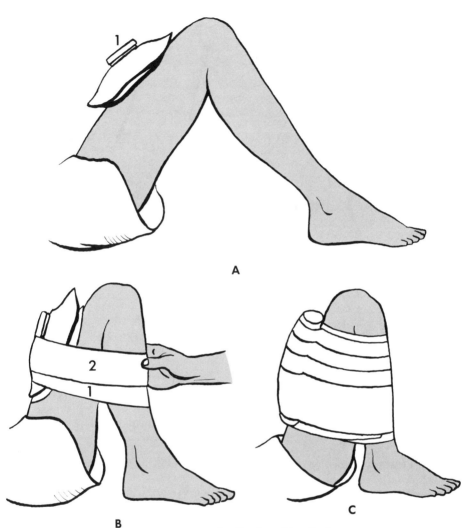

FIGURE 9–10 Application of Ice Pack.

APPLICATION OF ICE PACK (FIGURE 9–10)

Place ice pack on injured muscle (A). Press lower leg against the buttocks. With a 4 inch elastic bandage circle the leg and ice pack, overlapping each previous strip (B). Complete the bandage, anchoring the gauze in place with strips of adhesive tape (C).

Thigh Strain

Definition. A tear, or a rupture of the tendons or muscles in the region of the thigh. While a strain may occur in any thigh muscle, the hamstring group has the highest incidence of strains.

Symptoms

    Hemorrhage

    Pain

    Loss of function

    Discoloration a day or so after injury

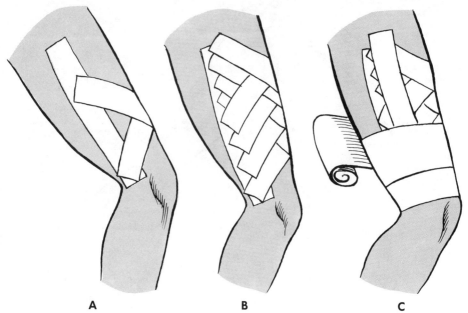

A   B   C

FIGURE 9–11 Taping for Strained Quadriceps Muscle.

Treatment

Ice packs for one to 48 hours, depending upon severity of injury
Pressure bandage
Rest area during the time ice packs are administered
Apply heat treatment after swelling ceases
Whirlpool
Protective taping for play
Analgesic packs

TAPING FOR STRAINED QUADRICEPS MUSCLE (FIGURE 9–11)

Place a 7 to 8 inch anchor strip on each side of the thigh. With 2 inch adhesive tape, start on the outside of the knee, crossing up and over the quadriceps to the inside of the leg. Repeat from the inside of the knee to the outside of the leg, forming a criss-cross pattern (A). Continue criss-crosses until the entire area between the anchor strips is covered (B). Secure the criss-crosses with an anchor strip of adhesive tape on each side of the thigh. Encircle the leg in a gauze bandage (C).

TAPING FOR PULLED HAMSTRING MUSCLE (FIGURE 9–12).

Place an anchor strip on each side of the thigh. With 2 inch adhesive tape, start at the lower end of the outside anchor strip and cross up and over the injured muscle to the inside anchor strip. Repeat from the inside to the outside anchor strip, forming a criss-cross (A).

Continue the criss-cross until the area between the two anchor strips is covered. Secure the criss-crosses with an anchor strip of tape on each side of the thigh (B). Encircle the leg in a 3 or 4 inch gauze bandage (C).

Scalp and face

Lacerations

Definition. Usually a crushing or tearing injury to the scalp or head.

Black Eye

Definition. A contusion of the area surrounding the eye.

Symptoms
> Redness
> Local tenderness
> Swelling
> Discoloration of skin throughout following days
> Possible clogged lymph system
> Fluids in tissues

Treatment
> Cold packs for at least an hour
> Heat (infrared) after swelling ceases (second day)
> Hot moist packs
> Consult physician if lymph system clogged
> Light massage

Foreign Bodies in the Eye

Definition. An object lodged in the eye or under the eyelid.

Symptoms
> Pain
> Disability of the eye
> Involuntary tears

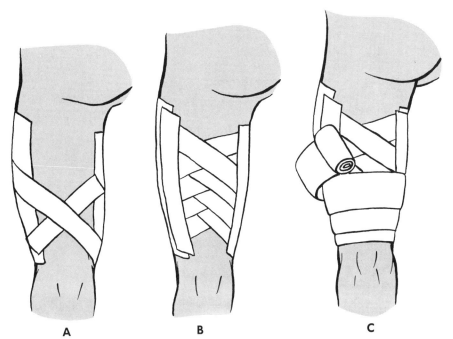

A   **B**   **C**

FIGURE 9–12 Taping for Pulled Hamstring Muscle.

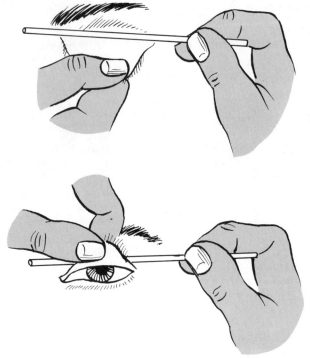

FIGURE 9-13   Removing Foreign Objects from Upper Eyelid.

Treatment
    Close eye until pain lessens
    Avoid "rubbing object out"
    Avoid removing object with fingers
Removal procedure for **upper** lid (Figure 9-13):
    Athlete looks down
    Grasp eyelashes and pull upper eyelid over the lower lid (tears
    produced may remove object)
    Place applicator stick over the eyelid
    Turn lid back over the stick
    Lift the object out with a cotton swab
Removal procedure for **lower** lid:
    Grasp eyelashes or depress the tissue of the lower lid
    Lift object out with a cotton swab
After removal of object:
    Flush eye with boric acid solution
    Ointment used if necessary
    Refer to physician if complications arise
    Concussions
Definition. A blow to the head which may or may not result in a loss
of consciousness.

Symptoms
> Headache
> Feeble pulse
> Clammy skin
> Loss of color
> Unconscious

Treatment
> Smelling salts—ammonia fumes
> Cold cloth to neck and forehead
> Test coherence of athlete when conscious
> May resume play if normal
> Wake every two hours during night if severe case
> Consult physician
> Rest—from one day up to the entire season, depending upon seriousness of injury

Shoulder

Shoulder Strain
Definition. Minor or severe damage to the muscles or tendinous structure of the shoulder joint.

Symptoms
> Local tenderness
> Pain
> Swelling

Treatment
> Cold packs until hemorrhage subsides
> Heat treatments after swelling ceases
> Ultrasonic treatments
> Protective taping may be necessary

Contusion of the Elbow
Definition. A bruise to any part of the area surrounding the elbow joint, usually the result of a fall or a blow to the arm.

Symptoms
> Pain may be slight
> Discoloration
> Swelling may be present
> Fluids may accumulate at the site

Treatment
> Aspiration of fluids
> Injection of hyaluronidase
> Cold packs for at least 24 hours (until swelling subsides)
> Elastic bandage over arm with elbow at right angle
> Heat treatment on second day (after swelling ceases)
> Sling to immobilize elbow

Wrist and hand

Contusion of the Wrist
Definition. A bruise in the area of the wrist, frequently the result of a blow delivered by another person when the hand lies extended on the playing surface.

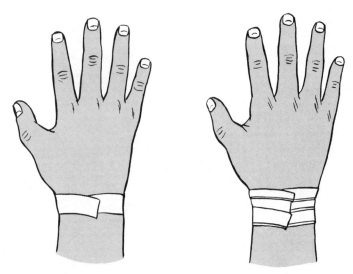

FIGURE 9-14   Taping a Sprained Wrist. Technique One.

Symptoms
    Local pain
    Tenderness in area
    Swelling
    Hemorrhage
    Discoloration
Treatment
    Ice pack until swelling subsides
    Compression bandage
    Heat on second day or after hemorrhage ceases
    Elastic bandage for mild contusion
    Forearm splint (if pain is present when the forearm is pronated
    or supinated, extend the splint above the elbow)
    Sprained Wrist
Definition. An injury to the tissues or ligaments of the wrist, usually
caused by falling on a hyperextended wrist.
Symptoms
    Swelling
    Tenderness
    Inability to flex the wrist
    Absence of pain or irritation over navicular bone
Treatment
    Ice packs for 24 hours or until swelling subsides
    Compression bandage for 24 hours
    Heat therapy after swelling ceases
    Analgesic packs
    Immobilize wrist
    Surgery if severe
    TAPING A SPRAINED WRIST
    Technique One (Figure 9-14)

Flex the wrist toward the injury and spread the fingers. Using 1 inch adhesive tape, encircle the wrist, starting with the center of the strip on the palm-side of the hand, and extending the tape upward and around both sides of the wrist. Apply two additional strips in the same manner, overlapping the previous strip by half an inch.

TAPING A SPRAINED WRIST

Technique Two (Figure 9–15)

(A) Wrap an anchor strip of 1½ inch tape around the wrist (1) and an anchor strip of 1 inch tape around the fingers (2). (B) Hyperextend the wrist (3), then place three strips of tape on the back of the hand: (4) on top of the two anchors; (5) on the little finger side of the hand to the inside of the wrist; and (6) on the thumb side of the hand to the outside of the wrist (C).

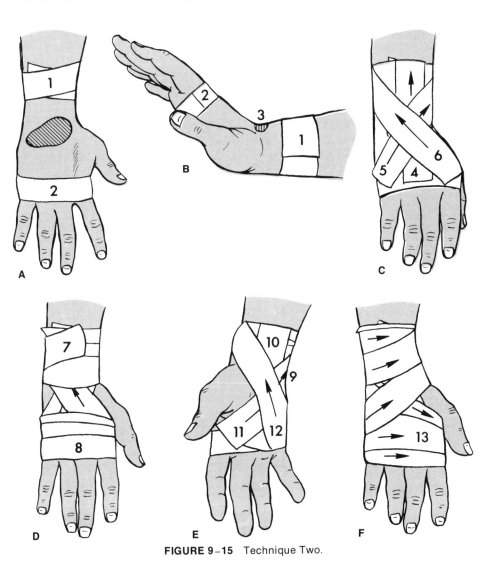

FIGURE 9–15 Technique Two.

Apply three strips of anchor tape above the wrist and three strips below the wrist (D). Apply tape over the anchors on the palm of the hand in the same manner as strips four, five, and six (E). Anchor tape around the wrist, over top of the hand, and around the palm (F).

Finger or Thumb Sprains

Definition. An injury to the tissues or ligaments of a finger or the thumb usually caused by jamming the digit.

Symptoms
> Pain
> Marked swelling
> Hemorrhage
> Tenderness

Treatment
> Ice packs until hemorrhage ceases
> Compression bandage
> Whirlpool after swelling subsides
> Hot packs
> Protective strapping
> Splint to immobilize, if necessary
> Surgery in severe cases

TAPING A SPRAINED THUMB (FIGURE 9–16)

Hold the thumb in a slightly spread position. Place five strips of tape across the thumb, covering the back and palm of the hand. Each strip should overlap the previous strip by half an inch (A). Encircle the thumb with two strips of tape. Start on top of the wrist, progressing toward the palm of the hand, around the thumb and to the inside of the wrist (B). Secure bandage with several strips of tape around the wrist.

TAPING A SPRAINED FINGER FOR PLAY (FIGURE 9–17)

With 1 inch tape, encircle the injured finger and the next finger. Secure by wrapping another strip of tape over the tape extending between the two fingers.

Contusion of the Hand

Definition. A bruise to any part of the hand, usually caused by hitting the hand or by another player kicking or stepping on the hand.

Symptoms
> Pain
> Swelling
> Bleeding
> Abrasion possible
> Laceration possible

Treatment
> Wash area with soap and water
> Ice packs until swelling subsides
> Elastic bandage
> Whirlpool after second day
> Ultrasonic treatment
> Protective taping for play

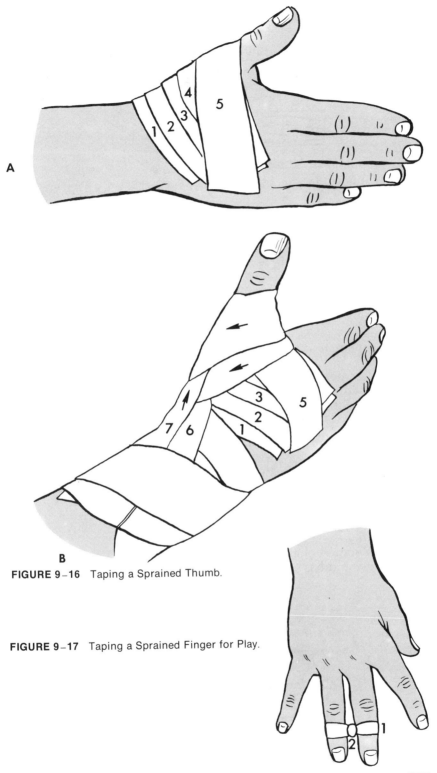

FIGURE 9-16 Taping a Sprained Thumb.

FIGURE 9-17 Taping a Sprained Finger for Play.

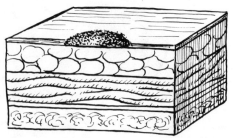

FIGURE 9-18   Cross-Section of Layers of Skin Showing Abrasion.

Infection of Finger Tip
Definition. The growth of germs in an area on the fingers, usually following an injury.
Symptoms
  Pain
  Swelling
  Redness
  Pus
  Heat in area
Treatment
  Sterilize needle or scalpel and drain area
  Warm saline dressings
  Protect with pad and dressing

Abrasions and lacerations

Abrasions (Figure 9–18)
Definition. "Floor burns"—A scraping injury to any part of the body, usually caused by an abrupt contact with the playing surface.
Symptoms
  Bleeding
  Swelling
  Discoloration of area
  Skin wound has a scraped appearance

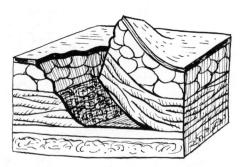

FIGURE 9-19   Cross-Section of Layers of Skin Showing Laceration.

Treatment
    Wash hands
    Irrigate area with water
    Ice pack to reduce swelling
    Direct pressure to reduce bleeding
    Sterile dressing
    Inspect daily for infection
Laceration (Figure 9–19)
Definition. A crushing or tearing injury, usually exposing the under-
lying muscle.
Symptoms
    Bleeding
    Swelling
    Discoloration of area
    Tissue damage
Treatment
    Wash hands
    Irrigate area with water
    Ice pack to reduce bleeding
    Sterile dressing
    Inspect daily for infection

GLOSSARY

Air Dribble—A dribble, formerly referred to as the juggle, in which the player throws, tosses or taps the ball into the air then regains possession of or contacts the ball before it touches the floor or another player.

Assist—A pass which leads directly to a basket.

Backboard—A rectangular or fan shaped surface on which an 18 inch basket is attached.

Backcourt—The half of the court where the opposing team's basket is located.

Banked Shot (Backboard Shot)—A shot in which the ball strikes the backboard then rebounds into the basket.

Basket—A goal, scoring either 1 or 2 points, or the object through which the ball is thrown.

Blocked Shot—A successful attempt by a player to prevent an opponent from completing a shot for the goal.

Blocking—A personal foul that impedes the progress of an opponent with or without the ball.

Blocking Out—A technique used to gain a position on the court between the basket and an opponent in order to rebound the ball.

Bounce Pass—A technique in which the ball contacts the floor and rebounds to a teammate.

Charging—A personal foul committed by a player with the ball who moves her body or the ball against an opponent with an established path.

Cutting—The use of techniques such as fakes, stops, pivots, turns and reverses to elude an opponent or drive for the basket.

Dead Ball—A ball which is not in play (clock is not running, except after a field goal).

Double Foul—A simultaneous infraction of the rules by two opponents against one another.

Double Pivot—A technique in which two players are positioned inside or outside the key, near the basket.

Double Team—A strategy in which two teammates guard one opponent.

Dribble—The act of advancing the ball by a series of bounces.

Drive—A maneuver by an offensive player entailing dribbling the ball while running toward the basket in order to score.

Fake or Feint—A technique designed to elude an opponent.

Fast Break—An offensive strategy in which the offense attempts to bring the ball into the scoring area before the defense can set up.

Field Goal—A score of two points awarded to a player who successfully shoots the ball over the basket rim and through the net.

Foul—An infringement of the rules resulting in the opponents being awarded one or more free-throws.

Free-Throw—An unguarded attempt for a goal from a line 15 feet in front of the basket.

Freezing—The technique of holding the ball and delaying the game, with no attempt to score.

Give and Go—An offensive maneuver whereby a player passes to a teammate and cuts for the basket, expecting to receive a return pass.

Hand-off—The act of handing the ball to a teammate.

Jump Ball—A method of having an official put the ball into play by tossing it between two opponents in one of the restraining circles.

Lay-up—A shot executed by a player laying the ball against the backboard so that it rebounds into the basket or drops just over the rim.

Outlet Pass—The first pass made after a successful defensive rebound.

Pass—Rolling, handing, tipping, bouncing or throwing the ball to a teammate or another player.

Pick and Roll—An offensive maneuver occurring when a player first screens for a teammate who has the ball, then executes a reverse roll and moves toward the basket.

Pivot—A technique for eluding an opponent by moving the body and stepping one or more times on one foot while keeping the other foot stationary.

Player-to-Player—A form of defense in which players are responsible for guarding one particular opponent.

Post Position—The position near the basket usually occupied by the pivot player or center.

Press—A type of strategy in which the defense assumes a close guarding position.

Rebound—A ball which bounces off the backboard or basket. Also, the process of obtaining a ball striking the backboard or basket.

Sagging—When players in player-to-player defense who are away from the ball do not play their opponents closely but move closer to the basket.

Screen—A technique used to block or delay an opponent, or to free or protect a teammate.

Switching—The act of two guards changing assigned forwards.

Trap—A maneuver occurring when two defensive players attempt to stop an offensive dribbler and prevent a successful pass.

Tip-in—The process of hitting or tapping the ball through the basket, usually following a missed field goal.

Traveling—An illegal method of progressing the ball with more than one step without passing, shooting or dribbling.

Triple-Threat Position—The position of a player with the ball who is ready to either pass, dribble or shoot the ball.

Violation—An infringement of the rules for which the opponents are awarded the ball out-of-bounds.

Zone—A defensive system in which each player is responsible for a specific area of the court.

BIBLIOGRAPHY

Baisi, N.: Coaching the Zone and Man-Man Pressing Defense. Englewood Cliffs, N.J., Prentice-Hall, Inc., 1961.
*Basketball Guide – 1970. Division for Girls' and Women's Sports. American Assoc. for Health, Physical Education, and Recreation. 1201 16th St. N.W., Washington, D.C. 20036
Bee, C. F.: Zone Defense and Attack. New York, Ronald Press, 1942.
Bell, M.: Women's Basketball. Dubuque, Iowa, William C. Brown Co., 1964.
Bike Sports Trail: Three trainers talk about basketball injuries. Vol. 22, No. 5. Oct.–Nov., 1968.
Brown, L.: Offense and Defense Drills for Winning Basketball. Englewood Cliffs, N.J., Prentice-Hall, 1965.
Colson, J. H. L., and Armour, W.: Sports Injuries and Their Treatment. London, Stanley Paul and Co., 1970.
Cooper, J. M., and Siedentop, D.: The Theory and Science of Basketball. Philadelphia, Lea and Febiger, 1969.
Cramer, J.: The First Aider. Vol. 38, Nos. 6, 7, 8, 9, 12. Gardner, Kansas, Nov., 1968–Mar., 1969.
Davis, B.: Aggressive Basketball. West Nyack, N.Y., Parker Publishing Co., 1969.
D. G. W. S.: Basketball Guides. Washington, D.C., AAHPER.
Dolan, J. P., and Holliday, L.: Treatment and Prevention of Athletic Injuries. 3rd ed. Danville, Ill., Interstate Printers and Publishers, Inc., 1967.
Garstang, J. G.: Basketball the Modern Way. New York, Cornerstone Library, 1963.
Harkins, M.: Successful Team Technique in Basketball. West Nyack, N.Y., Parker Publishing Co., 1966.
Henderson, J.: Emergency Medical Guide. New York, McGraw Hill Book Co., Inc., 1963.
Juckers, E.: Cincinnati Power Basketball. Englewood Cliffs, N.J., Prentice-Hall, Inc., 1962.
Klass, C., and Arnheim, D.: Modern Principles of Athletic Training. St. Louis, The C. V. Mosby Co., 1963.
LaGrand, L.: Coach's Complete Guide to Winning Basketball. West Nyack, N.Y., Parker Publishing Co., 1962.
McGuire, F.: Team Basketball Offense and Defense. Englewood Cliffs, N.J., Prentice-Hall, Inc., 1966.
Meyer, R.: Basketball. Englewood Cliffs, N.J., Prentice-Hall, Inc., 1967.
Morehouse, L., and Rasch, P.: Sports Medicine for Trainers. 2nd Ed. Philadelphia, W. B. Saunders Co., 1963.

---

*For more information on changes in rules, see earlier editions of the guide, 1907–present.

Mundell, C.: Triple-Threat Basketball. West Nyack, N.Y., Parker Publishing Co., 1968.

Neal, P.: Basketball Techniques for Women. New York, Ronald Press, 1966.

Newell, P., and Benington, J.: Basketball Methods. New York, Ronald Press, 1962.

Newsom, H.: Basketball. Dubuque, Iowa, William C. Brown Co., 1961.

O'Donoughue, D. H.: Treatment of Injuries to Athletes. Philadelphia, W. B. Saunders Co., 1965.

Pinholster, G.: Illustrated Basketball Coaching Techniques. Englewood Cliffs, N.J., Prentice-Hall, Inc., 1960.

Richards, J.: The Scramble for Winning Basketball. West Nyack, N.Y., Parker Publishing Co., 1968.

Rubin, R.: Attacking Basketball's Pressure Defenses. Englewood Cliffs, N.J., Prentice-Hall, 1966.

Ryan, A.: Medical Care of the Athlete. New York, McGraw Hill Book Co., Inc., 1962.

Samaras, R. T.: Blitz Basketball. West Nyack, N.Y., Parker Publishing Co., 1966.

Santos, H. G.: How to Attack and Defeat Zone Defenses in Basketball. West Nyack, N.Y., Parker Publishing Co., 1967.

Schaafsma, F.: Women's Basketball. Dubuque, Iowa, William C. Brown Co., 1966.

Sharman, B.: Sharman on Basketball Shooting. Englewood Cliffs, N.J., Prentice-Hall, Inc., 1965.

Strack, D. H.: Basketball. Englewood Cliffs, N.J., Prentice-Hall, Inc., 1968.

Teague, B.: Basketball for Girls. New York, Ronald Press, 1962.

The Coach: Original Basketball Rules (1891) Make No Provisions for Complexities of Modern Game. River Grove, Ill., Wilson Sporting Goods, Sept.–Oct., 1966.

The Coaching Clinic: Best of Basketball. West Nyack, N.Y., Parker Publishing Co., 1966.

INDEX